INSTITUTE OF MODERN LANGUAGES RESEARCH
UNIVERSITY OF LONDON

BITHELL SERIES OF DISSERTATIONS
VOLUME 42

Intercultural and Intertextual Encounters in Michael Roes's Travel Fiction

INSTITUTE OF MODERN LANGUAGES RESEARCH

BITHELL SERIES OF DISSERTATIONS

Launched in 1978 by the then Institute of Germanic Studies, the Bithell Series of Dissertations is designed to help young scholars publish recent work of high quality which has been accepted for the award of a research degree by a University in the United Kingdom or the Republic of Ireland. Volumes 14 to 41 were published in conjunction with the Modern Humanities Research Association. From 2015 onwards, publication has been resumed by the Institute of Modern Languages Research (IMLR). For a list of previous volumes in the series, see http://modernlanguages.sas.ac.uk/publications/bithell-series-dissertations/.

Theses for possible inclusion in the series are considered by the Bithell Editorial Board twice annually, in May and November. Recommendations for theses to be considered should be made by the supervisor and/or examiner(s), should be accompanied by a copy of the Examiners' Report and Abstract, and sent to Dr Godela Weiss-Sussex at the Institute of Modern Languages Research, University of London, Senate House, Malet Street, London WC1E 7HU (email: godela.weiss-sussex@sas.ac.uk).

Intercultural and Intertextual Encounters in Michael Roes's Travel Fiction

by

Seiriol Dafydd

Institute of Modern Languages Research
2015

Published by the

Institute of Modern Languages Research
School of Advanced Study, University of London
Senate House, Malet Street, London WC1E 7HU
http://modernlanguages.sas.ac.uk

First published 2015

ISBN 978 0 85457 242 7

ISSN 0266-7932

CONTENTS

ACKNOWLEDGEMENTS

I am grateful to the AHRC for the scholarship that made this research project possible.

I would like to thank Professor Julian Preece, my primary supervisor, wholeheartedly for all the encouragement and advice he has given me, and for being so ready to share his enthusiasm and expertise. I am grateful to Dr Brigid Haines and Dr Tom Cheesman for their comments on drafts of the thesis. I would also like to thank other members of staff in the Modern Languages Department at Swansea, especially Dr Katharina Hall, Professor Duncan Large and Dr Sophie Smith. I am also indebted to lecturers who have since left Swansea for inspiring me in my academic endeavours: Professor Rhys W. Williams and Dr Mererid Hopwood. Thank you also to Dr Annette Bühler-Dietrich, who made it possible for me to spend a period of research at Stuttgart University. I would like to extend my particular thanks to Dr Anne Simon for her meticulous editing work as this volume was being prepared for publication.

I am very grateful to Michael Roes, who kindly sent me a copy of one of his films and agreed to meet me in person to discuss his work. It has been a great pleasure and privilege to get to know the writer behind the books.

I would like to say a big thank you to my fellow postgraduate students in the German Section of the Modern Languages Department in Swansea, whose company and support I have greatly enjoyed and appreciated over the last few years. I owe a great debt to my parents, who have unfailingly encouraged me in my academic studies. Diolch yn fawr! And last, but certainly not least, thank you to Janina, who has been a ray of sunshine on even the rainiest of Swansea days.

NOTE ON REFERENCING

References to Roes's primary works are given in brackets with the following abbreviations:

Jizchak: Versuch über das Sohnesopfer (Berlin: Gatza, 1992) [*J*]

Cham: Ein Symposion (Berlin: Gatza, 1993) [*C*]

Lleu Llaw Gyffes (Berlin: Gatza, 1994) [*LLG*]

Leeres Viertel. Rub' al-Khali: Invention über das Spiel (Frankfurt am Main: btb, [1996]1998) [*LV*]

Durus Arabij/Arabische Lektionen (Frankfurt am Main: Eichborn, 1997) [*DA*]

Der Narr des Königs: Madschnun al-Malik. Ein Schelmenstück (Frankfurt am Main: Gatza bei Eichborn, 1997) [*NK*]

Der Coup der Berdache (Berlin: Berlin Verlag, 1999) [*CB*]

Haut des Südens: Eine Mississippi-Reise (Berlin: Berliner Taschenbuch Verlag, [2000] 2002) [*HS*]

David Kanchelli (Berlin: Berlin Verlag, 2001) [*DK*]

Nah Inverness (Berlin: Parthas, 2004) [*NI*]

Kain: Elegie (Berlin: Parthas, 2004) [*K*]

Weg nach Timimoun (Berlin: Matthes & Seitz, 2006) [*WT*]

Krieg und Tanz (Berlin: Matthes & Seitz, 2007) [*KT*]

Perversion und Glück (Berlin: Matthes & Seitz, 2007) [*PG*]

Ich weiß nicht mehr die Nacht (Berlin: Matthes & Seitz, 2008) [*IWN*]

Die Fünf Farben Schwarz (Berlin: Matthes & Seitz, 2009) [*FFS*]

Geschichte der Freundschaft (Berlin: Matthes & Seitz, 2010) [*GF*]

Engel und Avatare [with Hinderk Emrich] (Berlin: Matthes & Seitz, 2011) [*EA*]

Die Laute (Berlin: Matthes & Seitz, 2012) [*L*]

Die Legende von der Weißen Schlange (Berlin: Matthes & Seitz, 2014) [*LWS*]

INTRODUCTION

The journey motif reaches back to the very beginnings of literature and travel narratives are central pillars of the Western canon. Homer's *Odyssey*, Chaucer's *Canterbury Tales* and Cervantes's *Don Quixote* are all structured around protagonists and their journeys. The journey lends itself to narration; voyages promise excitement, adventure and the exceptional. Michel de Certeau goes so far as to state that '[e]very story is a travel story – a spatial practice'.[1] Over the course of the twentieth century, travel was democratized and large swathes of the Western population were able to venture on journeys of their own. Technological advances and the mechanisms of globalization have made the world, if not smaller, then certainly more traversable. People now enjoy far greater freedom and opportunity to travel to foreign countries. As European cities have become increasingly multicultural, encounters with foreign cultures have also become a constituent of life at home. This multicultural presence, felt by some to be a threat, by others an opportunity, has instigated a discussion on intercultural encounters that is becoming increasingly important and urgent.[2] Despite, or perhaps precisely because of, this greater opportunity to encounter other cultures both at home and abroad, a proliferation of both factual and fictional travel narratives line the shelves of European bookshops. The fascination of the reading public with the unfamiliar is seemingly unending.

This book investigates a specific aspect of travel literature – the fictional travel novel – and one practitioner of that sub-genre – the contemporary German author Michael Roes (b. 1960). The analysis focuses on two main areas of research. The first concerns Roes's representation of intercultural encounters: what is Roes's conception of an encounter between representatives of different cultures? How do his stagings of such encounters differ from those of other authors? And what constitutes a successful encounter, if such a thing can be believed to exist? The second area of interest in this study concerns Roes's intertextual methodology. Each of the four novels chosen as case studies is highly intertextual. This study aims to identify those intertextual references that are of greatest significance and to discern how and why Roes refers to

1 Michel de Certeau, *The Practice of Everyday Life*, trans. by Steven Randall (Berkeley: University of California Press, 1984), p. 115.

2 Cf. Arpad A. Sölter, 'Die Einbeziehung des Fremden: Reflexionen zur kulturellen Fremdheit bei Simmel, Habermas und Huntington', in *Der fremde Blick: Perspektiven interkultureller Kommunikation und Hermeneutik*, ed. by Ingo Breuer and Arpad A. Sölter (Bolzano: Sturzflüge, 1997), pp. 25–52 (p. 33).

other writers and their texts as he composes his own. The final aim of the study is to identify whether a connection exists between Roes's engagement with interculturality in all its facets and his utilization of intertextuality. Through close reading of the intertextual references, I seek to establish in what ways, if any, they illuminate the reader's understanding of the intercultural encounter.

The novels chosen for close analysis are prime examples of the way Roes constantly writes about real experiences while engaging with 'pre-texts' of a literary, philosophical or popular-cultural nature. I place my analysis of *Leeres Viertel. Rub' al-Khali: Invention über das Spiel* (1996), *Haut des Südens* (2000), *Weg nach Timimoun* (2006) and *Geschichte der Freundschaft* (2010) within the framework of Roes's *oeuvre* and within the wider context of travel literature of various kinds. This introduction is divided into four parts beginning with an overview of Roes's work. The second part places this *oeuvre* within the wider context of historical and contemporary travel literature, both factual and fictional. Part three offers an examination of Roes's ideas on intercultural encounters alongside a range of other theoretical approaches to encounters between Self and Other. I conclude with a review of contemporary theories and practices of intertextuality which are relevant to the individual chapters that follow.

Michael Roes

Roes is protean and versatile in his creative output. As well as being a prolific novelist, he has published volumes of essays, poetry and plays, and he has directed a number of films. Of the twelve novels he has published, only one, *Ich weiß nicht mehr die Nacht* (2008), is set entirely in Germany. Roes's *oeuvre* is unfluctuating in its engagement with foreign peoples and cultures, his focus is directed towards the rest of the world. The individual works are studies not only of foreign cultures but also of the interaction between cultural representatives. Roes has drawn inspiration from a wide and diverse range of cultures, from the North American Indians (*Der Coup der Berdache*, 1999) to contemporary China (*Die Fünf Farben Schwarz*, 2009; *Die Legende der Weißen Schlange*, 2014), and from Welsh mythology (*Lleu Llaw Gyffes*, 1994) to the Islamic world (*Leeres Viertel*, 1996; *Weg nach Timimoun*, 2006; *Geschichte der Freundschaft*, 2010; *Die Laute*, 2012). Perhaps none of Michael Roes's works epitomizes his interest in processes of intercultural communication quite as much as his film *Someone is Sleeping in my Pain: Ein west-östlicher Macbeth* (2001). In this film Roes takes one of the most famous plays of English literature, set in Scotland, and relocates the action to the unlikeliest of places – Yemen. His work as a whole is characterized by openness, investigation and experimentation, as evinced by the international, trans-historical and interdisciplinary nature of his intertextuality. His vision of intercultural learning is one of active exchange, an experience that must be sought and in which one must give as well as take: 'Man reist als jemand, der etwas mitbringt: die eigene Kultur; als jemand, der etwas will, nämlich den Dialog und eine Art Zusammenarbeit. [...] Meine Utopie ist die gemeinsame Arbeit'.[3]

Roes was born in Rhede (Westphalia) in 1960 and was brought up in the nearby city of Bocholt. He studied Psychology, Philosophy and German Literature at the Freie Universität Berlin, writing his final dissertation on the theme of marginal groups (1985). He went on to gain a doctorate (1991) in Philosophy with a thesis on the motif of the sacrifice of sons (see below). During this period he also worked as an assistant director at Berlin's Schaubühne and at the Munich Kammerspiele. Roes's interest in travel literature derives from his anthropological training, but his is a polymathic approach that combines elements from art history, philosophy, literary studies and even the sciences. These interests find their expression in his creative output. This is apparent not only in the range of subject matter addressed in his *oeuvre* as a whole but also within individual works. The recent volume *Engel und Avatare* (2011) is a perfect example of Roes's dynamic interdisciplinary approach. Co-authored by the psychiatrist and philosopher Hinderk Emrich (b. 1943), it centres on the motif of the avatar and the increasing virtualization of the world. Subjects covered include the internet and its influence on human psychology, Facebook and the peculiarities of social media, and the increasing atomization of society. The discussion touches on areas such as neurobiology, sociology and philosophy and exposes the divide between scientific and cultural studies as artificial.

The first three volumes published by Roes can be regarded as a loose trilogy, connected by their common theme of 'fathers and sons'. *Jizchak: Versuch über das Sohnesopfer* (1992) is based on the above-mentioned doctoral research. The volume is a genre-defying combination of art criticism (Caravaggio's *Sacrifice of Isaac* is the main focus), travel (an account of a journey in Israel) and anthropology. His second volume, *Cham: Ein Symposion* (1993), is a play which similarly engages with a biblical son perceived to have been wronged by his father. The play revolves around the curse put on Cham by his father Noah. The father, drunk on wine and lying nude in his tent, is observed by the son. His ambiguous transgression is to have seen his father's nudity: 'Nichts verzeihen patriarchen weniger als blozsgestellt zu werden' (*C*, p. 79). The third volume in the trilogy, and Roes's first novel, is *Lleu Llaw Gyffes* (1994). It takes

3 *Krieg und Tanz* (Berlin: Matthes & Seitz, 2007), p. 127. See the Bibliography for the title abbreviations of Roes's works henceforth used in the text.

a new departure by offering an example (taken from the Welsh mythology of *The Mabinogion*) of a son who suffers at the hands of his mother. Arianrhod inflicts curse after curse upon her son, but here the father-figure (Gwydion is actually the uncle) offers care and guidance and stands in direct contrast to the fathers in the previous two works. The 'trilogy of the sons' will be discussed again in more detail in the chapter on *Weg nach Timimoun*, a novel in which Roes deals with the theme of injustice against Algerian sons.

The first chapter of this book, on *Leeres Viertel. Rub' al-Khali* (1996), is the longest, reflecting the novel's importance within Roes's *oeuvre*. The novel brought Roes to the attention of Germany's reading public, winning him the prestigious 'Bremer Literaturpreis' in 1997; it remains the only work by Roes to attract extensive critical interest from the academy. *Leeres Viertel* is composed of two parallel diaries by travellers to Yemen, one set at the beginning of the nineteenth century and the other at the end of the twentieth. Both narrators are anthropologists interested in traditional Arab games. As they travel the Arab Peninsula, they experience the alienating foreignness of the culture and strive to engage meaningfully with the people. Long before the attention of the West turned once again towards the Islamic world in the wake of the 9/11 terrorist attacks,[4] Roes is depicting an attempt to build bridges between the Eastern and Western cultural spheres. Roes published two related works resulting from his year-long stay in Yemen: *Madschnun al-Malik: Der Narr des Königs* (1997) and *Durus Arabij/Arabische Lektionen* (1997). The former is another play based on an ancient Yemeni myth about a royal fool and the latter is his first volume of poetry that evokes the encounter with Arab culture, demonstrating Roes's utilization of a range of artistic forms even as he engages with the same intercultural themes and material.

The cluster of publications that followed has as its inspiration journeys to the USA which Roes undertook in the late 1990s. The three 'American' novels are *Der Coup der Berdache* (1999), *Haut des Südens* (2000) and *David Kanchelli* (2001). *Der Coup der Berdache* is both crime thriller and an ethnological document. Traditional expectations of a detective novel are undermined, however, and the novel's central concern is the deconstruction of binary gender models. Gender, in its traditional form, is revealed to be an inflexible cultural construct. The American Indian berdache (third-gender figures who fulfil multiple gender roles, also known as 'two-spirit people') of the title, although common to traditional tribal life in North America, is portrayed as

4 This was, of course, not the first time that Western attention turned towards the Middle East. Western pilgrims have travelled to and written about the Islamic world since before the Crusades. Cf. Nina Berman, *German Literature on the Middle East: Discourses and Practices, 1000–1989* (Ann Arbor: University of Michigan Press, 2011), pp. 24–32.

an example of 'progressive' gender counter-identity. The novel is a powerful example of the way Roes's fiction is frequently informed by and constructed around theoretical concepts, in this case post-structuralist gender theories. He engages with theories of gender performativity such as Judith Butler's but interweaves these into a detective narrative that leaves the reader bedazzled.

In *Haut des Südens*, Roes continues along a parallel line, with an examination of race that reveals that concept, too, to be a cultural construct rather than a biological essence. This deconstruction depends upon literary references to classic American novels. The highly intertextual travelogue narrates a journey through the Deep South on the trail of America's literary giants (Melville, Twain and Faulkner). Roes's narrator compares classic literary depictions with the contemporary state of race relations and finds that very little has changed since Twain's time. Taking the anti-racist stance one important step further, the novel reveals race to exist only insofar as it is a cultural model which continues to hold power over the collective imagination.

The third 'American' novel, *David Kanchelli*, depicts a dystopian neo-colonial world of the not-too-distant future. Published shortly before the 9/11 terrorist attacks, it portrays a world divided into two camps: East and West, rich and poor, colonizers and colonized. The title character is modelled on Roger David Casement, to whom the novel is also dedicated; and the parallels between the historical and fictional figures are clear. Both uncovered (neo-) colonial exploitation; both supported revolts against the ruling powers at home; and both are 'discredited' by personal diaries which reveal (homo-) sexual promiscuity deemed unacceptable in the society of the time. Roes's novel is thus a political document that simultaneously attacks Western neo-imperial abuses and comments on continuing discrimination on the basis of sexuality.

In 2004, Roes published a novel that continues his engagement with Yemen. *Nah Inverness* is a fictionalized narration of Roes's experience filming *Someone is Sleeping in my Pain: Ein west-östlicher Macbeth* with Yemeni tribesmen as lay actors. The director in the novel is an American unaccustomed to Arab ways and traditions, not a German like Roes with extensive knowledge of the region. Numerous intercultural difficulties arise to frustrate the director's creative project and the novel is Roes's most pessimistic in terms of the possibilities for intercultural understanding. This reflects perhaps the wider political context of the post-9/11 period in which America and its allies were engaged in a war in Iraq and relations between the West and the Islamic world were strained. Roes persists in his attempts to forge an intercultural dialogue but his work reflects the increased difficulty of such exchange in light of increased tension between the West and the Arab world.

In 2006, Roes published his first novel on Algeria, *Weg nach Timimoun*. The novel borrows elements from Aeschylus's *Oresteia* but relocates the action to the modern-day Maghreb. The protagonist, Laid, is called to return to his hometown, Timimoun, to avenge his father by killing his mother. This intertextual construct is analysed in detail in the third chapter of the book. Following on from the appropriation of Greek mythology in *Weg nach Timimoun*, *Ich weiß nicht mehr die Nacht* (2008) is a contemporary retelling of the Phaedra myth set in Bocholt, the provincial German city in which Roes grew up. Roes explains his adaptations of ancient myths as 'eine Reaktion auf eine Verzettelung der Welt, auf einen permanenten Informationsüberfluss. Durch die Mythen möchte ich die Konzentration auf die zentralen Dinge lenken'.[5] At a time in which words, sounds and images are circulated in excessive abundance, Roes attempts to rise above a postmodernist concern with triviality. In this respect, mythology functions in his work as archetypal maps that have retained their power to illuminate aspects of contemporary life.

In 2010 Roes published *Geschichte der Freundschaft*, another highly intertextual novel that engages with the lives of the young men of Algeria. A German traveller befriends an Algerian student and they return to Berlin where they live together. The intercultural encounter is here shown to cross borders, occurring not only abroad but now also at home. The references to cultural and philosophical works on friendship (Montaigne, Nietzsche, Foucault and many others) are intertextual keys to understanding the complex intercultural friendship between the two characters. Roes advances an innovative representation of male sexuality, rejecting 'mainstream' gay identity and preferring instead a more fluid concept of friendship that includes sensual and sexual elements.

Responding perhaps to China's emergence as a global economic powerhouse, Roes turns his attention in *Die Fünf Farben Schwarz* (2009) to the Far East. The novel's protagonist is Viktor Holz, an academic who leaves Leipzig for Nanjing to take up a guest professorship at the university there. He abandons himself to the alienating forces of Chinese culture, letting go of the assumed certainties of his own culture that he had brought with him. As in many of his other novels, Roes combines here a focus on interculturality with a highly intertextual approach. Interspersed throughout the novel is a collection of meditations on the topic of death that refer to thinkers such as Derrida, Spinoza and Montaigne. At the end of the novel, Holz faces his own

5 Andreas Resch, 'Sisyphosarbeit am Mythos', *taz*, 12 January 2010, www.taz.de/1/archiv/digitaz/artikel/?ressort=ku&dig=2010%2F01%2F12%2Fa0157&cHash=13a03790379bcd0dfa13e30908c5a59a [accessed 25 February 2013].

death at the hands of a depraved gang wielding chainsaws. Whether this is real or a product of the protagonist's hallucinating mind remains unclear, suggesting a typical Western fear of the Chinese Other and a breakdown in the face of overwhelming Otherness.

Die Laute (2012) sees Roes returning to his major theme of intercultural encounters with a story that bears some similarities to *Geschichte der Freundschaft*. The novel is told in multiple strands, each telling the story of Asis, a Yemeni man, at different stages of his life. *Die Laute* and the three novels that precede it all feature Arab or Chinese migrants in Europe. This indicates a recent change in Roes's writing from being predominantly concerned with Western travellers in far-away locations to a growing engagement with migration in the opposite direction. Reflecting the increasing permeability of borders in a globalized world, Roes's work acknowledges and thematizes the presence of the migrant in Europe, a presence which is often ignored or demonized.

Considering the breadth of Roes's literary interests and the intellectually demanding nature of his books, it is surprising that his profile in Germany remains relatively low. After the success of *Leeres Viertel*, he appears to have attracted progressively less critical attention, although perhaps the nomination of *Die Laute* for the 'Deutscher Buchpreis' of 2012 was a sign that this was changing.[6] As a prolific author who engages with intellectual themes and ideas even as he is composing compelling narratives, Roes arguably deserves more renown. He is regarded mainly as a writer concerned with the theme of interculturality and is often grouped with writers such as Hubert Fichte and Hans Christoph Buch, whose work is also intercultural and anthropological in nature.[7] However, the originality of Roes's writing extends more broadly and lies in his incorporation of complex theories from disparate fields into absorbing narratives. He provides innovative representations of gender, race, sexuality, and of the dynamics of intercultural encounters throughout his work.

Michael Roes is a noteworthy figure in the context of the contemporary literary scene. As one critic put it, there is hardly another contemporary

6 As is so often the case, the prize was awarded to a novel that engages with post-War German history. Ursula Krechel's *Landgericht* took the prize of €25,000 for a story about a German Jew returning from exile in Cuba after the end of the Second World War.

7 Cf. Christoph Schmitt-Maaß, 'Erbrechen oder Einverleiben? Zwischen eigenmotivierter Fremdforschung und Gefährdung des Subjekts: Ethnographie im Spannungsfeld von Wissenschaft, Poesie und Autobiographie', *Monatshefte*, 100 (2008), 191–212; and *Das gefährdete Subjekt: Selbst- und Fremdforschung in gegenwärtiger Ethnopoesie* (Heidelberg: Synchron, 2011); Alexander Honold, 'Der ethnographische Roman am Ende des 20. Jahrhunderts: Fichte und Roes', in *Räume der literarischen Postmoderne: Gender, Performativität, Globalisierung*, ed. by Paul Michael Lützeler (Tübingen: Stauffenberg, 2000), pp. 71–95.

German author who uses the novel 'so intensiv als Gattung unbeschränkter Möglichkeiten'.[8] His work differs from that of the new generation of 'neue Lesbarkeit' writers, who display a 'Lust am Erzählen' and 'keinerlei Ambitionen, als Gewissen der Nation in Erscheinung zu treten oder gar in die politische Arena zu steigen'.[9] Whereas this generation has moved away from a tradition of writing that was regarded as 'heavy, overly complex and staid',[10] Roes's works are intellectually demanding and not always easily readable. That has been perceived at times as a weakness, with some reviewers arguing that the academic in Roes is pulling the carpet from under the novelist's feet.[11] This study, however, argues that Roes's creative application of his scholarly interests is what distinguishes him as a writer and represents his original contribution to contemporary German literature. The four novels examined in this study are far more than common travel books. Roes exploits the freedom offered by the fictional novel form to explore areas of interest that range from mythology to philosophy, from linguistics to gender studies. The novels function as windows onto foreign cultures, but they also provide a framework within which the reader can come to understand his or her own culture in a new way. They are works of literature that challenge the reader to keep an open mind, invite a revision of firmly-held beliefs, and demand intellectual engagement not only with what is foreign, but also with important matters closer to home.

While *Leeres Viertel* has been comprehensively discussed in academic works, his remaining novels remain little discussed. This study begins the work of correcting this imbalance by expanding the focus to include Roes's more recent novels and aspires to serve as a catalyst for further studies on various works by this author. Studies on *Leeres Viertel* include examinations of the novel as literary anthropology,[12] of intertextuality,[13] representations of

8 Karsten Herrmann, 'Ein (Werk-) Porträt des Michael Roes', http://culturmag.de/rubriken/buecher/michael-roes-im-portrat/14846 [accessed 9 June 2014].

9 Volker Hage, 'Die Enkeln kommen', *Der Spiegel*, 11 October 1999, www.spiegel.de/spiegel/print/d-14906942.html [accessed 26 February 2013].

10 Beth Linklater, 'Germany as background: global concerns in recent women's writing in German', in *German Literature in the Age of Globalisation*, ed. by Stuart Taberner (Birmingham: University of Birmingham Press, 2004), pp. 67–88 (p. 69).

11 Steffen Richter, 'Das Grauen, das Grauen ... geht weiter', *Die Welt*, 15 December 2001, www.welt.de/print-welt/article493010/Das-Grauen-das-Grauen.html [accessed 25 February 2013].

12 Michaela Holdenried, 'Ketzerische Bemerkungen zu Michael Roes' ethnologischen Roman *Rub' al-Khali*', in *Ethno/Graphie: Reiseformen des Wissens*, ed. by Peter Braun and Manfred Weinberg (Tübingen: Gunter Narr, 2002), pp. 355–66; Honold, 'Der ethnographische Roman'; Klaus R. Scherpe, 'Europas "rettende Liebe"? Erfundene Ethnographie von Michael Roes', in *Auslassungen: Leerstellen als Movens der Kulturwissenschaft*, ed. by Natascha Adamowsky and Peter Matussek (Würzburg: Königshausen & Neumann, 2004), pp. 109–16; Schmitt-Maaß, *Das gefährdete Subjekt*, pp. 18–44.

13 Axel Dunker, '"Als wisse ich endlich Alles oder doch wenigstens mehr vom Oriente als die Orientalen selbst": Zu Michael Roes' *Rub al-Khali. Leeres Viertel. Invention über das Spiel*',

masculinity,[14] postmodern Orientalism,[15] and constructions of the self.[16] Two academic articles have been published on *Haut des Südens*, each focusing on different aspects. Rytz examines the metaphor of the skin in the novel,[17] while Simons's study of the intertextuality of German books on America includes an analysis of *Haut des Südens*.[18] To the best of my knowledge, no academic work has been published on *Weg nach Timimoun*, although it was, like *Leeres Viertel* and *Haut des Südens*, reviewed widely in the press. *Geschichte der Freundschaft* was reviewed by only one major newspaper and is yet to be the subject of academic study.

Travel Literature: Fact, Fiction, and Everything In-Between

The four works analysed in this study are novels and are therefore to be read as fiction. Calling them novels, however, is a little perfunctory. Roes's fictional accounts of journeys are clearly fashioned from his personal experience. As von Martels observes: '[...] often it is subject to discussion whether we may still speak of travel writing, for instance, where the distinction between travel writing and fiction becomes small, and the novel comes into being'.[19] Roes turns travel fact into travel fiction. In doing so he creates an enigmatic space in which he is free to exploit the advantages of both the fictional novel and the non-fiction travel account.

The boundary between fact and fiction is notoriously porous in the broad field of travel literature. This study follows Jan Borm and defines travel literature 'as an overall thematic category (and not as a genre) that includes

in *Ins Fremde Schreiben: Gegenwartsliteratur auf den Spuren historischer und fantastischer Entdeckungsreisen*, ed. by Christof Hamann and Alexander Honold (Göttingen: Wallstein, 2009), pp. 203–25; Christoph Schmitt-Maaß, '"mäandernd, ornamentalisch, ohne progression?": Intertexualität in Michael Roes' Freibeutertext *Leeres Viertel* (1996)', *Revista de Philología Alemana*, 15 (2007), 95–109.

14 Robert Tobin, 'Postmoderne Männlichkeit: Michael Roes und Matthias Politycki', *Zeitschrift für Germanistik*, 12 (2002), 324–33.

15 Todd Kontje, *German Orientalisms* (Ann Arbor: University of Michigan Press, 2004), pp. 231–37.

16 Schmitt-Maaß, *Das gefährdete Subjekt*, pp. 219–27.

17 Juliane Rytz, 'Die Metaphorik der Haut in Michael Roes' *Haut des Südens*', in *Haut – Zwischen Innen und Außen: Organ – Fläche – Diskurs*, ed. by Villigster Werkstatt Interdisziplinarität (Berlin; Münster: Lit, 2009), pp. 57–67.

18 Oliver Simons, '"Amerika gibt es nicht": On the Semiotics of Literary America in the Twentieth Century', *German Quarterly*, 82 (2009), 196–211 (pp. 206–08).

19 Cf. Zweder von Martels, 'Introduction', in *Travel Fact and Travel Fiction: Studies on Fiction, Literary Tradition, Scholarly Discovery and Observation in Travel Writing*, ed. by Zweder von Martels (Leiden: Brill, 1994), pp. xi–xviii (p. xi).

works of non-fiction and fiction'.[20] This can include fiction that features travel, factual travel accounts or travelogues, travel guides such as the *Lonely Planet* or *Baedeker* series, medieval pilgrimage narratives, photographic books, letters from abroad, maps and even documents of colonial administration. As Jonathan Raban notes, this broad field:

> is a notoriously raffish open house where very different genres are likely to end up in the same bed. It accommodates the private diary, the essay, the short story, the prose poem, the rough note and polished table talk with indiscriminate hospitality.[21]

Within this 'open house', those works by Roes analysed in this book can be loosely termed travel fiction – that is, fictional writing, usually in the form of a novel, that is concerned to a significant extent with travel and intercultural encounters.

However, it is not travel fiction as described above that first comes to mind when one thinks of travel literature, but the travelogue or *Reisebericht*. Defined humbly by Robyn Davidson as 'a non-fiction work in which the author goes from point a to point b and tells us something about it',[22] the travelogue is a genre ruled by a 'non-fiction dominant'.[23] Readers approach a travelogue expecting true stories about a journey, information about an unfamiliar culture, and discoveries of remote (but real) countries that they would otherwise never encounter. However, since travelogues contain an 'inevitable element of fiction',[24] it is more realistic to read modern travelogues as 'fictions of factual representations'.[25] The travel writer must select which events to narrate, thereby imposing a sense of cohesion upon the narrative that was not a feature of the journey. Such omissions are complemented by additions, for example when authors reconstruct conversations that cannot have been recorded as they were taking place.[26] Other fictionalizing features employed by travelogue writers, even when writing about real events, include 'free indirect style,

20 Jan Borm, 'Defining Travel: On the Travel Book, Travel Writing and Terminology', in *Perspectives on Travel Writing*, ed. by Glenn Hooper and Tim Youngs (Aldershot: Ashgate, 2004), pp. 13–26 (p. 19).

21 Jonathan Raban, *For Love & Money: Writing – Reading – Travelling 1968–1987* (London: Picador in association with Collins Harvill, 1988), p. 253.

22 Robyn Davidson, 'Introduction', in *The Picador Book of Journeys*, ed. by Robyn Davidson (London: Picador, 2001), pp. 1–7 (p. 3).

23 Borm, 'Defining Travel', p. 17.

24 Borm, 'Defining Travel', p. 15.

25 Patrick Holland and Graham Huggan, *Tourists with Typewriters: Critical Reflections on Contemporary Travel Writing* (Ann Arbor: University of Michigan Press, 2000), p. 10. Holland and Huggan draw here on Hayden White's term.

26 Borm, 'Defining Travel', p. 15.

scenic construction, present-tense narration, prolepsis, iterative symbolism, etc.'.[27] Moreover, as the genre has evolved over the centuries it has become increasingly acceptable, or even desirable, for the travel writer to narrate the journey in a subjective manner. Enlightenment travellers prioritized 'fact-finding and empirical enquiry into the wider world, [...] fashion[ing] themselves on the page principally as observers, and as "Cartesian" selves or subjectivities, detached from the scenes that they survey'.[28] However, after the publication of Laurence Sterne's fictional *A Sentimental Journey* (1768) it became common for travellers to include descriptions of subjective reactions to foreign places, even in non-fiction travelogues.

Even taking into account the expectations a modern readership has concerning the stylistic features and subjective content of a travelogue, the genre is infamous for manipulations, fabrications and outright deceptions. As Peter J. Brenner writes:

> Reisende genießen seit je einen schlechten Ruf. Nicht nur Reisende lügen, aber ihr Verhältnis zur Wahrheit wurde stets im besonderen Maße angezweifelt. Der Reisende als Lügner und der Reisebericht als eine Gattung, deren Wahrheitsgehalt wenig Vertrauen verdient, gehören zu den Topoi, welche die Reiseliteratur seit ihren antiken Anfängen begleitet haben.[29]

Among the numerous tellers of tall tales in the ancient world, Antiphanes of Berga has been called 'de[n] Inbegriff des lügenden Reisenden'.[30] He reported northern lands where the air was so cold that speech would freeze in the speaker's mouth. His name became synonymous with fabrication and fabulation: 'Die Bergäische Geschichte [...] wurde zum terminus technicus für eine erlogene Reisegeschichte'.[31] However, travellers in the pre-modern era faced a perplexing problem even when remaining strictly within the boundaries of truth. They were confronted with a predicament as they attempt to describe their journeys, since 'these [foreign] people and places may be so far beyond the ken of the audience, and may appear so strange or exotic, that they beggar belief back home'.[32] Even honest and factual accounts contained reports of such unusual peoples and practices that the untravelled masses

27 David Lodge, *The Practice of Writing* (London: Penguin, 1997), p. 8.

28 Thompson, *Travel Writing*, p. 117.

29 Peter J. Brenner, 'Die Erfahrung der Fremde: Zur Entwicklung einer Wahrnehmungsform in der Geschichte des Reiseberichts', in *Der Reisebericht: Die Entwicklung einer Gattung in der deutschen Literatur*, ed. by Peter J. Brenner (Frankfurt am Main: Suhrkamp, 1989), pp. 14–49 (p. 14).

30 Christophe Bourquin, *Schreiben über Reisen: zur ars itineraria von Urs Widmer im Kontext der europäischen Reiseliteratur* (Würzburg: Königshausen & Neumann, 2006), p. 71.

31 Bourquin, *Schreiben über Reisen*, p. 71.

32 Thompson, *Travel Writing*, pp. 65–66.

found it impossible to believe them, thus undeservedly damaging further the traveller's already tarnished reputation.

Following in the footsteps of classical accounts of fabulous lands and medieval reports of mythical beasts, the reputation of the modern travel writer remains questionable. Bruce Chatwin's two remarkable and innovative works of travel literature, *In Patagonia* (1977) and *The Songlines* (1987), have both attracted criticism due, in part, to their 'hybrid form' of fact and fiction.[33] Patagonian residents featured in Chatwin's book claimed that conversations recounted by the author were embellished or did not take place.[34] An Australian art dealer 'who saw herself portrayed negatively' in *The Songlines* considered taking legal action against the author.[35] In Chatwin's defence, he did fight a long and ultimately futile battle with his publisher to have the latter title categorized under the label of fiction rather than travel writing. One of Chatwin's acquaintances says of him that he 'was quite genuinely incapable of distinguishing fact from fiction. It wasn't a pretence'.[36] For a purportedly lying traveller, he was open about the liberties he took in adapting literary forms to suit his needs. Discussing his approach to writing about travel he famously told Paul Theroux: 'You have to embroider [...]. I don't believe in coming clean'.[37]

Robert Gernhardt playfully engages with the motif of the 'lying traveller' in his *Die Madagaskar-Reise: Ein Bericht* (1980). The straightforward title suggests a travelogue like many others. So, too, does the opening line of the book: 'Nie werde ich jenen hellen Junimorgen vergessen, an dem ich das erste Mal der Küste Madagaskars ansichtig wurde'.[38] In addition to the text, the book contains numerous drawings made by the author of sights encountered on his journey. As the reader begins to suspect from the very first page, however, the journey never took place. Gernhardt reveals in an afterword (as if the reader had not long suspected that something were amiss) that the book is somewhat of a hoax. He has never seen the coast of Madagascar other than in pictures,

33 Alison Russell, *Crossing Boundaries: Postmodern Travel Literature* (New York: Palgrave, 2000), p. 86.

34 Nicholas Shakespeare, *Bruce Chatwin* (London: Vintage, 2000), p. 316.

35 Russell, *Crossing Boundaries*, p. 87.

36 Shakespeare, *Bruce Chatwin*, p. 210.

37 Quoted in Casey Blanton, *Travel Writing: the Self and the World* (New York: Routledge, 2002), p. 103. Paul Theroux gives an account of his conversation with Bruce Chatwin in this interview with George Plimpton at The Poetry Centre in New York in 1989: 92Y/*The Paris Review* Interview Series: Paul Theroux, The Poetry Center, New York, 18 December 1989, www.theparisreview.org/audio/6017/92y-emthe-paris-review-em-interview-series-paul-theroux-paul-theroux [accessed 27 August 2014].

38 Robert Gernhardt, *Die Madagaskar-Reise: Ein Bericht* (Frankfurt am Main: Zweitausendeins, 1980), p. 8.

travelogues and in his mind's eye. The bizarre drawings were made at home during moments of 'gebremste[r] Verstand'.[39] His confession, although coming late in the text, lifts him above the charge of being a conventional travel liar and his work becomes a commentary on the genre of travel writing. According to Ulla Biernat, Gernhardt's 'groteske Vermischung' of truth and fantasy:

> zielt in *Die Madagaskar-Reise* nicht nur auf den Topos vom *travel liar* und die Frage nach der Authentizität eines jeden Reiseberichts. Sie verdeutlicht die Selektivität und Willkür jeder Fremdwahrnehmung sowie die Unangemessenheit der begrifflichen Konzepte, die ein Reisender an die Fremde heranträgt.[40]

For Gernhardt, the preconceptions about tourist destinations carried in the minds of travellers inevitably lead to textual and photographic representations that fail to recognize the truth about the country visited. As a result, most literary or photographic portrayals of those foreign countries can automatically be regarded as travel fictions. Gernhardt claims that his approach arrives at a truth deeper than the superficial images and impressions taken home by thousands of tourists: '[V]erglichen mit dem, was heutige Reisende normalerweise an Bildern heimbringen, sind meine Zeichnungen wenigstens ehrlich, ja wahrheitsgetreu. Der photographierende Tourist wird immer lügen, und wenn er sich auf den Kopf stellt'.[41] Travel writers of the 1980s were attempting to utilize new ways of representing encounters with the foreign. As the examples of Chatwin and Gernhardt show, fictional elements become an integral part of the writer's arsenal:

> In der Fiktion kann die bekannte Fremde wieder fremd gemacht werden – nicht in platten quasi-realistischen, einem essentialistischen Wirklichkeitsbegriff verhafteten Abbildungen wie standardisierten Touristenfotos; sondern in verfremdenden Bildern und Textstrategien, die zwar das 'wirkliche' Madagaskar nicht darstellen, aber die Alteritätserfahrung *sui generis* einfangen.[42]

39 Gernhardt, *Die Madagaskar-Reise*, p. 221.

40 Ulla Biernat, *"Ich bin nicht der erste Fremde hier": Zur deutschsprachigen Reiseliteratur nach 1945* (Würzburg: Königshausen & Neumann, 2004), p. 155.

41 Gernhardt, *Die Madagaskar-Reise*, pp. 220–21. Walter Eder also regards the invention of photography as having had a detrimental effect on authentic engagement with other cultures: 'Das [fremde] Land wurde zunehmend mit diesen aus dem räumlichen Zusammenhang gerissenen Bildern identifiziert. [...] [und es] entstand bei den Reisenden der Eindruck, es genüge, diesen Standardsatz von abgebildeten Objekten zu besuchen, um sich dem Land zu nähern, ja vielleicht gar es kennengelernt zu haben' (Walter Eder, 'Zu Hause in der Fremde?: Der Verlust der Raumerfahrung als Verlust des Erfahrungsraums beim Reisen', in *Das Fremde: Erfahrungsmöglichkeiten zwischen Faszination und Bedrohung*, ed. by Ortfried Schäffter (Opladen: Westdeutscher Verlag, 1991), pp. 158–72 (p. 164)).

42 Biernat, *"Ich bin nicht der erste Fremde hier"*, pp. 156–57.

In the postmodern era the articulation of truth becomes a relative matter. The confidence of earlier explorers that the truth about a foreign way of life can be contained in reports, observations and statistics has long disappeared. In its stead come experimentation with form and a blending of the factual and the fictional that is at times playful, at other times gravely earnest.

If the supposedly factual genre of the travelogue has at times failed to meet some readers' expectations of truthfulness, how can readers approach a fictional novel that recounts journeys to countries far afield? In her study of contemporary Anglophone travel writing, Debbie Lisle describes a hierarchy in which the travelogue is 'understood as *inferior* to the novel [...]. Travelogues will never achieve the status of the novel because the travel writer's imagination is always handcuffed to the narration of brute facts'.[43] The travelogue, although always popular with the reading public, has been and remains a much-maligned genre in certain circles. Even in the age of high imperialism the travelogue was disparaged, regarded by Gustav Flaubert as a 'low form of literature', on the same level as 'news items'.[44] For some it is a mode of writing that has inherited the loaded legacy of colonialism and it represents 'a refuge for complacent, even nostalgically retrograde, middle-class values'.[45] Lisle's argument that fictional novels about travel may be more truthful than allegedly non-fiction travelogues is not dissimilar to Robert Gernhardt's: 'To write fiction is to finally disown the ball and chain of fact and luxuriate in a superior genre where facts and truths can be rendered according to the writer's imagination'.[46] With the travelogue deemed a dubious genre, fiction featuring a travelling protagonist offers the potentially fruitful combination of fiction's freedom grounded in the experience of real-life encounters with other cultures. As long as the work makes clear its fictional status, expectations of factuality are naturally looser and it is taken for granted that the novelist is creating a fictional world, a figment of the imagination.

Notwithstanding Debbie Lisle's enthusiasm for the novel and her suspicion of the travelogue, a certain caution is advisable when dealing with narrations of journeys presented as fiction. It can well be argued that the world of

43 Debbie Lisle, *The Global Politics of Contemporary Travel Writing* (Cambridge: Cambridge University Press, 2006), p. 30.

44 Quoted in Davidson, *The Picador Book of Journeys*, p. 4. Davidson does not provide a source for the quotation, which seems to come from *Flaubert in Egypt*, trans., ed. & introd. by Francis Steegmuller (Harmondsworth: Penguin, 1996; first published: Chicago: Academy Chicago Publishers, 1979), p. 6. According to Steegmuller, the quotation actually stems from a friend of Flaubert, Maxim Du Campe, but no source is given.

45 Holland and Huggan, 'Preface', *Tourists with Typewriters*, pp. vii–xiv (p. viii).

46 Lisle, *The Global Politics of Contemporary Travel Writing*, p. 49.

fiction-publishing is populated with just as many 'second-rate talents'[47] as that of factual travel writing. Employing the genre of fiction is no panacea for the issues surrounding the representation of travel and the foreign cultures thus encountered. Lisle's charge that 'travel writers spend much of their time crossing cultural and national borders [but] fail to address the intricate and ambiguous power relations at work in these sites'[48] can likewise be levelled at writers of fiction. There lies within fiction the potential for reproducing national stereotypes just as much as in the allegedly factual travelogue. Furthermore, fictional works are often not engaged with the people and cultures of the country in which they are set. Nina Berman's study of German literature on the Middle East shows how fiction's engagement with that region is most often self-absorbed and 'directly motivated by a quest to understand German history'.[49] More troubling still is the 'tendency [of German writers] to portray the Middle East as a space of abjection'.[50] Berman cites Wolfgang Hildesheimer's *Masante* (1973) and Ingeborg Bachmann's *Der Fall Franza* (1978) as examples of novels that employ the Middle East as an abstract setting for the psychological turmoil of their protagonists, with Hildesheimer's novel featuring 'not a single Middle Eastern protagonist'.[51] This is a similar criticism to that made by Chinua Achebe of Joseph Conrad's *Heart of Darkness* (1901): 'Africa [is used] as setting and backdrop which eliminates the African as human factor [...] reducing Africa to the role of props for the break-up of one petty European mind'.[52] The danger in such cases is that Africa and the Middle East become an exoticized stage upon which the European protagonists deal with their own preoccupations.

The travelogue and the travel novel share a long history.[53] The constants between travel fact and travel fiction are such that it will prove useful to borrow from theories and criticism on the travelogue in this study of travel fiction. However, despite the similarities that they share, it is productive to attempt a definition of the travel novel, as distinct from its 'factual' cousin. A vast

47 Paul Fussell, *Abroad: British Literary Travelling Between the Wars* (Oxford: Oxford University Press, 1980), p. 212.

48 Lisle, *The Global Politics of Contemporary Travel Writing*, p. 9.

49 Berman, *German Literature on the Middle East*, p. 216.

50 Berman, *German Literature on the Middle East*, p. 217.

51 Berman, *German Literature on the Middle East*, p. 217.

52 Chinua Achebe, *Hopes and Impediments: Selected Essays* (New York: Doubleday, 1989), p. 12.

53 Percy G. Adams claims that 'prose fiction and the travel account have evolved together, are heavily indebted to each other, and are often similar in both content and technique'. Cf. Percy G. Adams, *Travel Literature and the Evolution of the Novel* (Lexington: University Press of Kentucky, 1983), p. 279; Reinhardt Heinritz, '"Fremde Wildnis": Über den neuen deutschsprachigen Reiseroman', *Jahrbuch Deutsch als Fremdsprache*, 17 (1991), pp. 72–93 (p. 73).

number, if not all, novels contain an element of travel, whether it be an epic train journey or a much shorter taxi ride through a city. For the purposes of this study a more limited definition of the travel novel is necessary. Only texts which are structured to a considerable extent around a protagonist's journey will be considered travel fiction. To this may be added the characteristic that many travel novels thematize the intercultural encounters that occur during the journey, although, as Nina Berman has shown, this is not always the case.

A brief glance at recent travel fiction in German reveals a genre that is popular with both writers and the reading public. Some examples from post-1945 German fiction include Max Frisch's *Homo Faber* (1957), Uwe Timm's *Morenga* (1978), Sten Nadolny's *Die Entdeckung der Langsamkeit* (1983) and Ilija Trojanow's *Der Weltensammler* (2006). As the three most recent titles of the four attest, the travel narrative is often also a historical novel – a trend that is reflected in Roes's *Leeres Viertel* (1996). Further examples are Thomas Stangl's *Der einzige Ort* (2004) and Daniel Kehlmann's *Die Vermessung der Welt* (2005). A number of such historical novels engage with European (and often specifically German) colonial activities in Africa, for example Alex Capus's *Eine Frage der Zeit* (2007).[54] A further sub-category can be detected in the proliferation of novels that feature a contemporary narrator who follows in the footsteps of a historical forebear, a category to which *Leeres Viertel* again belongs. By combining two narrative strands and contrasting two temporal planes the narratives gain a depth that allows the author to engage with past travellers and their textualized voyages.[55] Examples include Christoph Ransmayr's *Das Schrecken des Eises und der Finsternis* (1984), Raoul Schrott's *Finis Terrae* (1995), Alex Capus's *Munzinger Pascha* (1997), Felicitas Hoppe's *Pigafetta* (1999), and Markus Werner's *Der ägyptische Heinrich* (1999). In each of these cases the forebear is a real historical figure from the Golden Age of European exploration and high imperialism. How truthful the story of the contemporary traveller following in his footsteps might be, is always less clear and it becomes the reader's task to attempt to distinguish fact from fiction.

Another important development in the field of German travel fiction since the 1970s is the post-colonial novel. With roots in the *Studentenbewegung* of 1967 to 1968 and in the anti-Vietnam War protests of the same period, these novels are inevitably driven by a desire to question and change political relations between the First and Third Worlds. The focus of some

54 Cf. Dirk Göttsche, 'Der neue historische Afrika-Roman: Kolonialismus aus postkolonialer Sicht', *German Life and Letters*, 56 (2003), 261–80; and 'Hans Christoph Buch's *Sansibar Blues* and the Fascination of Cross-cultural Experience in Contemporary German Historical Novels about Colonialism', *German Life and Letters*, 65 (2012), 127–46.

55 The critical volume *Ins Fremde schreiben*, ed. by Christoph Hamann and Alexander Honold, gives an excellent overview of this category of fictional works.

novels, most notably Uwe Timm's *Morenga*, is on expanding the process of *Vergangenheitsbewältigung* about complicity in Nazi crimes to include the national guilt stemming from Germany's colonial activities in Africa. In comparison to France and Great Britain, Germany's empire was relatively small, late, and of short duration. It is perhaps no surprise that the post-colonial German novel includes more examples of works that engage with present-day relations between the developed and the developing world. Paul Michael Lützeler, one of the foremost critics in the field, includes Roes's *Leeres Viertel* in a list of key texts of the genre, alongside names such as Hans Christoph Buch, Hubert Fichte and Urs Widmer. Lützeler summarizes the attitude of the post-colonial traveller, saying:

> Die Autorinnen und Autoren gestehen Unsicherheiten, Irritationen, mögliche Irrtümer und die Begrenztheit ihrer Erfahrung ein. Sie wissen, daß ein eurozentrischer Blickwinkel den Zugang zu den Problemen der Dritten Welt erschwert, sind sich aber gleichzeitig darüber im klaren, daß sie bei ihren Reisen europäische Denk- und Verhaltensweisen nur revidieren, nie aber ganz aufgeben können bzw. wollen.[56]

He then outlines the nature of the inter-cultural encounter in such works:

> Sie konturieren Schwierigkeiten der Verständigung und bemühen sich, fremde Perspektiven, die aus anderen Religionen, Traditionen und Interessen resultieren, zu begreifen. Damit befinden sie sich in jenem diskursiven 'dritten Raum', in dem nach Homi Bhabha Vertreter anderer Kulturen mit Repräsentanten des Westens in einen Dialog treten, in dem es möglich wird, homogene Identitätsmodelle durch solche kultureller Hybridität zu ersetzen. Beim Dialog der Kulturen soll es nicht um eine dialektische Auflösung der Widersprüche in einer Synthese gehen, sondern um ein Verständnis, das Differenz profiliert, anerkennt und toleriert.[57]

Post-colonial writers attempt to re-imagine and restructure the relationship between the former colonial powers and their erstwhile subjects. They challenge the assumption of Western cultural and intellectual supremacy and question the colonial practices and discourses of the past that have continued into the present. Concurrent with this abandonment of privilege, the voice of the oppressed is sought out and the binary opposites of ruler-ruled are called into question. At its most basic, post-colonialism:

> means realizing that when western people look at the non-western world what they see is often more a mirror image of themselves and their own assumptions

56 Paul Michael Lützeler, *Postmoderne und postkoloniale deutschsprachige Literatur: Diskurs – Analyse – Kritik* (Bielefeld: Aisthesis, 2005), p. 100.

57 Lützeler, *Postmoderne und postkoloniale deutschsprachige Literatur*, p. 100.

> than the reality of what is really there, or of how people outside the west actually feel and perceive themselves.[58]

Hand-in-hand with such realizations comes a renegotiation of the Western traveller's position – he or she is, all of a sudden, vulnerable. This post-colonial context will be helpful when considering Roes's work.

The level of factuality, truthfulness and accuracy in different works of travel fiction ranges widely, with some writers (with Michael Roes among them) drawing extensively from personal experience of travel in their novels. At the other end of the spectrum, authors write about countries that they have never visited, most famously Karl May. In fact, Roes regards May as a ludicrous example of an author writing about places he has never seen, saying that in such cases it has more to do with 'Projektionen [...] , also mit Fantasieorten und nicht mit realen Orten'.[59] Michael Roes spends a considerable amount of time in the countries he writes about before publishing. His experience of travelling and living in these countries anchors the fictional representation firmly in fact. Despite the licence to imagine and create that is conferred on an author of fiction, Roes's novels reflect his extensive knowledge of life in the foreign countries visited. In German, experience (*Erfahrung*) and travel (*fahren*) are etymologically linked, sharing the Indo-Germanic root *per* which is also to be seen in the word *Gefahr*.[60] Dietz Lange states: 'Die Grundbedeutung von "erfahren" ist "reisen um etwas zu erkunden". [...] zunächst ist wichtig, daß man durch "Fahren" "erfahren" wird'.[61] As reflected in the development of this group of German words, travelling means gaining experiences and encountering dangers. To narrate these experiences in fictional form can be regarded as writing against what Walter Benjamin called the fall in the value of experience. Benjamin wrote in the essay 'Der Erzähler':

> Es ist, als wenn ein Vermögen, das uns unveräußerlich schien, das Gesichertste unter den Sicheren, von uns genommen würde. Nämlich das Vermögen, Erfahrungen auszutauschen. Eine Ursache dieser Erscheinung liegt auf der Hand: die Erfahrung ist im Kurse gefallen. Und es sieht aus, als fiele sie weiter ins Bodenlose.[62]

58 Robert J. C. Young, *Postcolonialism: A Very Short Introduction* (Oxford: Oxford University Press, 2003), p. 2.

59 Jens Nommel and Michael Roes, 'Im Gespräch über die eigenen Grenzen', http://handlungsreisedialog.blogwerft.de/2007/12/13/michael-roes/ [accessed 4 November 2009].

60 Dietz Lange, *Erfahrung und die Glaubwürdigkeit des Glaubens* (Tübingen: Mohr Siebeck, 1984), p. 8.

61 Lange, *Erfahrung und die Glaubwürdigkeit des Glaubens*, p. 8.

62 Walter Benjamin, 'Der Erzähler', in *Gesammelte Schriften*, ed. by Rolf Tiedemann and Hermann Schweppenhäuser, 12 vols, II, pt. 2 (1977), pp. 438–65 (p. 439).

One way of resisting this decline is to travel, to gain experience of the world and thereby gather stories to pass on to an audience. Benjamin cites the saying: 'Wenn einer eine Reise tut, so kann er was erzählen'. Roes, for one, seems to have taken such advice to heart and has travelled widely, collecting stories and experiences that he relays in his fictional work. In a postmodern age increasingly characterized by 'simulation' and 'hyperreality', real experience is a rich mine from which a wealth of material for fictional adaptation can be extracted.

As part of his doctoral research on the topos of the *Sohnesopfer*, Roes spent periods of time in the Negev Desert in Israel. He was awarded his PhD by the Freie Universität Berlin in 1991, publishing the volume *Jizchak. Versuch über das Sohnesopfer* (1992) based on this research. He later spent a year conducting ethnological research in Yemen in preparation for the volume *Leeres Viertel*, which he also submitted as his *Habilitationsschrift*. *Nah Inverness* (2004) is a novel that draws on Roes's experience of directing a film adaptation of *Macbeth* in the same country. Numerous stays in Algeria resulted in the novel *Weg nach Timimoun* (2006) and the feature film *Timimoun* (2005); a further novel set in Algeria, *Geschichte der Freundschaft*, was published in 2010. Roes's literary travel works display a consistent interest in and engagement with contemporary issues in the regions in which they are set. Both *Leeres Viertel* and *Weg nach Timimoun* feature historically accurate portrayals of civil wars, in Yemen and Algeria respectively, as a political backdrop to the plots of the novels. *Geschichte der Freundschaft* has as its background the political protests that erupted in the Kabyle region of Algeria as the Berber population demanded legal status for its minority language. Roes lived in New York for six months before publishing *Der Coup der Berdache*, and undertook a journey along the Mississippi in preparation for writing *Haut des Südens*, in which the narrator visits locations associated with the greats of American literature. He spent three months in Nanjing carrying out research for the novel *Die Fünf Farben Schwarz*, declaring that to attempt to write about China without ever having been there would be ludicrous. This dedication to researching the locations and cultures that serve as a backdrop to his novels reveals a desire to be true to those cultures and to represent them as faithfully as possible to a German audience.

The resulting tension produced by the hybridization of fact and fiction, and the realistic representation of life in fiction, has at times been a matter of some confusion for literary critics working on Roes's *oeuvre*. In *Leeres Viertel*, for example, the narrator of the 1994 strand is kidnapped by a desert tribe, an episode that Klaus R. Scherpe takes as fact.[63] Another commentator on the novel

63 Scherpe, 'Europas "rettende Liebe"?', p. 113.

disagrees,[64] and regards the episode as a fictional element that distinguishes the protagonist from the author. Roes appears to deliberately obscure matters when he has his narrator ask: 'Und wenn wir, anstatt zu reisen, jene abenteuer wirklich nur erfänden? Wären sie unwahrer als die tatsächlich erlebten abenteuer?' (*LV*, p. 723). Whether the author really was kidnapped is perhaps less important than the realization that such confusion is perhaps an appropriate element in fictional travel narratives. By creating fictional accounts of real worlds, the travel fiction author is allowing the reader to travel in imagined worlds that are in many ways more real than we may at first imagine.

The four texts chosen as the main focus of this study – *Leeres Viertel*, *Haut des Südens*, *Weg nach Timimoun* and *Geschichte der Freundschaft* – all share a number of features. They all include journeys set outside Europe and, with the exception of *Haut des Südens*, these journeys take place in the Arab world. Roes is interested in travelling to countries that are culturally far-removed from his own. His journeys take him to the extreme desert landscapes of Yemen and Algeria, sparsely populated areas with vastly different cultures. Even the novels set in more populated areas attest to Roes's interest in people who occupy the edges of society – the unemployed youth of Algeria; the immigrant in Berlin; the disenchanted, discriminated African-Americans of the Deep South. This reflects the position and character of the narrator in Roes's works: he is almost always an outsider himself, both at home and in the places he visits.

The encounter with other cultures is the main theme of Roes's *oeuvre* and it is a theme that will be addressed more thoroughly in a separate section of this introduction. For now it suffices to state that the journey, and the intercultural encounter that ensues, constitutes a major structuring framework in each of these novels. Even the narrator of *Weg nach Timimoun*, a young Algerian man travelling through his own country, encounters elements of his own culture as unfamiliar. Roes, however, rarely uses the conventional circular structure in which the traveller sets off from home, travels the world, staying in various destinations, before returning home with a greater understanding of himself and the world. This pattern (A – B – A) is particularly visible in the genre of the travelogue and is regarded by some as a particularly colonial approach to writing:

> Colonial travel literature is structured by a circular itinerary, which begins and ends in the *métropole*, perceived as the centre and origin of all journeys. The outward journey emerges as necessarily southward; the privileges of travelling, watching and writing are restricted to the white European.[65]

64 Dunker, '"Als wisse ich endlich Alles"', p. 206.

65 Charles Forsdick, Feroza Basu and Siobhán Shilton, *New Approaches to Twentieth-Century Travel Literature in French: Genre, History, Theory* (New York: Peter Lang, 2006), p. 121.

Roes's works show a more ambiguous picture. *Leeres Viertel*, for example, is structured in a simple A – B pattern: there is no journey home. The protagonists' encounter with Yemeni culture (for the fates of both the anonymous 1994-narrator and Schnittke are left unexplained) will apparently be an indefinite one, with both characters willingly dissolving into their host culture and abandoning their Western identities. The journey featured in *Weg nach Timimoun* is structured in a diametrically opposite way. It is a journey back from an adopted city to the childhood home (B – A). *Haut des Südens* begins in St. Louis, Missouri and the reader never learns how the narrator has travelled there from Germany. This is the beginning of a journey along the Mississippi which leads to an enigmatic ending that suggests a dangerous crossing of the Atlantic will be attempted: (B – C – D?). Finally, *Geschichte der Freundschaft* features a plot that takes the narrator back and forth between Germany and Algeria (via Mali), in a B – C – A – B structure. Analysing structures in this manner reveals that Roes's journeys are formatted in a distinctive way; they reveal an interest in people and cultures that goes beyond that of the conventional travel writer. The author travels repeatedly to Algeria and to Yemen and this is reflected in his creative output. As a result of these repeated and often lengthy visits, his work displays a more nuanced understanding than that of many travelogues. Despite their label as fiction, Roes's works could be said to contain just as much 'truth' as explicitly non-fiction titles by other travel writers.

Intercultural Encounters

Michael Roes's theoretical statements regarding intercultural encounters are relatively uncomplicated; his conception of engagement with other cultures is practical and unpretentious. His alter-ego in *Leeres Viertel* writes: 'Die direkteste art, den anderen zu verstehen, ist, ihn als begehrenswert zu empfinden und ihm ein bewusztsein dieses wertes zu vermitteln' (*LV*, p. 800). Klaus Scherpe admires this directness, saying about the novel: 'Ein Text wie dieser, der frei ist vom interkulturellen Schmus einer "Hermeneutik des Fremden", von wohlfeiler Toleranz und suggestiver Globalisierungsrhetorik, sollte uns eben darum am liebsten sein.'[66] Despite this apparent simplicity, it will prove useful to consider some theoretical positions with regard to intercultural encounters, and to reflect on how these relate to Roes's ideas, before beginning with the analysis of the individual novels.

66 Scherpe, 'Europas "rettende Liebe"?', p. 115.

It can of course be claimed that there is no such thing as an 'intercultural encounter', the term being too ambiguous and indeterminate. In practice, such encounters are always specific events that occur when two people meet: 'Nicht kulturen begegnen einander, sondern gesichter, gerüche, stimmen' (*LV*, p. 800).[67] Roes's conception of such encounters is corporeal, as the discussion below regarding the importance of the body will reveal. Moreover, an individual can never claim to represent his or her culture in its entirety, since one's cultural group or nationality is only ever one aspect of a more complex identity. Other aspects that can be of equal or greater importance include gender, occupation, class, sexual orientation and interests. Equally, no culture is homogenous. Not all Germans are the same, neither are all Algerians. The differences between two people of the same nationality can be greater than the differences between two people from different nations who share a common interest or profession. To complicate matters further, one inevitably encounters changes and inconsistencies within individuals over a period of time. Ryszard Kapuściński (1932–2007), the Polish journalist and author of literary reportage, argues that everybody, including the foreign individuals encountered on a journey, is a constantly changing combination of two main elements:

> [T]his relationship existing within each of us, between the person as individual and personality and the person as bearer of culture and race, is not immobile, rigid or static, not fixed inside him for good. On the contrary, its typical features are dynamism, mobility, variability and differences in intensity, depending on the external context, the demands of the current moment, the expectations of the environment or even one's own mood and stage of life. [...] So every encounter with the Other is an enigma, an unknown quantity – I would even say a mystery.[68]

As a result, both parties in any encounter would do well to acknowledge that an unstable core is at the centre of any engagement, an unpredictability which Roes, as I argue below, actively seeks.

Otherness is a relational quality. For something or someone to be foreign or 'Other', there must be a self that is making the comparison. Ortfried

67 Compare with Helmut Rez, Monika Kraemer and Reiko Kobayashi-Weinsziehr, 'Warum Karl und Keizo sich nerven: Eine Reise zum systematischen Verständnis interkulturellen Missverständnisse', in *Interkulturelle Kommunikation: Methoden, Modelle, Beispiele*, ed. by Dagmar Kumbier and Friedmann Schulz von Thun (Reinbeck: Rowohlt, 2006), pp. 28–73: 'Nicht Kulturen begegnen einander, nicht Kulturen missverstehen und bekämpfen oder verstehen und wertschätzen sich. Es sind individuelle Menschen, und diese können sich – unter anderem – in ihrer Kulturzugehöhrigkeit unterscheiden' (pp. 30–31).

68 Ryszard Kapuściński, *The Other*, trans. by Antonia Lloyd-Jones (London: Verso, 2008), pp. 14–15.

Schäffter outlines a typology that delineates four patterns of structural characteristics that such intercultural comparisons can exhibit. Identifying these structures of interpretation, especially in relation to interpreting Otherness, is important because they can become repressive, especially in cases 'wenn sie sich als natürliche Ordnung verstehen und folglich den ihnen zugrunde liegenden Interessenstandpunkt zu einer objektiven oder universellen Sicht verabsolutieren'.[69] The first of Schäffter's structural frameworks for engagement with Otherness is labelled 'Fremdheit als Resonanzboden des Eigenen'. In this mode of encounter the Other is regarded as the origin or source of the Self: 'das von mir zwar Unterschiedene, aber der gleichen Wurzel Entstammende'.[70] Aspects of this mode of encounter can be detected in *Leeres Viertel*, where Schnittke and his companions take on the anthropological mission of finding the Ark of the Covenant. This undertaking constitutes nothing less than the search for the common origins of Western and Eastern cultures and religions.[71] This is the 'Erfahrungsmodus [...] in dem die fernöstlichen Kulturen als Kindheit Europas gedeutet wurden',[72] according to which Eastern cultures are regarded as the origins of Western civilization.

In Schäffter's second mode, the Other is regarded as the counterfoil to the Self: the two poles are clearly separate and easily distinguishable: 'das Fremde [erhält] den Charakter einer Negation der Eigenheit und zwar im Sinne von gegenseitiger Unvereinbarkeit'.[73] Here, the Other is regarded as a threat to the Self's sense of identity or existence, such as is sometimes the case with anti-immigrant hysteria. This threat, paradoxically, concurrently assists in the creation or maintenance of a strengthened sense of Self as it defends itself against the perceived danger. In both these manifestations, this mode embodies an inherently hostile essence in which the Other takes on the aspect of an enemy. Summarizing, Petra Dietsche writes: 'Die Anderen werden nicht in ihrer Unvergleichbarkeit wahrgenommen, sondern sie sind das, was man selbst nicht ist'.[74] Samuel P. Huntington's well-known conception of the 'clash of civilizations' is a perfect example of this adversarial mode of encounter: 'We

69 Ortfried Schäffter, 'Modi des Fremderlebens: Deutungsmuster im Umgang mit Fremdheit', in *Das Fremde: Erfahrungsmöglichkeiten zwischen Faszination und Bedrohung*, ed. by Ortfried Schäffter (Opladen: Westdeutscher Verlag, 1991), pp. 11–42. Also available online at http://ebwb.hu-berlin.de/team/.../III_19_Modi_des_Fremderlebens_Endv.pdf [accessed 11 January 2013]. The quotation is found on p. 4 of the pdf document.

70 Schäffter, 'Modi des Fremderlebens', pdf document, p. 5.

71 Cf. Kontje, *German Orientalisms*, p. 236.

72 Schäffter, 'Modi des Fremderlebens', pdf document, p. 7.

73 Schäffter, 'Modi des Fremderlebens', pdf document, pp. 7–8.

74 Petra Dietsche, 'Einleitung', in Petra Dietsche, *Das Erstaunen über das Fremde* (Frankfurt am Main: Peter Lang, 1984), pp. 5–11 (p. 5).

know who we are only when we know who we are not and often only when we know whom we are against'.[75]

The third category, 'Fremdheit als Ergänzung', represents a more sophisticated mode of engagement than the first two and takes into consideration the internal differentiation that exists within any person or cultural group, such as was mentioned above: 'Die Produktivität dieser Ordnungsstruktur beruht daher nicht auf der Herstellung einer internen Eindeutigkeit und in der schützenden Abgrenzung des Eigenen nach außen, sondern in der Regelung von Prozessen einer Verinnerlichung des Äußeren und einem Entäußern von Innerem'.[76] In this mode, the engagement with Otherness is an opportunity for learning, development and exchange: 'Das Fremde erhält für ein dynamisches Ordnungsgefüge die Funktion eines externen Spielraums, der entwicklungsfördernde Impulse und strukturelle Lernanlässe erschließen hilft und in dem auch unvorhersehbare Entwicklungen möglich werden'.[77] Schäffter's description of Otherness as a 'Spielraum' in which one can engage and be transformed reflects a position similar to that of Roes. The latter writes about intercultural communication in similar terms: 'Spiel [ist] nicht nur ein bei*spiel*haftes Konzept, Probleme und Möglichkeiten interkulturellen Verstehens aufzuzeigen. Es eröffnet auch Perspektiven, Verständigungsprozesse zwischen Fremden in Gang zu bringen und zu vertiefen' (*KT*, p. 41). Important in both cases is the 'Entdeckung bislang ungeahnter Möglichkeiten'.[78] In this mode of engagement, the Self encounters the Other and is open enough to undergo a process of transformation. Exactly what kind of transformation cannot be known in advance and there is a danger that such interactions lead the Self 'zu einer systemsprengenden Überforderung'.[79] I return to this point when making the distinction between travel and tourism below; for now it suffices to note that this mode of engagement is very relevant to an analysis of Roes's conception of intercultural encounters.

Schäffter's fourth and final category, 'Fremdheit als Komplementarität', is distinct from the first three because it does not relate Otherness to aspects of the Self's identity. The emphasis here is on recognition of the Other's radical difference and on the validity of a multitude of competing perspectives. As Schäffter explains:

75 Samuel P. Huntington, *The Clash of Civilizations and the Remaking of World Order* (New York: Simon & Schuster, 1996), p. 21.

76 Schäffter, 'Modi des Fremderlebens', pdf document, p.10.

77 Schäffter, 'Modi des Fremderlebens', pdf document, p. 11.

78 Schäffter, 'Modi des Fremderlebens', pdf document, p. 11.

79 Schäffter, 'Modi des Fremderlebens', pdf document, p. 12.

> Im Deutungsmuster komplementärer Fremdheit werden Schwellenerfahrungen nicht mehr als Verlockung zu einer umfassenden und dadurch letztlich inflationären Ausweitung des Innen aufgefasst, sondern als Zwang zur Anerkennung einer radikalen gegenseitigen Differenz, als Sensibilität für gegenseitige Fremdheit.[80]

The acknowledgement of one's own culturally rooted perspective (e.g. Eurocentrism) and the recognition of the Other's indeterminability result in a position that compels the Self 'das Fremde als Fremdes [zu] belassen'.[81] This mode of engagement is reflected in episodes of Roes's novels in which narrators express despair at the overbearingness of their own cultural conditioning,[82] and the variations in the way people from different cultures come to a transcultural understanding.[83] Acceptance of radical forms of difference is also an important aspect of Roes's position. As Matthias Kroß argues, Roes rejects outright universalist positions such as the one put forward by Jürgen Habermas's school, because 'sie in ihrem Universalismus die Vielfarbigkeit der kulturellen Divergenzen im Laugenbad der eurozentrischen Rationalität zur Achromie der Vernunft entfärben'.[84] For Roes, an essential aspect of the intercultural encounter lies in recognizing the differences between peoples and cultures and abiding with that unsettling experience of alterity.

The above typology offers a productive perspective with which to assess different kinds of engagement with Otherness. Considering the revolution in technology over the course of the twentieth century, it might be assumed that a comparable evolution in intercultural understanding would come to pass, both in quantitative and qualitative terms. That appears not to have been the case. Despite the dramatic growth of the tourism industry over the last century and a half, it has been argued that the number of Westerners who encounter other cultures in a meaningful way remains a small proportion of those who set off abroad.[85] The distinction is often made between tourists and travellers. The word 'tourist' carries unflattering connotations of sheep-like herds well-insulated from the alienating forces of Otherness. In contrast, the traveller's engagement with other cultures is usually thought to be dynamic, intense, and of long duration. Roes summarizes this difference by claiming that:

80 Schäffter, 'Modi des Fremderlebens', pdf document, pp. 13–14.

81 Schäffter, 'Modi des Fremderlebens', pdf document, p. 15.

82 'wie sehr ich meiner eigenen kultur noch verhaftet bin' (*LV*, p. 459).

83 'Auch wenn ich sie verstehen lernen könnte, wie sollte sie je mich verstehen lernen?' (*LV*, p. 147).

84 Matthias Kroß, 'Die Poetik des Fremden', in Michael Roes, *Perversion und Glück. Poetikvorlesungen* (Berlin: Matthes & Seitz, 2007), pp. 87–116 (p. 94).

85 Cf. Eder, 'Zu Hause in der Fremde?', p. 162; Hans Magnus Enzensberger, 'Eine Theorie des Tourismus', in Hans Magnus Enzensberger, *Einzelheiten 1: Bewußtseins-Industrie* (Frankfurt am Main: Suhrkamp, 1962), pp. 179–205.

> Tourismus und Reise sind Gegenbegriffe. Der klassische Reisende will sich dem Fremden aussetzen, der klassische Tourist will sich vom Vertrauten erholen, indem er in der Ferne vertraute Umstände aufsucht. Tourismus heißt Zerstreuung statt Konzentration, Abschalten statt Aufmerksamkeit, Entspannung statt Anstrengung (*KT*, p. 126).

Roes claims that he is not criticising tourism (*KT*, p. 134), merely making a distinction between two forms of travel. Other writers have been more choleric with regard to tourism. Writing in 1950, Gerhard Nebel described tourism as 'eine der großen nihilistischen Bewegungen, eine der großen westlichen Seuchen'.[86] In his well-known essay 'Eine Theorie des Tourismus' (1958), Hans Magnus Enzensberger claimed that Nebel had failed to identify the real problem with the phenomenon of tourism. Outlining the aporia of the industry from an anti-capitalist perspective, Enzensberger claims that it has never been and never will be able to provide the freedom that it promises to its customers: 'Der Tourismus zeigt, daß wir uns daran gewöhnt haben, Freiheit als Massenbetrug hinzunehmen, dem wir uns anvertrauen, obschon wir ihn insgeheim durchschauen'.[87]

Tourism is concerned with recreation and not with true encounters with Otherness. Walter Eder, arguing that modern tourists largely insulate themselves from their foreign surroundings, outlines what is lost as a result:

> Das Risiko, durch neue Erkenntnisse sein Weltbild verändern zu müssen, ist minimal. Er kann eben das vermeiden, was den Wert des Reisens als Weg zu einer tieferen Selbstwahrnehmung ausmachte und die eigene Identität am tiefsten prägte, nämlich aus unausweichlichen und notwendigen Erfahrungen mit der Bevölkerung des Reiselandes zu lernen, seine mitgebrachten Überzeugungen und Werte zu überdenken und in der fremden und befremdlichen Umgebung gleichwohl das Vernünftige und Respektable zu erkennen und anzuerkennen.[88]

By remaining separated from the culture of the country visited, the tourist denies him or herself not only the possibility of learning but also of changing long-held, culturally conditioned beliefs. As Eder suggests, there is an element of risk in true intercultural encounters – one risks having experiences that will forever change one's outlook on life. Regarded in this way, the traveller is a vulnerable figure, since the Self that began the journey is unlikely to return home. This appears to be particularly true when the intercultural encounter happens within the framework of anthropological research, such as in *Leeres Viertel*. The intensity and duration of the period of study leave their mark. Claude Lévi-Strauss

86 Gerhard Nebel quoted in Enzensberger, 'Eine Theorie des Tourismus', p. 182. No page reference is provided by Enzensberger.

87 Enzensberger, 'Eine Theorie des Tourismus', p. 205.

88 Eder, 'Zu Hause in der Fremde?', p. 168.

speaks of a 'chronic restlessness' and 'psychological maim[ing]' that result from the anthropologist's engagement with alterity.[89] Paul Rabinow talks of anthropological fieldwork as a 'difficult and trying experience' during which neither the 'subject [the anthropologist] nor the object [the informant] remain static'.[90] There is, of course, an ethical problem here. The traveller consciously chooses to set off on a journey and the anthropologist freely decides to pursue that profession. In contrast, the residents of the countries travelled or studied do not always volunteer to be the object of the traveller's gaze. The changes that occur in the people or their societies as a result of the arrival of uninvited foreign guests may not always be desirable or desired. Roes acknowledges this inequality but does not offer an answer to the problem: 'rechtfertigt dieses interesse [des anthropologen] den wissenschaftlich-voyeuristischen einbruch in das möglichst unberührte, ungewarnte, unvorbereitete untersuchungsfeld? [...] Glaube ich wirklich, mit guten vorsätzen dem grundsätzlichen dilemma zu entkommen[?]' (*LV*, pp. 239–40).Nevertheless, Michael Roes regards the vulnerability and potential transformation of the traveller as a desirable and integral part of travel: 'Wenn ich reise, lasse ich mich vollkommen darauf ein, was mir widerfährt – körperlich, fast masochistisch'.[91] The transformation that results from such openness is a threat but also an opportunity. This exemplifies Schäffter's third type of intercultural engagement, 'Fremdheit als Ergänzung'. It is an active exchange that entails a certain risk of a 'systemsprengend[e] Überforderung'.[92] Talking in comparable terms, the narrator of *Geschichte der Freundschaft* discusses travel as illness: 'Überlebt der Körper die Infektion, geht er gestärkt aus der Krise hervor. Die Kontaminierung mit Fremdem führt zu einer gesteigerten Immunabwehr, aber auch zu Hybridbildungen, Bastardisierungen, Fehllesungen. Sie machen Entwicklung erst möglich' (*GF*, p. 298). According to Roes, growth and development of this kind can only result from regarding travel as work and not as pleasure:

> Ich finde es fast tragisch, die Suche nach dem Glück als Sinn einer Reise oder als Lebenssinn zu definieren. [...] Ich suche beim Reisen die Erfahrung des sich Verirrens, des Schmerzes, der Krankheit. Das Lebendigsein als bewußte Erfahrung mit geschärften Sinnen (*KT*, p. 128).

89 Claude Lévi-Strauss, *Tristes Tropiques*, trans. by John and Doreen Weightman (London: Jonathan Cape, 1973), p. 55.

90 Paul Rabinow, *Reflections on Fieldwork in Morocco* (Berkeley: University of California Press, 1977), p. 39 and p. 73.

91 Jens Nommel and Michael Roes, 'Im Gespräch über die eigenen Grenzen', http://handlungsreisedialog.blogwerft.de/2007/12/13/michael-roes/ [accessed 4 November 2009].

92 Schäffter, 'Modi des Fremderlebens', pdf document, p. 12.

For Roes, confusion, misunderstanding and physical discomfort are valuable impulses for intercultural communication. In contrast, happiness induces contentedness, which becomes a hindrance: 'Wer glücklich ist, muß nicht nachdenken, muß sich nicht verändern' (*KT*, p. 129). Such statements clearly delineate Roes's conception of travel as a taxing undertaking that is far-removed from the experience sought by the typical tourist. Far from seeking pleasure, luxury or amusement, Roes regards travel as a serious endeavour that entails conscious effort and a great deal of discomfort. His conception of real travel is therefore also simultaneously an indirect critique of tourism as an unconscious and unproductive enterprise which avoids engagement with foreign cultures.

Roes's emphasis on physical phenomena such as pain and illness is significant and he regards the body as being of primary importance in intercultural communication. Outlining his basic theoretical position on intercultural encounters, he states:

> Meine Grunderfahrung ist, daß es zwischen den Menschen ohnehin mehr Gemeinsames als Trennendes gibt, daß Unterschiede also relativ oberflächlich sind. Was trennt, das sind die Sprachen, die Mythen. Was wir gemeinsam haben, sind elementare körperliche Erfahrungen: Geburt, Hunger, Schmerz, Glück. Das sind die tieferen Erfahrungen (*KT*, p. 127).

This comment reveals a position that lies somewhere between a universalist and a relativist understanding of cultures and the interaction between their representatives. The universalist position states that all cultures share fundamental, common elements, norms that transcend cultural, national and racial divides. In contrast, proponents of relativism claim that any 'area of human experience which is cultural rather than biological is potentially subject to variation across cultures, precisely because such behaviour is learned rather than biologically determined.'[93] Roes's position combines elements of both universalism and relativism in a way reminiscent of Johann Gottfried Herder's concept of 'enlightened relativism', as outlined in *Auch eine Philosophie der Geschichte zur Bildung der Menschheit* (1784–91): 'By assuming a common origin of all human life in spite of its manifest varieties, Herder successfully combines notions of universalism and cultural relativism, identity and difference.'[94] Roes's position shares much with Herder's: he refuses to negate the differences between himself and the Other, but at the same time

93 Richard J. Evanoff, 'Universalist, relativist, and constructivist approaches to intercultural ethics', *International Journal of Intercultural Relations*, 28 (2004), 439–58 (p. 445).

94 Carl Niekerk, 'The Romantics and other cultures', in *The Cambridge Companion to German Romanticism*, ed. by Nicholas Saul (Cambridge: Cambridge University Press, 2009), pp. 147–61 (p. 148).

he insists that different cultures have much more in common than that which divides them. Roes thereby firmly and self-consciously places himself within the tradition of cosmopolitan thought, whose 'simple but by no means trivial claim is that, despite all our differences, humankind is effectively one and must be understood as such'.[95]

Such a position would appear to suggest a relatively optimistic view of the possibility for successful encounters between representatives of different cultures. With the body functioning as a bridge between people, the only barriers remaining are language and culture. This understanding is reflected in Roes's fiction, albeit with a subtle differentiation that reflects the complexity of real life. The awareness of the importance of the body on the part of the contemporary narrator of *Leeres Viertel* is heightened when he engages in a Yemeni ritual dance. The physical movements bring him closer to the culture he is studying in a manner that transcends intellectual understanding. Paradoxically, however, the body also signifies his difference from the locals as he repeatedly falls ill with tropical illnesses. This example demonstrates how Roes's fictional depictions are often more nuanced and ambiguous than the theoretical positions he advances in his essays. In places, the fictional work shows ineffectual communication even when involving the body as a means of intercultural bridge-building. My chapter on *Leeres Viertel* compares the partial success that novel's narrator enjoys when using the body as a tool of communication with examples of less successful encounters taken from Roes's *Nah Inverness* and Uwe Timm's *Morenga*. In the case of Timm's German protagonist, the body and physical movement are precisely what separate him from African people and their culture. He admires the graceful, natural movements of an African dance ritual but is incapable of duplicating that agility, which marks him as an outsider and putting an end to the process of assimilation into the foreign tribe.

Roes regards the value of language in processes of intercultural communication as dubious. 'Es gibt ein wissen, das mit sprache nicht hinreichend beschrieben werden kann' (*LV*, p. 445), says the narrator of *Leeres Viertel*, pointing towards the limited scope of language as a tool for communication. The narrator of *Geschichte der Freundschaft* considers language to be full of potential complications: 'Vor allem in den Worten liegen die Missverständnisse' (*GF*, p. 172). In one essay, Roes states that, 'Jedes Verständigungsproblem ist immer auch ein Sprachproblem' (*KT*, p. 42). Roes regards language as an imperfect communication system, even within one cultural group. Instances of miscommunication are inevitable considering

95 Robert Fine, *Cosmopolitanism* (London: Routledge, 2007), p. xvii. See also David Adams and Galin Tihanov (eds.), *Enlightenment Cosmopolitanism* (London: MHRA and Maney, 2011).

the subtleties and imprecisions that are inherent to language. One theorist of interculturality claims that: 'Alles Verstehen findet über Sprache statt: Als solches ist es überhaupt nur möglich. Damit ist es aber gleichzeitig auch begrenzt: Sprache schneidet immer – d.h. strukturell – etwas von dem, was sie darstellt, ab; sie vermag die Realität nicht vollständig zu repräsentieren'.[96] Roes would presumably disagree with the first part of the above statement, arguing instead that communication also happens on other levels. The second part of the quotation, however, describes the central problem: language is not a direct representation of reality and words do not have a stable, inherent meaning. Despite this precariousness, Roes identifies one intriguing example of a situation in which language use becomes a more conscious, and therefore more reliable, endeavour. In cases of intercultural communication where one or both partners are conversing in a foreign tongue, the heightened awareness of the potential for misunderstanding assists the speakers to overcome the language barrier: 'Fast scheint die grundsätzliche Schwierigkeit, einander zu verstehen, bewußter – und damit lösbarer – zu sein, wenn der andere tatsächlich eine *Fremd*sprache spricht. In dieser Begegnung ist es selbstverständlich, sich zu vergewissern, richtig verstanden worden zu sein' (*KT*, p. 42). Ironically, it is precisely when the fallibility of language is most acute that Roes regards language as being most efficient. It is only when awareness of the limitations of language is heightened that it becomes a reliable communication tool.

The encounter with Otherness is often, if not always, an event that triggers insights into the Self. Psychoanalytical approaches to intercultural encounters take this further and claim that 'das Fremde, das es wahrzunehmen und zu verstehen gilt, nicht nur – vielleicht nicht einmal in der Hauptsache – außerhalb unserer Person, sondern *in uns selbst* liegt'.[97] The encounter with the Other then becomes an encounter with repressed aspects of the Self. In Roes's work, the protagonist-narrators are not only interested in encountering the Other, they are almost always Others themselves. They are, not unlike the author himself, intellectuals, artists, writers and thinkers. Their sexuality and gender identity also set them apart from the mainstream. Most of Roes's narrators are gay men, but they usually distance themselves from conventional gay identities. The characters are often outsiders of various kinds within their own cultures, as well as 'Other' within the societies they are visiting. This perception of living outside the norm within their own cultural sphere appears to be what impels

96 Jürgen Kramer, 'Das Verstehen fremder Kulturen: Möglichkeiten und Grenzen aus ethnologischer, hermeneutischer und psychoanalytischer Sicht', in *Fremdheitserfahrung und Fremdheitsdarstellung in okzidentalen Kulturen: Theorieansätze, Medien/Textsorten, Diskursformen*, ed. by Bernd Lenz and Hans-Jürgen Lüsebrink (Passau: Rothe, 1999), pp. 37–53 (p. 50).

97 Kramer, 'Das Verstehen fremder Kulturen', p. 49.

them to inquire about the cultural and racial Other in countries far afield. The encounter with Otherness can be said to have begun well before setting off on the journey, since the investigation into alternative identities, mindsets and cultures is a constant pursuit at home too. This recognition of the 'Fremde in uns'[98] not only assists in the understanding of the Other, it is perhaps what sows the seed of interest in the cultural Other to begin with.

Intertextuality

Roes's works of travel fiction abound with literary allusions and his *oeuvre* invites analysis from an intertextual angle. Not only do the novels include numerous individual references and quotations, some also borrow plots and share thematic interests with classic works of literature. Knowledge of these pre-texts, coupled with an understanding of the intertextual practices of the author, is extremely valuable when reading Roes's work and approaching his novels in this way offers rich analytical potential. This book seeks to determine what principles or concepts lie behind the intertextual borrowing and aims, ultimately, to draw links between intertextuality in these works and Roes's vision of cosmopolitan interculturality. How do the texts with which Roes engages illuminate our understanding of the intercultural encounter? A critical assessment of this kind will necessarily confront the question regarding the nature of Roes's reading matter. Not surprisingly, he refers to a range of German writers (Nietzsche, Goethe, Lichtenberg, and a host of German travel writers such as Carsten Niebuhr). He also refers to numerous Western writers of other nationalities (Aeschylus, Montaigne, Cervantes, Melville, Faulkner, and English travel writers such as T. E. Lawrence), making his intertextuality truly international. It is, however, a distinctly Western intertextuality. Although Roes does refer to some non-Western literature,[99] his main points of reference are Western. The analysis that follows will attempt to establish the implications of this intertextuality for the staging of the intercultural encounter.

Roes's choice of intertexts is not only international, but trans-historical, drawing upon ancient, Early Modern and contemporary sources. He focuses less on history than on transcending historical boundaries in the search for thematically appropriate material and ideas. It could be argued that most

98 Kramer, 'Das Verstehen fremder Kulturen', p. 49.

99 Examples of Roes's non-Western references include a discussion of Yemeni theatrical tradition in *Leeres Viertel*, references to the Moroccan author Mohamed Choukri and the Kabyle singers Si Moh and Lounès Matoub (*Geschichte der Freundschaft*), Ibn Battuta and Hafis (*David Kanchelli*), and the Chinese authors Lu Xun and Yu Hua (*Die Fünf Farben Schwarz*).

practitioners of intertextuality move freely across the boundaries of the epochs as they look back in time for pre-texts that open up a more expansive field of vision. In Roes's case, however, this is particularly pronounced, confirming that myth, the classical tradition and the history of ideas exert a strong influence on the author and his position with regard to modernity and contemporary society. Roes exhibits a particular tendency to refer to and quote from texts dating from the Age of Enlightenment and the Age of Empire, periods of intense geographical and intercultural exploration. The main chapters of this book explore the ways in which Roes engages with these various sources and uses them to exhibit his own place within the Western literary and anthropological tradition. Roes's intertextual strategies and the manner in which he juxtaposes sources make great demands on the reader and their effect depends upon the reader having an understanding of what those paradigms were to begin with. At times Roes transforms or rejects the pre-texts and paradigms which he cites; at other times his admiration for his sources (Carsten Niebuhr being a prime example) shines clearly.

Before approaching the specific pre-texts in the individual chapters, a brief overview of relevant theories of intertextuality is presented in this section. After sketching out the origins of the term, I proceed to outline the main theories and typologies that are drawn upon in the main chapters. The section concludes with a brief description of how Roes's works exemplify or resist these theories and practices. It will prove useful to define at the outset what exactly is meant by the term intertextuality. I take it to mean any connection that exists between one text and a pre-existing text. Quotation, allusion, parody, homage and imitation are but a few of the specific means authors have at their disposal when referring to previous literary works. By employing such techniques, writers may evoke a sense of a shared literary heritage or, conversely, instigate a critique of preceding works. The practice of literary allusion and quotation has been widespread since the beginnings of literature but it was only in the 1960s that Julia Kristeva introduced the term 'intertextuality' to literary criticism. Since then, the term has been contentiously debated, with theorists such as Harold Bloom, Roland Barthes, Michael Riffaterre and Gérard Genette advancing competing definitions.[100] Post-structuralist theorists such as Kristeva and Barthes regard language as inherently intertextual and they ascribe a significance to the term that is not limited to the field of literature. Developing Bakhtin's concepts of dialogism and polyphony, Kristeva advances a concept of intertextuality in which:

100 Brigid Haines, 'The reader, the writer, her narrator and their text(s): intertextuality in Christa Wolf's *Störfall*', in *Christa Wolf in Perspective*, ed. by Ian Wallace, *German Monitor*, 30 (Amsterdam: Rodopi, 1994), pp. 157–72 (p. 158).

> the intertextual dimensions of a text cannot be studied as mere 'sources' or 'influences' [...]. The text is a *practice* and *productivity*, its intertextual status represents its structuration of words and utterances that existed before, will go on after the moment of utterance, and so are, in Bakhtin's terms, 'double-voiced'.[101]

According to post-structuralists, authors do not need explicitly to include quotations or allusions to qualify as intertextual. Since all writers are also readers, every new text is always a montage of linguistic units from previously extant texts. As H. Porter Abbott explains:

> Just as a language pre-exists any narrative that is written in that language, so too do all of a narrative's other features precede it, from its overarching genres to its minute turns of phrase. They come out of a pre-existing cultural web of expressive forms. Seen in this way, narratives have no borders but are part of an immense, unfolding (and hence ever-changing) tapestry.[102]

Roland Barthes, developing Kristeva's concept of intertextuality, famously announced the 'death of the author', stating that each 'text is a tissue of quotations drawn from the innumerable centres of culture'.[103] The concept of original literary production had become problematic and the status of the author as controlling figure was challenged. According to post-structural theory, the author, rather than producing original representations of the world, is 'reduced to providing the site or space for the interplay of texts'.[104]

The position adopted by this study is more aligned with structuralist approaches to intertextuality and is concerned with concrete examples of intertextual practices consciously employed by authors. Moving down from the elevated plane of post-structural theory:

> [i]n this structuralist version of intertextuality the author retains authority over his text, the unity and autonomy of the text remain intact, and the reader does not get lost in a labyrinthine network of possible references but realizes the author's intentions by decoding the signals and markers inscribed into the text.[105]

This book is concerned with questions such as the following: how do authors appropriate the work of other authors? Why choose to refer to a specific text,

101 Graham Allen, *Intertextuality*, 2nd edn (London: Routledge, 2011), p. 35.

102 H. Porter Abbott, *The Cambridge Introduction to Narrative* (Cambridge: Cambridge University Press, 2008), p. 101.

103 Roland Barthes, 'The Death of the Author', *Image – Music – Text*, trans. by Stephen Heath (London: Fontana, 1977), p. 146.

104 Manfred Pfister, 'How Postmodern is Intertextuality?', in *Intertextuality*, ed. by Heinrich F. Plett (Berlin; New York: Walter de Gruyter, 1991), pp. 207–24 (p. 212).

105 Pfister, 'How Postmodern is Intertextuality?', p. 210.

be it a classic of the canon or a piece of modern popular fiction? What specific practices are relevant when analysing works of travel fiction? In the attempt to answer these questions, the work of the following theorists and critics will be useful and will be reference points over the course of the main chapters.

This book adopts the intertextual typology outlined in the work of the French theorist Gérard Genette, most notably in the volume *Palimpsests: Literature in the Second Degree* (1982, English translation 1997). Where most other theorists use the term intertextuality, Genette uses 'transtextuality', which he takes to mean the 'textual transcendence of the text [...] defined roughly as "all that sets the text in a relationship, whether obvious or concealed, with other texts"'.[106] Within transtextuality, Genette identifies five sub-categories that inevitably overlap to some degree. Genette names his first category (rather confusingly) 'intertextuality', which covers instances of quotation and plagiarism. It is defined in a limited sense as 'the actual presence of one text within another'.[107] Numerous examples of Genette's 'intertextuality' are to be found in Roes's work since he often includes marked and referenced quotations in his novels. Genette's second category, the 'paratext', refers to aspects of the text that exist outside the body of the text proper: titles, prefaces, appendices, blurbs and book covers. These paratextual elements assist the reader by indicating ways of approaching a literary work. Genette dedicated a book-length study to the topic in *Paratexts: Thresholds of Interpretation* (1987, English translation 1997). Genette's third category is 'metatextuality', which he describes as the '*critical* relationship par excellence'.[108] This category includes texts that comment on or criticize other texts and is exemplified by academic literary criticism. Roes's essay-novel, *Haut des Südens*, is a good example of this kind of transtextuality. Genette dedicates the bulk of the volume *Palimpsests* to an analysis of the fourth type of transtextuality, which he terms 'hypertextuality'. This he defines as:

> any relationship uniting a text B (which I shall call the *hypertext*) to an earlier text A (I shall, of course, call it the *hypotext*), upon which it is grafted in a manner that is not that of a commentary.[109]

Hypertextuality does not depend on quotations, but exists rather as a relationship between the formal structure or thematic sphere of two works. An example of this is Roes's *Weg nach Timimoun*, a hypertext that could not exist as it does without the existence of its hypotext, Aeschylus's *Oresteia*.

106 Gérard Genette, *Palimpsests: Literature in the Second Degree*, trans. by Channa Newman and Claude Doubinsky (Lincoln: University of Nebraska Press, 1997), p. 1, quoting himself.

107 Genette, *Palimpsests*, p. 2.

108 Genette, *Palimpsests*, p. 4.

109 Genette, *Palimpsests*, p. 5.

Genette's fifth category is 'architextuality'. He defines this type as a literary work's generic appellation, which encompasses generic conventions, expectations and transgressions. Genette describes this as 'the most abstract and implicit [category] of all'.[110] Although they overlap at times, Genette's clear typology will prove useful as we examine specific examples of transtextual literary relationships. Despite my reliance on Genette's analysis, unless otherwise stated I use the term 'intertextuality' in the broader sense where Genette uses 'transtextuality'. When referring to what Genette calls intertextuality, I use appropriate specific descriptions such as 'quotation' or 'allusion'.

Manfred Pfister's work on intertextuality is also of great relevance to the analysis presented in this book. His studies on specific intertextual practices cover postmodern intertextualities (1991) and the intertextuality of travel literature (1993 and 2006). Both of these areas are pertinent in a discussion of Michael Roes's fiction, which often centres on travel itineraries and displays postmodern aesthetic characteristics. While not exclusive to postmodernism, Pfister regards intertextuality as its 'very trademark'. Postmodern authors believe that 'originality in these late days of history can only reside in a novel dealing with second-hand material [...] repeat[ing] endlessly and in ever new ways what has been thought and said before'.[111] Much of Roes's work is an engagement with 'second-hand material' and he is, in some specific ways, an exemplary postmodern intertextualist. He has rewritten Greek mythology, produced a Yemeni film adaptation of *Macbeth*, and his novels are peppered with thematically relevant allusions. By referring so conspicuously to other texts, his work draws attention to its own status as a text, marking itself as metatextual (in a different meaning to that of Genette). This move toward metatextuality may appear to be a move away from mimesis, or truthful representations of reality, but 'yielding to literariness' can also be regarded as a means of 'overcoming the gap between experience and language; [the] solution is to write a book about writing a book'.[112] Ironically, by foregrounding their own existence as texts, books about travel, especially novels, can be more honest in their representation of journeys than works that deny this (inter-) textual dimension.

I argue throughout this book that while Michael Roes's intertextual aesthetics often appear to be postmodern, he resists the political, moral and aesthetic abandonment of values so prevalent in postmodernism. For example,

110 Genette, *Palimpsests*, p. 4.

111 Pfister, 'How Postmodern is Intertextuality?', p. 209.

112 Heather Henderson, 'The Travel Writer and the Text: "My Giant Goes with Me Wherever I Go"', in *Temperamental Journeys: Essays on the Modern Literature of Travel*, ed. by Michael Kowalewski (Athens: University of Georgia Press, 1992), pp. 230–48 (p. 244).

it is often said that for postmodernists no distinction exists between high and low forms of culture: 'Postmodernism's serenely unconcerned juxtaposition of Pop and classics, of the media garbage of the present and the cultural refuse of the past, has as its very aim the levelling down of all traditional distinctions between high and low'.[113] The cultural references in *Geschichte der Freundschaft* are an example in which Roes is verging on this postmodern position: Batman and Robin are placed alongside Barthes and Foucault with no discernible distinction. In *Haut des Südens*, however, Roes bestows a value judgment on his literary sources: Mark Twain is regarded as morally foul while Herman Melville is deemed a praiseworthy model. Far from abolishing the distinction between intertextual sources, Roes in fact actually maintains the differentiation by favouring one set of intertexts over another.

This is a very different position to that of Raymond Federman, whose theory of postmodern intertextuality also informs parts of this study. Federman, an avowed postmodernist, refuses to reveal his sources, claiming that 'there are no sacred sources for thinking and writing'.[114] Although Roes almost always reveals his sources, Federman's essay on 'Imagination as Plagiarism' (1976) is illuminating when read alongside *Leeres Viertel*. The first chapter of this book reads the intertextuality of that novel as a postmodern game played with sources taken from Western travel writing on the Orient. Roes 'plagiarizes' a number of authentic travel accounts and inserts the textual haul into the historical strand of the novel. This theft is analysed within the context of Federman's term 'pla(y)giarism'. The theft is one of a number of textual games played by the author and these are linked in the analysis to the anthropological subject of the novel – traditional Arab games.

Another aspect of Manfred Pfister's work drawn upon in this book is his analysis of intertextuality in travel literature. According to Pfister, practitioners of the travelogue had regarded themselves for centuries as being ruled by a 'Programmatik des voraussetzungslosen Blicks, der sich nicht durch die Informationen und Vorgaben anderer Texte um die Fremdheit des Fremden bringen lassen will'.[115] Even at the beginning of the early 1990s, some travel writers continued to regard the travelogue as 'das letzte Refugium einer romantischen Unmittelbarkeitsästhetik, noch unangekränkelt vom postmodernen Bewußtsein der Verstrickung aller Erfahrung in textuell vermittelte Wahrnehmungsschemata und Erfahrungsdispositionen, der

113 Pfister, 'How Postmodern is Intertextuality?', pp. 218–19.

114 Raymond Federman, 'Imagination as Plagiarism [an unfinished paper…]', *New Literary History*, 7 (1976), 563–78 (p. 566).

115 Manfred Pfister, 'Intertextuelles Reisen, oder: Der Reisebericht als Intertext', in *Tales and "their Telling Difference": Festschrift für Franz K. Stanzel*, ed. by Herbert Foltinek, Wolfgang Riehle and Waldemar Zacharasiewicz (Heidelberg: Winter, 1993), pp. 109–32 (p. 110).

dialogischen Teilhabe jedes Textes an anderen Texten'.[116] Pfister's work on the intertextuality of travel literature sets out to correct this misconception. He identifies four categories of intertextuality commonly found in travel literature. The first category, 'verdrängte und negierte Intertextualität', refers to the attempt to conceal intertextual dependency by suppressing the presence of other texts within new travelogues.[117] This includes such examples of plagiarism as the thirteen pages of unmarked quotations in Tobias Smollett's *Travels through France and Italy* (1766). The historical strand of Roes's *Leeres Viertel* plays with this form of intertextuality by appropriating other travelogues and leaving the quotations unmarked. An appendix to the novel, however, draws attention to the theft and marks it as a postmodern process of playful textual production. Both Smollett and Roes are reliant on pre-texts, but whereas the former attempts to wipe away all textual traces of his predecessors, the latter ultimately acknowledges the influence of literary forebears.

Pfister calls the second category 'kompilatorische Intertextualität', which refers to travel books that include information from a range of referenced pre-texts: 'Hier wird der neue Text zum Supplement des Prätexts, das diesen erweiternd fortschreibt'.[118] This second category is more relevant to a study of eighteenth- and nineteenth-century travelogues than it is to an analysis of contemporary travel novels. However, the third category, 'huldigende Intertextualität', is of great relevance when reading *Haut des Südens*. Pfister describes as 'huldigend' any 'literarische Bildungsreise, die zu den Geburts-, Wirkungs- und Grabestätten berühmter Autoren führt'.[119] The narrator of *Haut des Südens* undertakes such a literary pilgrimage and visits locations associated with Mark Twain, Herman Melville and William Faulkner. However, the narrator's position with regard to Twain reveals itself to be more in accord with Pfister's fourth and final category of intertextual travel writing: 'dialogische Intertextualität'. This is a 'kritische[r] Dialog mit den Prätexten',[120] in which one travel writer corrects what he or she perceives as the erroneous views of a previous traveller. The relationship between two such texts is an 'antagonistischer und polemischer [Gestus]'.[121] The relationship of *Haut des Südens* to its main pre-texts, especially Twain, corresponds to Pfister's definition of the dialogic and polemic. The novel is concurrently a metatextual analysis (in Genette's terms) and a dialogic critique (in Pfister's) of a previously read text.

116 Pfister, 'Intertextuelles Reisen', p. 111.
117 Pfister, 'Intertextuelles Reisen', p. 112.
118 Pfister, 'Intertextuelles Reisen', p. 118.
119 Pfister, 'Intertextuelles Reisen', p. 120.
120 Pfister, 'Intertextuelles Reisen', p. 125.
121 Pfister, 'Intertextuelles Reisen', p. 126.

Based on studies such as those by Pfister and others (cf. Henderson), Ulla Biernat comes to the conclusion 'daß Intertextualität ein entscheidendes Kennzeichen der Gattung [der Reiseliteratur] ist'.[122] It is certainly the case that Roes's extensive writing on travel is almost always fundamentally intertextual. The extent and intensity of Roes's intertextuality suggests that he requires a pre-text as a framework around which he crafts his own. This dependency on previous literary works might strike some readers as evidence of creative poverty. In fact, the analysis of Roes's travel novels presented in this book reveals that the process of intertextual appropriation employed is different in each novel and is at times highly original. The innovation and ingenuity of the works lie, to a considerable extent, in the approach taken to recycling old material from various epochs. Each of the four novels chosen represents a different intertextual position. *Leeres Viertel* is a plagiaristic work, a 'Freibeutertext'[123] that ultimately confesses its parasitic character. The novel is partially composed from its pre-texts in quotations that constitute what Genette termed 'intertextuality'. *Haut des Südens* also contains many quotations, but these are incorporated into the novel in a way reminiscent of an academic essay. The novel's transtextuality is thus best regarded as metatextual in Genette's definition of the term. Moreover, evidence is presented in the second chapter of this book to support the view that this transtextual relation becomes at times a hypertextual one to illustrate Roes's admiration of Melville's *Moby Dick*. The relationship of *Weg nach Timimoun* to its main intertext is more complex. No quotations from the *Oresteia* are included, but Roes's novel is dependent on the Greek play for its meaning and its existence. Roes's novel is the hypertext and the *Oresteia* is the hypotext. The nature of this hypertextual relationship is elucidated in the third chapter. Finally, *Geschichte der Freundschaft* is a hybrid that includes various kinds of intertextuality. It is 'intertextual' in Genette's sense, incorporating as it does numerous quotations from a range of sources. It also contains a metatextual aspect, displaying a relationship with its intertexts that is like a commentary. The transtextuality is oriented around the novel's central theme and the narrative engages with the theories and examples presented in the separate sections of quotation.

An important aspect of intertextuality is the reader's active involvement. For any intertextual reference to be effective, it must be recognized by the reader. Whenever a reader identifies an intertextual allusion, he or she brings additional meanings and connotations to a text – sometimes ones not even deliberately intended by the author. Conversely, when a reader fails to notice a reference, meaning is lost and the power of the passage does not register in full.

122 Biernat, *"Ich bin nicht der erste Fremde hier"*, pp. 19–20.
123 Schmitt-Maaß, '"mäandernd, ornamentalisch, ohne progression?"', p. 95.

It is necessary here to make some qualifications. In this book, I aim to detect and analyse the most important of Roes's many intertextual references and practices. Applied to such highly intertextual works, this goal is an ambitious undertaking. Due to their sheer number, it has been impossible to discuss every example of literary reference, quotation or allusion. Furthermore, it is possible that some references have passed undetected. This would not be surprising considering the erudition and breadth of knowledge displayed in Roes's work. This may be more pronounced with regard to works emanating from outside the Western cultural sphere, although it should be noted that Roes takes most of his reference points from the Western canon. This study proceeds now, however, to present close analytical readings of Roes's works, in the attempt to illuminate the author's approach to textual appropriation as a component of literary representations of intercultural encounters.

CHAPTER 1

Aspects of Play in *Leeres Viertel. Rub' al-Khali*

Michael Roes's *Leeres Viertel. Rub' Al-Khali: Invention über das Spiel* (1996) consists of two separate but closely related narrative strands, one set in the 1990s, and the other at the beginning of the nineteenth century.[1] The intercultural encounters portrayed in the novel are staged within a specifically anthropological context. Informed by recent theories of anthropology, the unnamed contemporary protagonist, arguably an alter ego of Michael Roes, is travelling in Yemen and carrying out research into traditional children's games in the period leading up to the civil war of 1994. The protagonist of the historical strand, on the other hand, Ferdinand Alois Schnittke, is an assistant to a group of ethnographers who are looking for ancient inscriptions, with the ultimate aim, which was unknown to Schnittke himself when they left Germany, of finding the Ark of the Covenant. The novel's narrative takes the form of two parallel sets of diary entries. Schnittke's diary is partly based on a compilation of authentic travel accounts, which are listed in an afterword. They range from Carsten Niebuhr's *Reisebeschreibung nach Arabien und andern umliegenden Ländern* (1774) to T. E. Lawrence's *Seven Pillars of Wisdom* (1936). Schnittke, a fictional character, is presented as a forerunner to the contemporary researcher who, according to the narrative conceit of the novel, has discovered an incomplete copy of Schnittke's diary in the Anna-Amalia-Bibliothek in Weimar. The contemporary anthropologist now follows in Schnittke's footsteps to the Arabian Peninsula and to the Empty Quarter of the novel's title, and the reader is invited to compare their experiences by reading extracts from their respective accounts.

This chapter approaches *Leeres Viertel* by first outlining the novel's status as a work of literary anthropology. I demonstrate how the contemporary narrator's deliberations on anthropological methods reflects the influence of theorists such as Clifford Geertz and James Clifford, who proposed new ways of writing

1 Based on details mentioned in the text, Christoph Schmitt-Maaß puts the date at between 1802 and 1805, but adds that Roes '[...] die Idee einer zeitlich eindeutigen Verortung [negiert]'. For example, Kaspar Hauser is mentioned in Schnittke's diary, despite the fact that Hauser as a historical figure only came to the public's attention in 1828 (Schmitt-Maaß, '"mäandernd, ornamentalisch, ohne progression?"', 99).

ethnography in the 1970s and 1980s. Following this contextualization, I analyse the presentation of the anthropological subject matter, namely traditional Arab games. In the age of postmodernism, play has penetrated every aspect of modern life. It is no longer the exclusive domain of children and many aspects of life not related to leisure activities are now described using the vocabulary of play. I argue that Roes presents travel as a playful activity in which the traveller is free to try out new modes of behaviour and thought. However, whereas the player of a game is free to return to ordinary reality at any time, the traveller risks experiencing a transformation that leaves him or her permanently changed. After analysing the dynamics of intercultural encounters in the first half of the chapter, the second half evaluates the intertextual aspects of the novel. I identify three main types of intertextuality: first, the contrapuntal *intra*textual relation between the historical and contemporary strand; second, the intertextual references to external texts; and, third, the playful level of intertextual 'plagiarism' in which unmarked quotations from real travel accounts are embedded into the novel. In closing, I argue that the novel's intertextuality takes on playful characteristics which reflect the anthropological subject matter. I read the process of intertextual borrowing as a game or, to borrow Raymond Federman's term, 'pla(y)giarism'.

Ferdinand Alois Schnittke, 'Comödiant, Kirchen- und Prospectmaler und Marionettentheaterdirector' (*LV*, p. 14) in Weimar, the centre of German culture at the time, leaves that city hoping to find relief from his emotional distress following the death of his wife and child. Schnittke also cites the animosity between himself and the director of the local theatre, the Weimarer Hoftheater, in one of many veiled references to Goethe in the novel (analysed in detail later), as another reason he needed to leave. Schnittke is employed as secretary on the ethnological mission by Baron Ernst Eugen de la Motte and Tertulio Liebtrud Schotenbauer. Other members of their party include Doctor Schlichter and the mute former slave Frere Jacque. Schnittke's diary is an exciting and colourful travelogue that often resembles an adventure story. Over the course of their travels, the group face numerous difficulties, including illness, arrest and incarceration. Doctor Schlichter dies in Jeddah after a fever. De la Motte is stabbed to death on the crowded streets of Sana'a (*LV*, p. 390), and Frere Jacque's body is never found after he is shot at night by an unidentified sniper in Beni Gahim (*LV*, p. 471). Schnittke and Schotenbauer are taken captive by a desert tribe and are held in a dungeon, where the latter dies after being stung by a scorpion. Schnittke, the expedition's last man standing,[2] escapes but can only survive in the harsh desert environment long enough to be rescued by his former captors. He is adopted by this tribe, the

2 Schnittke's story is very similar in this respect to Carsten Niebuhr's. All of Niebuhr's travel companions died during the 1761–67 expedition, leaving Niebuhr to complete the voyage alone and publish the scientific and ethnographic data collected.

Beni Lafitat, and takes on the name Ali Fard ibn Almani al Lafitat as a reflection of his status as a 'Neukabilen honoris causa' (*LV*, p. 763). At the close of his account it appears that he will marry into one of the tribal families, retain his adopted identity and remain there forever. Schnittke's diary is thus a 'going native' story, but while his new name signals his adopted kinship (Lafitat), it is also a reminder of his origins (Almani), suggesting the impossibility of completely relinquishing one's original cultural identity.

The contemporary anthropologist undergoes a similar journey but his account is drier, less sentimental and influenced by the latest anthropological theories. His diary notes are a juxtaposition of travel writing, which includes observations on daily life, lists of anthropological data and reflections on the theory of play. He also describes the physical and emotional difficulties he faces in the unfamiliar climate, and he records sexual encounters with local men. He travels first to the capital Sana'a and then to some of the towns and villages nearby, always observing the games that the children play. With a civil war brewing between the Yemeni government and supporters of the Yemeni Socialist Party, and with other Europeans leaving the country, the anthropologist takes increasing risks to continue his research in the outlying villages.[3] He is eventually taken hostage but is treated well by his captors and allowed to continue to work in the village where he is held. The tribe's leader vows to protect him and he in turn vows not to leave without permission. When the American Dick Barber from the Research Institute in Sana'a arrives to take him home, the young man chooses to stay, feeling an increasing sense of belonging at the edge of the Empty Quarter. The novel closes with the narrator remaining in the village of his captors, another instance of a Westerner 'going native'. By doing so, he challenges the dichotomy of Self and Other since it appears that he is no longer an anthropologist studying Yemeni society from the outside. 'Going native' raises questions about the colonial and neo-colonial order, systems whose 'Funktionieren die energische Abgrenzung von den "Anderen" [...] erfordert'.[4] Whether the contemporary narrator can assimilate entirely into his new environment, however, remains unclear at the end of the novel.

3 *Leeres Viertel* is different to other recent German novels on civil wars in the Middle East since it is the only novel, according to Paul Michael Lützeler, in which one finds 'einen Icherzähler, der mit Mühe Aspekte einer völlig fremden Kultur schätzen lernt. Aber auch bei ihm ist der kulturelle Gewinn einseitig'. German novels on Middle Eastern civil wars tend otherwise to be 'ernüchternde Dokumente einer nichtkommunikativen Kulturbegegnung' (Paul Michael Lützeler, 'Macht und Gewalt: Zu Romanen über Bürgerkriege im Nahen und Mittleren Osten von Kühn, Born, Kracht und Roes', in *Gewalt und kulturelles Gedächtnis: Repräsentationsformen von Gewalt in Literatur und Film seit 1945*, ed. by Robert Weninger (Tübingen: Stauffenberg, 2005), pp. 19–37 (p. 33)).

4 Hansjörg Bay, 'Going Native?: Mimikry und Maskerade in kolonialen Entdeckungsreisen der Gegenwartsliteratur (Stangl; Trojanow)', in *Ins Fremde Schreiben*, ed. by Christof Hamann and Alexander Honold, pp. 117–42 (p. 118).

Despite the two centuries separating these two characters and their fictional diary accounts they have a number of things in common. In each case a German man ventures to the Middle East with an apparently inquisitive and open mind. The two men take a very different attitude towards foreign cultures to those adopted by the majority of other Europeans in the novel. The nineteenth-century Schnittke's eagerness to make contact with the Arab population is in stark contrast to the lack of interest, indeed the 'typisch koloniale[r] Arroganz'[5] of his employers, who, it seems, are only there to carry out research into the ancient civilization of the country and take very little interest in the living populace. Similarly, the colleagues of the contemporary character at the Research Institute in Sana'a are isolated from day-to-day life, separated from the real world by the walls of their compound. Sharing a sensitivity to local customs, an interest in the traditions of the Arab world and a similar fate, their diary accounts closely intertwine. On their journeys they learn just as much about themselves as they do about an unfamiliar culture. However, crucially they are absorbed, at least partially, into that culture and at the end of the novel they both remain in the Yemeni desert, facing what is admittedly an uncertain future.

In the autumn of 1996, *Leeres Viertel* was a minor sensation in Germany's literary scene and was awarded the 'Bremer Literaturpreis' of 1997. Yet while the novel was widely reviewed in the German-language print media it had a mixed reception. Iris Radisch in *Die Zeit* hailed Roes's novel as the perfect antidote to the 'akuter Wirklichkeitsmangel' in the contemporary German book market. While other writers produce 'immer mehr Bücher mit immer mehr Stoff [...], den keiner der Autoren aus eigener Erfahrung, doch jeder aus eigener Lektüre, beisteuert', Roes has achieved an unusual fusion which combines both reading and real-world experience.[6] *Leeres Viertel* was widely perceived to be genre-defying, with Michael Braun applauding the 'kühne Gratwanderung zwischen den Gattungen', describing it as being 'zugleich Reise- und Abenteuerroman, umfangreiche anthropologische Materialsammlung, Ethnographie einer fremden Kultur, nicht zuletzt phantastische Legende und autobiographisches Fragment'.[7] Sybille Cramer in the *Neue Zürcher Zeitung* was equally enthusiastic, opining that the novel not only reconciles 'Wissen und Poesie', but is also a book which bears a political significance in terms of initiating a dialogue between East and West.[8]

5 Karsten Herrmann, 'Ein (Werk-) Porträt des Michael Roes', http://culturmag.de/rubriken/buecher/michael-roes-im-portrat/14846 [accessed 9 June 2014].

6 Iris Radisch, 'Das Ende der Spielzeit', *Die Zeit*, 4 October 1996, Section F, p. 1.

7 Michael Braun, 'Michael Roes: Leeres Viertel. Rub' al-Khali', *Die Woche*, 4 October 1996, p. 9.

8 Sybille Cramer, 'Jede Wirklichkeit hat ihre eigene Sprache', *Neue Zürcher Zeitung*, 7 November 1996, p. 33.

The description 'Roman' on the cover of the volume raised a few eyebrows, however, with Volker Hage in *Der Spiegel* particularly critical of this 'verkaufsfördernde, nicht eben originelle Trick'.[9] His was the most critical of all the reviews, claiming Roes 'hat keine Sprache', and sarcastically describing the style of the book as 'Deutsche Gegenwartsprosa pur'. Angela Praesent in the *Weltwoche*[10] argued that Roes's main theme was homo-erotic lust, and that the protagonist was an 'erotischer Tourist' who feigned interest in the foreign culture.[11] She proceeded to criticize the anthropological lists which are compiled and presented, she says, in just the same way as those of the ethnographers of the colonial period; and raised doubt about the narrator's research methodology and theory of play. Praesent then questioned whether the Schnittke sections, which were favoured over the contemporary sections by many other reviewers, are strictly necessary, describing them as a 'wackelige Montage' which combines both Baroque and Romantic styles with anachronistic vocabulary.

Questions concerning the form of the novel dominated discussions regarding the text. To what extent can a work that consists on the one hand of anthropological observations, and on the other of excerpts adapted from a number of authentic historical accounts, be regarded as a novel? In considering the movement between the two narrative strands, it is worth reflecting upon the significance of Roes's subtitle for the novel, *Invention über das Spiel*. 'Invention' is a musical term denoting short pieces in two-part counterpoint. The two narratives of *Leeres Viertel* can certainly be seen as in literary counterpoint to each other, especially since the two narratives at one point merge in a confusing union. The novel has also been likened to a fugue,[12] in which the various sounds interplay with and imitate each other.[13] This interpretation has interesting implications for a reading of *Leeres Viertel*. The

9 Volker Hage, 'Sprachlos in der Wüste', *Der Spiegel*, 25 November 1996, p. 220.

10 Angela Praesent, 'Ein erotischer Tourist im Jemen', *Weltwoche*, 9 January 1997, p. 35.

11 Christoph Schmitt-Maaß, in a book-length study of anthropological novels, refutes Praesent's claim, stating that the sexual scenes in the novel are highly ritualised: 'Den homoerotischen Sexualpraktiken und den ihnen vorausgehenden Aushandlungen kommt also eine bedeutungsstiftende Funktion zu, so dass von "Sextourismus" nicht die Rede sein kann' (Schmitt-Maaß, *Das gefährdete Subjekt*, p. 208).

12 Cramer, 'Jede Wirklichkeit', p. 33.

13 There are some fascinating parallels here with Raoul Schrott's novel *Finis Terrae* (1995), which also features a contemporary narrator who follows in the footsteps of a historical traveller. Schrott, posing as the volume's editor, presents the fictional travelogue by the historical figure Pytheas of Massalia and the diary account by the purely fictional Ludwig Höhnel, not only as authentic but also as 'eine Art Kontrapunkt' (Raoul Schrott, *Finis Terrae* (Munich: DTV, 1997), p. 13). Other features that the novels share include imitation of historical syntax, an indistinct boundary between fact and fiction, and a research interest in fields such as anthropology and archaeology.

two voices in the text are clearly individual voices and each narrator carves out a distinct identity for himself. Their literary approaches vary, but they meet a fate that is eerily similar and their idiosyncratic voices unite in a surprisingly harmonious, fugue-like way.

The two diary accounts are distinguished by characteristic orthography. Schnittke uses antiquated spelling which clearly identifies him as an Enlightenment intellectual. It has been noted that Roes at times goes too far in making Schnittke's language appear dated, resulting in a Baroque style, a mistake that nevertheless contributes to Roes's intention of making Schnittke and his time seem '"anders", als "fremd" – und damit als entfernt'.[14] Bizarrely, Roes pursues a similar strategy through the use of unorthodox spelling in the contemporary sections: nouns are left uncapitalized and the 'ß' is expressed by using 'sz'. In contrast to Schnittke's case, the reader does not know what has driven the modern narrator from Germany, but one can speculate that writing in this idiosyncratic orthography is a linguistic reflection of the narrator's alienation from his own culture.

To venture into metaphors of translation, the modern narrator is reading and translating a text (Yemen and its culture) for a German readership. In the way that he conveys his knowledge of the foreign culture to his German audience, he can be seen to adopt what Lawrence Venuti has described as a 'foreignizing' approach.[15] By bringing the reader away from the comforts of his home culture and of standard German orthography, and by 'making the reader of the translation travel abroad',[16] Roes is restraining the 'ethnocentric violence'[17] that is an inherent part of translation (or of writing about other cultures). Another aspect of this 'foreignizing' approach in *Leeres Viertel* is the use of Arabic script. The novel's title is bilingual, as is the title of a volume of poetry by Roes, *Durus Arabij. Arabische Lektionen* (1997), in which some of the German poems are published side-by-side with Arabic translations. Some Arabic script appears in *Leeres Viertel* untranslated. The novel's epigraph, for instance, is: 'إذا كان ما ستقوله ليس أجمل من الصمت فاصمت (Arabisches Sprichwort)' (*LV*, p. 6). This is an unusual manifestation of a 'paratext'[18] because the majority of the book's German readership will presumably be unable to understand it. To discover the meaning of the proverb, the reader would need to instigate an

14 Schmitt-Maaß, '"mäandernd, ornamentalisch, ohne progression?"', 107–08.

15 Lawrence Venuti, *The Translator's Invisibility: A History of Translation*, 2nd edn (London; New York: Routledge, 2008), pp. 83–124. Inspired in no small part by Friedrich Schleiermacher, Lawrence Venuti is the most famous modern proponent of the foreignizing approach to translation.

16 Venuti, *The Translator's Invisibility*, p. 84.

17 Venuti, *The Translator's Invisibility*, pp. 12–20.

18 Genette, *Palimpsests*, p. 3.

intercultural encounter of his or her own. The author of this work was reliably informed by a speaker of Arabic that the proverb translates as: 'If what you have to say is no better than staying silent, then stay silent'.

In the post-colonial context, writers from former colonies writing in English often use untranslated words. In such cases:

> [the] inserted language 'stands for' the colonized culture in a metonymic way, and its very resistance to interpretation constructs a 'gap' between the writer's culture and the colonial culture. The local writer is thus able to represent his or her world to the colonizer (and others) in the metropolitan language, and at the same time to signal and emphasize a difference from it.[19]

Roes, as a German traveller, is clearly writing from a different position but his use of a similar technique suggests an attempt to write from a post-colonial perspective. From a purely practical point of view, using untranslated words is a means of expressing ideas or describing things for which German has no equivalent. The effect, however, is to give the Arabic language a certain status or footing in the text and to expose the reader to the experience of alienation that contact with a foreign culture can engender. It highlights the huge cultural divisions with which the narrator is contending and signifies the alienation of the traveller as he attempts to come to grips with the unfamiliar surroundings. Of course, many instances of Arabic in *Leeres Viertel* are glossed or translated, thus bridging the divide for the reader. Without this 'domesticating' assistance the average reader might find the novel frustrating and put it down without having learned anything new. However, by including Arabic words, Roes creates a feeling of distance between his readership and the target (German) culture, and brings them subtly towards the source (Arabic) culture. Roes deliberately distances his narrator from the latter's *Heimat*, positioning him between two worlds. That experience is reported in a language that resists domesticating the experience of the Middle East for his German readership.

The Literary Turn in Anthropology

The anonymous contemporary anthropologist quotes Alfred Le Chatelier, a French Orientalist writing in 1904 about the aims of anthropological surveys in Morocco:

> wir wollen Marokkos Ursprünge ergründen, seinen Verzweigungen, seinen Konflikten und Bündnissen nachspüren; mit einem Wort, wir wollen jenes

19 Bill Ashcroft, Gareth Griffiths and Helen Tiffin, *Post-Colonial Studies: The Key Concepts*, 2nd edn (London: Routledge, 2007), p. 123.

> Terrain, in dem wir möglicherweise irgendwann zu intervenieren gezwungen sein werden, so umfassend wie möglich erforschen, so daß wir auf der Grundlage genauer Kenntnisse werden handeln können (*LV*, p. 240).

Anthropology in this respect is aggressive and manipulative, and is part of the wider colonial politics of the period. It is a perfect illustration of Edward Said's argument in his seminal work *Orientalism* (1978), according to which Western academic, scientific and literary discourse on the Arab world contributed to the West's domination over the East. Said goes on to call for a 'contemporary alternative to Orientalism' and for an approach to the 'study [of] other cultures and peoples from a libertarian, or a nonrepressive and nonmanipulative, perspective'.[20] The methods and aims of anthropology have changed considerably in the ninety years that separate Le Chatelier and the contemporary protagonist, causing the latter to distance himself from such predecessors. The contemporary anthropologist is, nevertheless, sensitive to the fact that his research may have an impact on the 'möglichst unberührte, ungewarnte, unvorbereitete untersuchungsfeld' (*LV*, p. 239). He reflects on his methodology, his motives and the unforeseeable consequences his presence may have on the people he is studying; and describes his presence in Yemen as a 'wissenschaftlich-voyeuristischen einbruch' (*LV*, p. 239). Yet, despite the fact that his anthropology is less invasive than that of Le Chatelier in Morocco, he recognizes that his research into traditional games in Arab culture is also manipulative: 'alle verhaltensweisen bleiben strategisch. Sie zielen darauf ab, die begegnung mit dem fremden zu einem kontrollierten, wiederhol- und überprüfbaren experiment zu machen' (*LV*, p. 240).

The narrator's doubts in *Leeres Viertel* reflect an increasing awareness in the field of anthropology since the 1970s that the discipline shares 'complex institutional connections with Western colonial expansion on the one hand, and a salvational belief in the power of pure science on the other'.[21] A number of theoretical responses to these problems have emerged since the 1970s as anthropology has searched for new approaches to the study of other cultures. One of the main figures in this regard is Clifford Geertz, who called for a refocusing of anthropological interest onto the literary and stylistic processes employed in the writing of ethnological narratives. No longer are anthropological texts to be regarded as transparent windows onto foreign cultures but rather as literary constructs. As James Clifford, another major figure in the debate surrounding the literary turn in anthropology, put

20 Edward Said, *Orientalism* (London: Penguin, 1978; 2003), p. 24.

21 Nigel Rapport and Joanna Overing, *Social and Cultural Anthropology: The Key Concepts* (London: Routledge, 2000), p. 237.

it, moving the focus onto 'text making and rhetoric serves to highlight the constructed, artificial nature of cultural accounts'.[22]

In the well-known essay 'Thick Description: Toward an Interpretive Theory of Culture' (1973), Geertz, drawing on Max Weber, regards culture as readable:

> [M]an is an animal suspended in webs of significance he himself has spun, I take culture to be those webs, and the analysis of it to be therefore not an experimental science in search of law but an interpretative one in search of meaning'.[23]

Geertz conceives of anthropology as an exercise in what he terms 'thick description', a textual rendering of 'a multiplicity of complex conceptual structures, many of them superimposed upon or knotted into one another, which are at once strange, irregular, and inexplicit'.[24] He moves the emphasis of anthropological research 'from the measuring of social structure to the interpretation of meaning'.[25] For Geertz, the anthropological insights gained in the field can thus only ever be regarded as interpretations of interpretations: that is, the anthropologist's inevitably partial understanding of the indigenous population's interpretation of its own cultural system.

Not only does Geertz regard the anthropologist's 'reading' and interpretation of a foreign culture as comparable to the task of the literary critic,[26] he also puts forward the idea that ethnographic texts are literary fictions 'in the sense that they are "something made," "something fashioned" – the original meaning of *fictiō* – not that they are false, unfactual, or merely "as if" thought experiments'.[27] In *Works and Lives: The Anthropologist as Author* (1988), Geertz analyses classic texts by four major twentieth-century anthropologists (Claude Lévi-Strauss, E. E. Evans-Pritchard, Bronisław Malinowski and Ruth Benedict) and concludes that these works became classics due to their stylistic and literary force. Roes has also stated that the literary quality of an anthropological account is crucial: 'Jeder gute Roman ist gute Ethnologie. Ich würde das sogar umkehren: nur dann ist Ethnologie gute Ethnologie, wenn sie auch ein guter Roman ist'.[28] The claim that anthropological texts are literary and fictional constructs has not been universally accepted in the

22 James Clifford, 'Introduction', in *Writing Culture: The Poetics and Politics of Ethnography*, ed. by James Clifford and George E. Marcus (Berkeley: University of California Press, 1986), pp. 1–26 (p. 2).

23 Clifford Geertz, *The Interpretation of Cultures* (London: Fontana, 1973; 1993), p. 5.

24 Geertz, *The Interpretation of Cultures*, p. 10.

25 Rapport and Overing, *Social and Cultural Anthropology*, p. 210.

26 Geertz, *The Interpretation of Cultures*, p. 9.

27 Geertz, *The Interpretation of Cultures*, p. 15.

28 Roes in interview with Christoph Schmitt-Maaß, *Das gefährdete Subjekt*, p. 285.

academy and the new focus on literary questions has been criticized by some as 'an unhealthy self-absorption; narcissistic and decadent; time-wasting and hypochondriacal'.[29] For Roes and other literary anthropologists, however, that increased acknowledgement of the literariness of anthropological texts is one means of coming to terms with the moral entanglement of representing foreign cultures textually.

Another solution put forward by Geertz and others to this moral dilemma is to 'admit that anthropology entails representing one sort of life in the categories of another'.[30] Paradoxically, the understanding gained of the foreign culture is communicated by the anthropologist in the language and cultural concepts of his or her own culture. This is an aporetic problem that the narrator of *Leeres Viertel* wrestles with in his diary:

> Entweder bleibe ich ganz in meinem wissenschaftlichen system dem anderen gegenüber, dann gibt es aber kein verständnis seiner sinnwelt, oder ich bemühe mich um ein verstehen aus seinem selbstverständnis heraus; dann musz ich aber meine wissenschaftliche darstellungsweise aufgeben (*LV*, p. 731).

He speculates that he would have to abandon all pretence of scientific integrity to gain any understanding of the Yemeni people. Whereas Geertz suggests that admitting to the Eurocentric nature of cultural accounts leads out of the theoretical impasse, Roes's narrator goes further and suggests that knowledge of another culture would ideally be gained and communicated through the foreign culture's conceptions of itself. He concedes, however, that his attempts to understand and explain foreign cultures are a part of a distinctly Western intellectual tradition and therefore will inevitably fail completely to comprehend other ways of thinking and being. This was the paradox that faced anthropologists writing at the end of the twentieth century: can knowledge about one culture be successfully transmitted in the language of another? Moreover, of all types of language, is the language of science the most appropriate to use whilst writing ethnography? The narrator of *Leeres Viertel* seriously doubts it: 'Keine sprache ist vollständig. Und von allen denkbaren ist die sprache der wissenschaft eine der beschränktesten' (*LV*, p. 731).

As debates over methods of writing ethnography evolved, the border with fiction became more 'gradual and shifting'.[31] In the German-speaking world Hubert Fichte (1935–86) is the best-known proponent of an anthropological literature, literary anthropology, or *Ethnopoesie*. Fichte's aim was not only

29 Rapport and Overing, *Social and Cultural Anthropology*, p. 239.

30 Rapport and Overing, *Social and Cultural Anthropology*, p. 239.

31 Kirin Narayan, 'Ethnography and Fiction: Where is the Border?', *Anthropology and Humanism*, 24 (1999), 134–47 (p. 143), quoted in Antonius C. G. M. Robben and Jeffrey A. Sluka, eds., *Ethnographic Fieldwork: an Anthropological Reader* (Malden: Blackwell, 2007), p. 493.

to unite ethnography and poetry, 'sondern beide Produktionen aus einem Kopf und einem Körper entstehen zu lassen, beide Formen menschlicher Kreativität situativ neu zu entwickeln'.[32] Fichte was certainly an anomaly on the German literary scene, a writer who followed his own agenda. His subject is the underdog or the outsider, be that in St. Pauli or in Belize. He combines the poetic, the journalistic and the ethnographic, and insists on a sparse, barren style. Numerous similarities exist between Fichte's ethnographic novels and Roes's *Leeres Viertel*, not least the inclusion of the protagonists' doubt over the ethics of their research and the narration of the sexual encounters with other men that they experience during their journeys. It should, however, be noted that Michael Roes distances himself from the term *Ethnopoesie* and has stated that 'Hubert Fichte [...] definitiv nicht zu meinen Vorbildern [gehört]'.[33] Roes regards the language and style in which Fichte presents his ethnographic discoveries as impoverished: '[...] sprachlich lassen mich seine Texte verdursten'.[34]

In the essay 'Ketzerische Bemerkungen für eine neue Wissenschaft vom Menschen' (written in 1976 and published in *Petersilie* in 1980), Fichte outlines his poetics of ethnopoetry. Like Clifford Geertz, he calls for the focus to be turned onto the methods and processes used to record ethnological knowledge:

> Anthropologie, Ethnologie, Ethologie und die ihnen verwandten Wissenschaften behandeln, unterschiedlich, Verhaltensweisen des Menschen.
>
> Unter "Logos" versteht man vor allem "Das Wort".
>
> Worte sind Verhaltensweisen.
>
> Schon hier ergibt sich eine Antinomie: Der Typus der Beschreibung und der Typus des Beschriebenen gehen unkritisch ineinander auf.
>
> Antinomien können nur poetisch ausgedrückt werden.[35]

Fichte regards the human sciences as 'wortgebunden'.[36] Attempts to describe other cultures without acknowledging the interconnectedness of the mode of representation and object of description are doomed to failure. It is a point also made by Geertz: '[T]he line between mode of representation and

32 Hans-Jürgen Heinrichs, 'Die authentische Beschreibung der fremden Kultur', in *Hubert Fichte: Materialien zu Leben und Werk*, ed. by Thomas Beckermann (Frankfurt am Main: Fischer, 1985), pp. 142–51 (p. 142).

33 Roes in interview with Schmitt-Maaß, *Das gefährdete Subjekt*, p. 285.

34 Roes in interview with Schmitt-Maaß, *Das gefährdete Subjekt*, p. 285.

35 Hubert Fichte, 'Ketzerische Bemerkungen für eine neue Wissenschaft vom Menschen', in *Petersilie* (Frankfurt am Main: Fischer, 1980), pp. 359–69 (p. 359).

36 Schmitt-Maaß, *Das gefährdete Subjekt*, p. 19.

substantive content is as undrawable in cultural analysis as it is in painting'.[37] According to Fichte, such a paradox can only be addressed by poetry, since the human sciences must utilize that which differentiates humans from animals: 'die poetisch komponierte Aussage'.[38] Like the narrator of *Leeres Viertel*, Fichte criticizes scientific jargon, describing it as an 'Ausdrucksweise des blanken Neokolonialismus. Er verhüllt Zusammenhänge, anstatt sie aufzudecken, er verdrängt seine ideologischen Reflexe, anstatt sie zu reflektieren'.[39]

In addition to increased awareness of the textual practices of anthropology, a move was instigated in the 1970s to include the anthropologist in the fieldwork account. Prior to these developments the anthropologist, after some introductory remarks about his or her arrival in the field, would largely remain absent from the text. As Paul Rabinow explains: 'An experiential "I was there" element establishes the unique authority of the anthropologist; its suppression in the text establishes the anthropologist's scientific authority'.[40] Since objectivity had come to be regarded as an impossibility, the only recourse for the honest ethnographer was to write in a manner that acknowledged this inherent subjectivity and to record personal biases and professional difficulties. Fichte, too, calls for the inclusion of the ethnographer in the written account, stating that he or she is just as much of an object of interest as the culture being researched:

> Ist es eine Schande, einzugestehen, dass man über die Woloff forscht, weil man schwul ist?
>
> Doch wohl nicht mehr!
>
> Auch das bedeutet ein ethnologisches Faktum, und es wäre Irreführung, es zu verschweigen.[41]

He then proceeds to urge anthropologists to include problems and difficulties faced abroad in their anthropological accounts:

> Ist es nicht aufschlussreich, neben jedem Hüpfschritt der Shia, die Schwierigkeiten des Ethnologen in Bahrain aufzuzeichnen, der an den selbstzerstörerischen Riten des Mouharram teilnehmen will?[42]

This call for self-reflexivity in anthropological reports is of great importance. There are earlier examples in which the anthropologist's subjective experience

37 Geertz, *The Interpretation of Cultures*, p. 16.
38 Fichte, 'Ketzerische Bemerkungen', p. 363.
39 Fichte, 'Ketzerische Bemerkungen', p. 360.
40 Paul Rabinow, 'Representations are Social Facts: Modernity and Post-Modernity in Anthropology', in *Writing Culture*, ed. by Clifford and Marcus, pp. 234–61 (p. 244).
41 Fichte, 'Ketzerische Bemerkungen', p. 362.
42 Fichte, 'Ketzerische Bemerkungen', p. 363.

is included in written accounts. Claude Lévi-Strauss famously begins his self-reflexive anthropological memoir *Tristes Tropiques* (1955) with the statement: 'I hate travelling and explorers'.[43] Laura Bohannan's decision to publish her anthropological novel *Return to Laughter* (1964) under the pseudonym Elenore Smith Bowen is a symptom of her time.[44] It was not until the 1970s that self-reflexivity became increasingly common. Paul Rabinow's *Reflections on Field Work in Morocco* (1977) is a self-reflexive text to which this study will return. In such works, the anthropologist does not attempt to minimize his or her presence in the account in an attempt to convey the impression of scientific neutrality. The researcher is present and, moreover, acknowledges that that presence may have an influence upon the people and society being studied.

The influence of the self-reflexive approach can be clearly observed in *Leeres Viertel*. The narrator combines the objective observations of the scientifically-minded ethnographer with the more personal, subjective narrative of the diarist. He records moments of emotional sensitivity and intense self-reflexivity. He reports a number of sexual encounters with Arab men, encounters which sometimes turn out to be fleeting, unfulfilling, or even dangerous.[45] He also describes the increasingly debilitating bouts of illness he suffers as well as their psychological repercussions. At times he expresses (as does Schnittke) his frustration at the division that persists between him and the Arab people and culture. In one diary entry the young anthropologist sees himself as being 'verhaftet' by his own culture, failing to open up to the 'neuen, fremden alltag' (*LV*, p. 459). He has furnished his apartment 'in vertrauter weise', and is surprised 'immer noch' by the physical contact Yemenis share. The verbs he uses make his estrangement clear: *beobachten*, *abwenden*, *entziehen*, *zurückschrecken*, *widersprechen*, *ausschlieszen* (*LV*, p. 459). The house is used as a metaphor, with the narrator seeing the *diwan* as a symbol for this distance between him and the Arab people. It is the 'grenzraum' (*LV*, p. 594), the room to which guests are invited. The guests will not, however, be invited any further into the home. The Western practice of showing a guest around the house on arrival is inconceivable. For the analytical mind of the narrator the house is 'nicht nur modell einer sozialen, sondern auch einer psychischen ordnung' in which 'die grenzen der begegnung und der anteilnahme zwischen mir und den anderen deutlich [werden]: Ich werde nur bis in den "diwan der seele" vorgelassen. Die inneren räume bleiben mir verschlossen' (*LV*, p. 594).

43 Lévi-Strauss, *Tristes Tropiques*, p. 17. A sentiment that is, perhaps, echoed in Schnittke's statement as he leaves Weimar: 'ich, der das Reisen über alle Maassen hasst' (*LV*, p. 11).

44 Clifford, 'Introduction', in *Writing Culture*, ed. by Clifford and Marcus, p. 13.

45 Cf. Paul Rabinow, *Reflections on Fieldwork in Morocco*, pp. 68–69, where he refers to a night spent with a prostitute.

The anthropologist's expression of despair informs the reader of his emotional state but affords at the same time an insight into life in the Arab countries, the architecture of their homes and the way they interact with each other and with foreigners.

Along with anthropology's realization that writing objective accounts of other cultures is impossible came the recognition that full and complete understanding is also inconceivable. As the narrator of *Leeres Viertel* comes to realize: 'Ein "objektives" oder auch umfassendes verstehen eines anderen wird es nie geben' (*LV*, p. 731). This realization is reflected in *Leeres Viertel* by an element of fragmentation. The narrator is aware that his account can only hope to convey a small part of the cultural life of the Yemeni people. Unanswered questions and ever-evolving theories support this impression of a work in progress, an incomplete but not unaccomplished depiction. The aim is no longer to portray a complete account of the culture in question, since that is deemed to be impossible. All that can be done is to present *impressions* of that culture in a series of observations, conversations and theoretical speculations. Hubert Fichte had already pointed in this direction in his 1976 essay:

> Das Fragment:
>
> Warum müssen wissenschaftliche Erzeugnisse vollständiger sein als ihr Vorwurf?
>
> Freiräume, Fehler, Lücken stellen die Frage nach Freiheit und Veränderung auf formale Art neu.[46]

Stephen A. Tyler, in his contribution to *Writing Culture*, also writes of the need to replace representation with evocation: 'A postmodern ethnography is a cooperatively evolved text consisting of fragments of discourse intended to evoke in the minds of both reader and writer an emergent fantasy of a possible world of common-sense reality'.[47]

Both Tyler and Fichte regard such fragmentation as going hand-in-hand with a 'plurivocal' ethnography in which the position of the ethnographer as the master of the text is challenged. The interview was one of Fichte's favoured forms of writing, a medium that allowed two voices to co-exist with equality in a text. Tyler's conception of a postmodern ethnology is one that 'privileges "discourse" over "text," it foregrounds dialogue as opposed to monologue, and emphasizes the cooperative and collaborative nature of the ethnographic

46 Fichte, 'Ketzerische Bemerkungen', p. 364.

47 Stephen A. Tyler, 'Post-Modern Ethnography: From Document of the Occult to Occult Document', in *Writing Culture*, ed. by Clifford and Marcus, pp. 122–40 (p. 125). The landmark volume includes nine meta-anthropological essays calling for reform in the poetics of cultural representation.

situation in contrast to the ideology of the transcendental observer'.[48] In *Leeres Viertel* conversations between the narrator and his anthropological informants are recounted, allowing the Yemeni characters to express their understanding of their own culture in their own words, albeit translated into German. Dialogue has, of course, always been a component of novels, but this kind of conversation is different in that it often features a question-and-answer format by means of which much anthropologically significant information is gathered. In a variation of this, the narrator discusses his findings and theories with a native Yemeni anthropologist, Professor Abdul Malik Al-Makrami of Sana'a University. The German anthropologist's developing theory of play is rejected by his Yemeni colleague (*LV*, p. 155), who objects to the polarization inherent in the German's understanding of the differences between Eastern and Western attitudes to play. The Yemeni anthropologist's indigenous standpoint assists the traveller in deepening his understanding of traditional Yemeni games. Whereas the 'natives' were previously only ever the objects of study, in *Leeres Viertel* it is clear that the Yemeni researcher influences the development of the German's work. Abdul Malik admits that his view of his own culture is also blinkered: 'Ihm fehle, trotz der stadtkindheit, der abstand, der "fremde blick", da die traditionelle lebensweise der wüstenbewohner für alle araber ein ursprungs- und vorbildmythos sei' (*LV*, p. 156). However, a dialogic exchange between partners can result in a multi-perspectival, more nuanced account that compensates for the shortcomings and prejudices of any individual.

Mikhail Bakhtin describes the novel as a genre still in development, a genre that has yet to reveal all its 'plastic possibilities'.[49] He also states that the novel 'squeezes out some genres and incorporates others into its own peculiar structure'.[50] The emergence of ethnopoetic literature could be regarded as an example of the novel's incorporation of another genre. It is an innovative development for both the novel as a genre and for anthropology as an academic discipline. It can well be argued that great literature has always been anthropological. As Roes argues in interview, citing Grimmelshausen's literary depiction of the Thirty Years' War in *Simplicius Simplicissimus*: 'Große Autoren sind große Ethnologen, weil sie Kultur sezieren, in Sprache umzusetzen verstehen und mit dem Leser in ein Gespräch kommen'.[51] However, it can also be seen to work the other way: anthropology has always been literary. That this has now been acknowledged allows courageous anthropologists to

48 Tyler, 'Post-Modern Ethnography', p. 126.

49 Mikhail M. Bakhtin, 'Epic and Novel: Toward a Methodology for the Study of the Novel', in *The Dialogic Imagination*, trans. by Caryl Emerson and Michael Holquist (Austin: University of Texas Press, 1981), pp. 3–40 (p. 3).

50 Bakhtin, 'Epic and Novel', p. 5.

51 Roes in interview with Schmitt-Maaß, *Das gefährdete Subjekt*, p. 286.

explore and experiment with new literary forms. *Leeres Viertel* is a product of, and a contribution to, the on-going debate surrounding the literary turn in anthropology. It is part of a movement in which the manner of conducting and writing ethnology is under scrutiny and in which the boundaries with fiction are less easy to define. On the one hand, it is a literary novel that deals with an anthropological subject, comparable to a number of Hubert Fichte's works and to Bruce Chatwin's *The Songlines* (1987). On the other hand, it is a work of anthropology that capitalizes on the new poetic, literary and self-reflexive freedom that was afforded to anthropologists writing in the late twentieth century: a fusion of fact and fiction that is at once literary and scientific.

'Das Spiel ist nicht Spielerey': The Anthropology of Play

The contemporary anthropologist portrays himself as an observer. He conducts research into play but admits that he is 'kein guter spieler' himself (*LV*, p. 170). His research into children's games takes him from the streets of the Yemeni capital Sana'a to the remotest regions at the edge of the great desert, the Empty Quarter. Over the course of his journey he observes a vast number of games that he lists and describes at various points in his diary. Taking an anti-modern stance, he limits the scope of his interest to traditional games and excludes computer games, sport, competitions, educational games and betting on the grounds that these are too similar to work activities ('ein computerspiel unterscheidet sich in seiner anwendung nicht von der computerarbeit' (*LV*, p. 320)) or are undertaken for some purpose or gain other than pleasure. The concept of play developed by the German anthropologist 'steht nicht nur im gegensatz zum ernst, sondern auch zur festigkeit, zur produktiven tätigkeit und zum gottgefälligen dasein' (*LV*, p. 224). He distinguishes two categories of characteristics that determine whether an activity is play, one internal to the player, the other external:

> *Zu inneren gesetzen* zähle ich spieltrieb, bewegungsdrang, experimentierfreude, lust am gemeinsamen handeln, an der aneignung der umwelt, den wunsch nach grenzerfahrungen [...] *Bestimmte umstände* sind freie zeit, zwangslosigkeit, das vorhandensein eines spielwunsches, eines spielraums, einer spielgruppe und, wenn nötig, von spielmaterial (*LV*, p. 321).

As a result of this discriminating, but in some respects, broad categorization, unexpected areas of culture are included as being defined by a spirit of play: dance, theatre, role-play, poetry and song (*LV*, p. 321). The narrator's understanding of play is therefore comparable to that of Johan Huizinga, whose classic study *Homo Ludens* (1938) examines elements of play in fields such as law, war, poetry and art.

Play is a notoriously difficult concept to define, although Huizinga's attempt is a useful place to begin:

> Summing up the formal characteristics of play we might call it a free activity standing quite consciously outside 'ordinary' life as being 'not serious', but at the same time absorbing the player intensely and utterly. It is an activity connected with no material interest, and no profit can be gained by it. It proceeds within its own proper boundaries of time and space according to fixed rules and in an orderly manner. It promotes the formation of social groupings which tend to surround themselves with secrecy and to stress their difference from the common world by disguise or other means.[52]

Roes briefly refers to play-concepts such as those formulated by Huizinga and other theorists and cultural historians such as Rorty, Freud, Mead and Piaget (*LV*, p. 304), which differ greatly, suggesting the impossibility of consensus. However, the anthropologist does not regard the difficulties of defining the term as a negative: 'Ich rede von spiel, ohne die grenzen genau umreiszen zu können. Das bedeutet nicht, dasz ich die grenzen nicht kennte [*sic*]' (*LV*, p. 445). He seems rather to suggest that it is this very indefinability of the term that makes it useful in daily life: 'Im alltäglichen sprachgebrauch ist möglicherweise die ungenauigkeit eines begriffs ein kriterium seiner brauchbarkeit' (*LV*, p. 445).

However, the narrator does put forward some ideas regarding the nature of play: games are played for no explicit purpose, except for enjoyment and pleasure; play is enclosed within a defined space and time; within the 'magic circle' of the game (court, field, yard) and within the period of time when the game takes place, the rules are binding. These rules differ from those that determine behaviour in real life and there is no need for them to make sense according to the logic that pertains outside the 'magic circle': '*Der sinn liegt allein innerhalb des spiels. Weil der sinn des spiels ein hergestellter und sein ablauf ein frei vereinbarter ist, können sie nicht in frage gestellt werden. Die regeln des spiels sind* unbedingt *bindend*' (*LV*, p. 303). Roes entitles an essay in the volume *Krieg und Tanz* 'Wahrheiten können wir leugnen, Spielregeln nicht': the game relies on the players' voluntary acceptance of the rules. This is a vital point, as Huizinga also emphasizes:

> These rules in their turn are a very important factor in the play-concept. All play has its rules. They determine what 'holds' in the temporary world circumscribed by play. The rules of a game are absolutely binding and allow no doubt. Paul Valéry once in passing gave expression to a very cogent thought when he said: 'No scepticism is possible where the rules of a game

52 Johan Huizinga, *Homo Ludens: A Study of the Play Element in Culture*, trans. by R. F. C. Hull (Boston: Beacon, 1955), p. 13.

> are concerned, for the principle underlying them is an unshakeable truth. [...]' Indeed, as soon as the rules are transgressed the whole play-world collapses. The game is over.[53]

Ironically Huizinga regards the spoilsport as a figure more loathed than the cheat: 'the latter pretends to be playing the game and, on the face of it, still acknowledges the magic circle [...] the spoil-sport shatters the play-world itself'.[54]

In *Leeres Viertel* the theme of travel is closely linked to the traditional children's games of Yemeni culture that are the focus of the contemporary protagonist's research. Just as a child is able to distance himself from '*alltagsverhalten*' (*LV*, p. 255) while playing a game, the journeying traveller is given an opportunity to experiment with new modes of behaviour, dress, and emotion. In effect the traveller is playing, taking on a role. Freed from the '*alltags-ich*' (*LV*, p. 256) he is no longer constrained by familiar surroundings. When a child adopts the rules of a game it enters a 'parallele[r] wirklichkeit', a realization that leads the narrator to question whether there exist 'so viele wirklichkeiten wie welt-anschauungen' (*LV*, p. 356). Seen in this way, the world becomes the sum of all possible realities in which 'wir wände, ja, zeiten beliebig durchschreiten, uns permanent verändern, wir selbst und zugleich ein anderer sein können' (*LV*, p. 357). Huizinga posits that 'play is not "ordinary" or "real" life. It is rather a stepping out of "real" life into a temporary sphere of activity with a disposition all of its own'.[55] I suggest that for Roes travel also fulfils this criterion: the world is a playground in which the traveller can choose to take on new identities and beliefs, leaving behind his previous identity.

In his essay 'Wahrheiten können wir leugnen, Spielregeln nicht', Roes elaborates on the link he perceives between play and intercultural encounters, saying that play is 'nicht nur ein bei*spiel*haftes Konzept, Probleme und Möglichkeiten interkulturellen Verstehens aufzuzeigen. Es eröffnet auch Perspektiven, Verständigungsprozesse zwischen Fremden in Gang zu bringen und zu vertiefen' (*KT*, p. 41). It is no surprise, then, that in *Leeres Viertel* the subject of the contemporary character's anthropological research is children's games; and yet in the field of anthropology, play has only become recognized relatively recently as a valid subject of study. In an article published in 1974 Edward Norbeck, a cultural anthropologist, suggests that the traditional Protestant work ethic has been responsible for the view that play is 'unseemly behaviour' and therefore not worthy of serious academic study.[56] To

53 Huizinga, *Homo Ludens*, p. 11.
54 Huizinga, *Homo Ludens*, p. 11.
55 Huizinga, *Homo Ludens*, p. 8.
56 Edward Norbeck, 'Anthropological Views of Play', *American Zoologist*, 14 (1974), 267–73 (p. 267).

anthropologists of the late-twentieth and early twenty-first centuries, such as Roes, play must seem like an ideal subject which presents itself as fertile ground for intercultural comparisons. Play is a feature of every culture on earth. It is, one could argue, one of the elements that Roes claims that 'wir gemeinsam haben' (*KT*, p. 127). However, although play is something all humanity has in common, each society plays different games, with different aims. That these 'specific forms of play are learned, culturally molded ways of behaving' points towards the conclusion that comparing the way different cultures play will provide valuable insights, especially taking into consideration Norbeck's opinion that 'the prevailing forms of play of any society [are] congruent with other elements of its culture'.[57] This is a similar point to the one I will make later in this chapter regarding the intercultural significance of dance: physical movement, dance and play are all universal phenomena but they manifest themselves in culturally specific forms.

The approach taken by the narrator in his study of the Arab games is comparative. He compares the games played by Arab children with play patterns of children in Europe and develops theories based upon these differences (*LV*, p. 155, p. 173, p. 191). At times he recognizes similarities between the games he observes and those he played during his childhood and theorizes that 'spiele [...] in allen kulturen offenbar ähnliche wesensmerkmale aufweisen [müssen], um von den kindern als spiel anerkannt und nachgespielt zu werden' (*LV*, p. 213). Schnittke, too, observes 'wie die Spiele auf der ganzen Welt die selbigen zu seyn scheinen' (*LV*, p. 96) after identifying a game played on the banks of the Nile as the same one that is played on the banks of the Ilm in Thuringia. This statement by the fictional Schnittke is taken and adapted by Roes from Carsten Niebuhr's real travel account of his voyage to the Arab peninsula and India in 1761–1767.[58] As men of the Enlightenment, Schnittke and his real-world model Niebuhr might be expected to tend towards such a universalist perspective.

It is no surprise that Yemen does not escape football's global domination, even if Yemeni children do not always conform to FIFA rules. However, the contemporary narrator is more reluctant than his predecessor to admit the universal nature of children's play, sensing a divide between children's games in Western societies and those in the traditional tribal societies of the Arab peninsula. While children's games in the West have become largely dependent on technology, time has, to some extent, stood still in the remoter areas of Yemen. Childhood in Arab society is much briefer than in the West, leading

57 Norbeck, 'Anthropological Views of Play', 268 and 271.

58 Carsten Niebuhr, *Reisebeschreibung nach Arabien und andern umliegenden Ländern* (Zurich: Manesse, 1997), p. 185.

the narrator to wonder whether the games Arab children play are simpler and less varied. In Arab countries he has identified a proliferation of games that imitate adult activities such as tribal warfare, hunting, plundering raids and legal trials. He goes on to speculate: '*Je komplexer sich eine gesellschaft darstellt, umso länger sind kindheit und jugend und um so differenzierter ihre spiele*' (*LV*, p. 155). This leads to an insightful discussion between the Western anthropologist and Abdul Malik, his Yemeni counterpart, who disagrees with him. Abdul Malik questions the validity of the Westerner's interpretation of the Arab children's 'nachahmungsspiele' as being less complex than Western children's 'regelspiele'. Just as in a traditional society, Western children imitate their elders when playing. In the West, however, the 'umfassende technisierung des alltags' (*LV*, p. 156) means that children's games are increasingly played on machines, a development that Abdul Malik sees as an impoverishment. This two-way anthropological analysis relativizes each position and reveals both to be culturally determined. Even empirical observations are interpreted through the prejudiced lens of one's own cultural apparatus but this relativized viewpoint leads to a more nuanced understanding.

Despite the impression the reader may form from the cataloguing of Arab games (e.g. *LV*, pp. 184–86, pp. 211–13), the researcher clearly does not conceive of play as simply the activity of playing a game as defined in contrast to other areas of human life such as work. Contrasting 'Spiel' with 'Ernst' or 'Arbeit' is only part of the definition. Play can also be regarded as 'a *mode of human experience* – a way of engaging with the world whatever one is doing'.[59] This broader definition of play as an attitude rather than a specific activity seems to be a Western concept. The narrator posits the theory that the West's post-industrial society '*die tendenz* [*hat*], *ihre strukturen und mechanismen als einen kontext von spielen zu begreifen* [...] *In einer nach wie vor traditionell strukturierten gesellschaft wie der jemenitischen wird das dasein tendenziell als folge von kämpfen begriffen*' (*LV*, p. 173). Dick Barber, the Head of the Research Institute in Sana'a, considers this application of the play metaphor to be 'der wirkliche grund für die überlegenheit des westens' (*LV*, p. 225). Barber quotes the Duke of Wellington as having said that he won the Battle of Waterloo on Eton's cricket grounds: 'Das bedeutet, dasz die briten ihr weltreich erobert haben, indem sie das erobern als sportlichen wettkampf begriffen, als fortsetzung des bereits in den schulen trainierten spielgeistes' (*LV*, p. 226). The Western powers' success in colonizing the world is regarded as resulting not only from highly sophisticated technology and weaponry but also from the equally sophisticated metaphor which reduces the conquest from a battle to a

59 Thomas M. Malaby, 'Anthropology and Play: The Contours of Playful Experience', *New Literary History*, 40 (2009), 205–18 (p. 208).

game. As a result colonialism is made harmless and the world is regarded as a playground where a competitive spirit will take you far. The application of the play metaphor in other spheres of life, or indeed to encompass the whole of life, is thus potentially problematic and linked to the contentious history of colonial expansion.

Roes draws parallels between play and travel. Attempting to break down traditional distinctions between the traveller as subject and the 'travelee'[60] as object, he conceives of travel as an 'Auseinandersetzung mit der Welt und mit mir, als eine Hoffnung, in der Forschen und Reisen zusammengehören, in der nicht einer den anderen zum Objekt macht' (*KT*, p. 127). In *Leeres Viertel* he expresses a parallel theory: 'Spielen bedeutet nicht nur, dasz ein spieler (mit) etwas spielt, es bedeutet auch, dasz etwas mit dem spieler spielt' (*LV*, p. 797; see also *KT*, p. 57). Both the traveller and the player must expect to be both subject and object at some point. This suggests a certain loss of control; and the privileged status enjoyed by the traveller does not go unchallenged. Roes seems to be comfortable with the vulnerability to which this leads,[61] explaining that just as one can 'play' with all that life has to offer, '[kann] das Leben [...] [auch] mit uns sein Spiel treiben. Plötzlich finden wir uns als Spielfigur eines größeren Spiels wieder, dessen Regeln wir nicht durchschauen und dessen Grenzen wir nicht erkennen' (*KT*, p. 57). Taken in the context of intercultural encounters this is, essentially, a recognition that the Other is also an active agent (not passive as Pratt's term 'travelee' suggests) and that the traveller should be open to the influences of outside forces.

Intercultural exchange in this context means change, a point made repeatedly by the American anthropologist Paul Rabinow in his *Reflections on Fieldwork in Morocco* (1977). Both the anthropologist and his informant inhabit the 'liminal, self-conscious world between cultures [...] , a difficult and trying experience' because it is 'unnatural'.[62] According to Rabinow neither the 'subject nor the object remain static'.[63] The anthropologist's informant from the host culture changes as a result of being forced to 'reassess his own sense

60 'Travelee' is a term coined by Mary Louise Pratt to describe the indigenous population with which the traveller comes into contact (Mary Louise Pratt, *Imperial Eyes: Travel Writing and Transculturation* (London: Routledge, 1992), p. 7). For a critique of the term, see Catherine Mee, 'European Travellers in Africa – The Negotiation of Identity', *Forum for Modern Language Studies*, 45 (2009), 378–89 (pp. 388-89).

61 In an interview with Jens Nommel, Roes even describes a 'fast masochistisch' tendency on his part to be open to such experiences; Jens Nommel and Michael Roes, 'Im Gespräch über die eigenen Grenzen', http://handlungsreisedialog.blogwerft.de/2007/12/13/michael-roes/ [accessed 4 November 2009].

62 Rabinow, *Reflections on Fieldwork in Morocco*, p. 39.

63 Rabinow, *Reflections on Fieldwork in Morocco*, p. 73.

of identity',[64] to provide insights and answers to the anthropologist's questions. The change that the anthropologist himself undergoes comes initially as a result of observation:

> In the dialectic between the poles of observation and participation, participation changes the anthropologist and leads him to new observation, whereupon new observation changes how he participates. But this dialectical spiral is governed in its motion by its starting point, which is observation.[65]

In *Leeres Viertel* the contemporary anthropologist is a reluctant participant to begin with but is drawn into this cycle of observation and participation. At one point he even becomes immersed in the spirit of play, and experiences '[u]nbändige spielfreude. Augenblicke vollkommener selbstvergessenheit. Keine fragen nach dem sinn dessen, was ich tue [...] Nichts schiebt sich zwischen die empfindung und das dasein' (*LV*, p. 653–4). He becomes involved in a 'dialogical exchange' as envisioned by Tzvetan Todorov, a dialogue which requires:

> exposure to an otherness which lies far beyond the self (without being totally incommensurable); [...] [and] a willingness to 'risk oneself', that is, to plunge headlong into a transformative learning process in which the status of self and other are continually renegotiated.[66]

In this regard travel is an experience from which the anthropologist returns home a changed person.

Schnittke, too, notices that changes have occurred in him since arriving in Arabia. Like Rabinow, he feels that his experiences have altered the manner in which he perceives his new surroundings. He insists that these changes are not superficial, but go to the core of the way he perceives the world. The extent of these transformations of the self are expressed by means of an architectural metaphor: 'Würde ich meinen Leib mit einem Haus vergleichen, so hätte sich nicht nur die Façade verändert, sondern das ganze Gebäude befände sich im Umbau. Fenster und Thüren werden erweitert, Geschosse aufgestockt, geheime Verbindungen zu anderen Gebäuden hergestellt' (*LV*, p. 89). This appears to be an extensive but not unwelcome change: the widening of the doors and windows suggests openness and receptiveness. An effect of this might be increased ability for exchange: receiving and giving, observing and participating become, as Rabinow notes, self-perpetuating cycles. Some of these changes may be clearly visible to others ('Geschosse aufgestockt'), others

64 Rabinow, *Reflections on Fieldwork in Morocco*, p. 120.
65 Rabinow, *Reflections on Fieldwork in Morocco*, p. 80.
66 Fred Dallmayr, *Beyond Orientalism: Essays on Cross-cultural Encounter* (Albany: State University of New York Press, 1996), p. xviii.

are more personal and concealed ('geheime Verbindungen'). This fundamental reorientation, expressed as a positive change in the metaphor of the house, is also perceived as psychological disorientation. Schnittke realizes that he has begun to see the world 'durch zwey Paar verschiedener Augen', a sensation that leads him to feel 'dem Irrsinn nahe' (*LV*, p. 94). Contact with Arab culture has taught him to re-evaluate his own culture, giving him a new perspective with which to interpret the world. With this gain, however, comes the loss of an established sense of identity and identification with his home culture. Profound engagement with the foreign culture can leave the traveller bereft and unstable.

Roes illustrates the parallels that exist between play and travel, stating that they both break away from '*alltagsverhalten*' (*LV*, p. 255). Entering into the state of play is a voluntary act that can be reversed at any time – one need only step out of the 'magic circle' to end the game. Roger Caillois states in *Man, Play and Games* (1958) that for an activity to be defined as play 'it is necessary that they [the players] be free to leave whenever they please, by saying: "I am not playing any more"'.[67] The traveller, too, is always free to end the 'game' by returning home. However, in this case the internal changes wrought by the journey remain long after he or she has arrived home. During the journey and during the period spent in the foreign country (the 'magic circle'), he or she may behave as if it were a game – experimenting with different actions, emotions, dress, modes of perception. However, this, as Schnittke and the contemporary narrator learn, leads to fundamental and irrevocable change. When the traveller exits the magic circle within which the journey takes place (the *temenos*)[68] – on the return home – these deep transformations will likely remain. This is perceived, on the one hand, as a danger but, on the other, as a rare and valuable opportunity. For the contemporary anthropologist a journey is a chance to change oneself permanently, to be concurrently Self and Other (*LV*, p. 357). Claude Lévi-Strauss agrees but sees the anthropologist as particularly vulnerable to this sense of displacement, more so than a 'mere' traveller:

> The conditions in which he [the anthropologist] lives and works cut him off physically from his group for long periods; through being exposed to such complete and sudden changes of environment, he acquires a kind of chronic rootlessness; eventually, he comes to feel at home nowhere, and he remains psychologically maimed.[69]

67 Roger Caillois, *Man, Play and Games*, trans. by Meyer Barash (Urbana and Chicago: University of Illinois Press, 2001), p. 6.

68 Huizinga, *Homo Ludens*, p. 77.

69 Lévi-Strauss, *Tristes Tropiques*, p. 55.

Extensive engagement with the Other can lead the anthropologist to become a different version of him or herself. Even when the 'game' has ended the consequences continue to be felt. Insofar as this is true, it is clear that play is not to be taken lightly: 'Das Spiel ist nicht Spielerey' (*LV*, p. 664).

Dance and Intercultural Encounters

Fundamental to Roes's thinking on interculturality is the concept that that which unites the human race is much greater than that which divides it. Thus Roes can be regarded as a modern representative of a cosmopolitan tradition that 'seeks to *reconcile* the idea of universal species-wide human solidarity with particular solidarities that are smaller and more specific than the human species'.[70] No matter where on earth he or she may live, every human being has one thing in common: a physical body. Language and culture may keep people apart, but the experience of physical sensations forms a bond deeper than the superficial factors that separate the human race. Roes explains: 'Der Körper ist das Vertraute, das uns Menschen Gemeinsame. In ihm liegt alle Hoffnung auf Verständigung, auf Begreifen, Annehmen und Hingeben begründet, denn diese eine Körper-Erfahrung teilen wir miteinander, allen unterschiedlichen Sprachen und Kulturen zum Trotz'.[71] According to Roes, when language is not a practical means of communication, when cultural barriers prevent understanding through conventional means, engaging the body in the process of communication increases the chance of a profound interchange. Shared physical sensations offer an opportunity to connect with others, especially those with whom one does not share a language or culture. In literature depicting intercultural encounters dance is one way in which characters from the West attempt to contact, befriend, and communicate with characters from Arab and, as one later example will show, African countries. Although it is a motif that recurs in travel literature it is not always portrayed as being a successful means of contact, which may come as a surprise considering Roes's faith in the power of the body to transcend cultural barriers.

At the end of *Leeres Viertel* the modern-day narrator is dancing the traditional *bar'a* war dance with Ahmed, a dance which is normally only danced by Yemeni tribesmen. Paradoxically the *bar'a* is not 'technically described by the term generally translated as dancing (*raqs*)',[72] since the word *raqs* carries

70 Robert Fine, *Cosmopolitanism* (London: Routledge, 2007), p. 15.

71 Michael Roes and Rachid Bouytayeb, 'Der eifersüchtige Gott: Ein Gespräch', *Merkur*, 64 (2010), 228–41 (p. 236).

72 Najwa Adra, 'Dance and Glance: Visualizing Tribal Identity in Highland Yemen', *Visual Anthropology*, 11 (1998), 55–102 (p. 61).

connotations of frivolity. The *bar'a* is 'one of the most important tribal markers in Yemen'[73] and its performance is a symbol of loyalty: it shows, on the one hand, a readiness to fight one's enemies and, on the other, a willingness to protect one's own people. The narrator's participation in this ritual would seem to suggest that he has finally been admitted into the 'diwan der seele' (*LV*, p. 594), the inner sanctum of Arab society. He enters into the spirit of the dance and experiences a heady ecstasy, reflected in his diary account by fluid sentences that are sometimes ungrammatical or left incomplete. The euphoria that he experiences whilst dancing the *bar'a* symbolizes the temporary transcending of cultural barriers via the universal medium of the body. He is afforded an insight into this new culture and feels part of it: 'Tanz ist poesie, *der körper selbst die sprache*, kein festgebanntes bild kein so bin ich sondern so will ich sein, ein krieger der den kampf wie einen tanz besteht voll leichtigkeit und zuneigung' (*LV*, p. 802, my italics). Here the body becomes the language with which the dancers speak. Not only do the two men, the German protagonist and Ahmad, his Yemeni friend, communicate through the medium of dance, they also draw the observing crowd of men into the ritual: 'die zuschauenden männer feuern uns mit rhythmischen klatschen und zurufen an doch vergisz sie tanz für sie doch vergisz sie' (*LV*, p. 802). The protagonist briefly experiences the elation that successful interaction with people from vastly different cultures can offer. Through the ritual of the war dance he is granted a glimpse of mystical unity with the Other. Theory, observation, and deliberation fall aside, leaving only pure and direct experience. Yet after the dance the narrator is exhausted, plagued as he is by illness. His body, despite having spent many months in Yemen, has not adapted to the overwhelming demands made upon it by life in the desert. In this instance the body indicates the narrator's difference from the tribesmen.[74] As the day draws to an end, and the warriors of the tribe go off to war, the reader may suspect that a chasm still exists between the narrator and the Arab culture: 'Beim anbruch der dämmerung ist alles vorbei. Die männer klopfen sich den staub von den röcken, steigen mit knapper geste oder gruszlos in ihre geländewagen und fahren in ungeordnetem haufen und ohne licht in die wüste hinaus' (*LV*, p. 803). His 'peak experience' (to borrow Abraham Maslow's term in psychology) ends as suddenly as it began, leaving the narrator alone in the emptiness of a desert far from his homeland, his fate still in the hands of his captors.

73 Adra, 'Dance and Glance', 78.

74 Roes acknowledged in an interview after his return from Yemen 'daß auch der Körper westlich ist. Ich hatte, als ich zurückkam, 15 Kilo Gewicht verloren und sehnte mich nach dem Wechsel der Jahreszeiten, die mich besonders im Winter so gestört hatten' (Marko Martin, 'Objektivität ist Lüge: Michael Roes, Völklerkundler und Literat', *Der Tagesspiegel*, 28 January 1997, p. 24).

The motif of the dance recurs in Roes's novel *Nah Inverness* (2004). Jessy, an American actor involved in the *Macbeth* production being filmed in Yemen, is also a dancer and is eager to stage a performance in a hall in Sana'a. He has choreographed a 'Zurück- oder Wiederholung seiner eigenen Kindheitserfahrungen in Harlem, wo er vor allem sich selber und seine Mutter darstellt' (*NI*, p. 213). In contrast to the dancing episode in *Leeres Viertel*, in which the protagonist was seeking to understand the Yemeni tribesmen and their culture through the medium of dance, this is a situation in which the Westerner is seeking to perform his own dance. Rather than seeking to understand, he is seeking to be understood. Asked whether the Yemeni public will understand his representation of a New York childhood through the medium of dance, he replies: 'Ich glaube, daß es mehr Ähnlichkeiten als Unterschiede zwischen einer Kindheit in Harlem und einer hier in Sanaa gibt. Ich rede über ein Mutter-Sohn-Verhältnis. Und die Sprache, in der ich rede, ist universal, nämlich eine des Körpers' (*NI*, p. 213). The language here is very similar to that used by Roes in the interviews quoted above, but whereas in the interviews Roes's conviction concerning the potential of the body to overcome barriers of communication shines through, the novel is unmistakeably pessimistic. Jessy's planned performance is never realized, partly for financial reasons and partly because of Yemeni attitudes towards dance. He is dismayed by the realization that in Yemen the only dances performed publicly are the festive *raqs* dance and the *bar'a* war dance. He is told that the only women he will find dancing in the Arab world are the prostitutes and belly dancers in Cairo and Beirut nightclubs.

Jessy's failure to carry out his dance project is foreshadowed by an incident that reveals Yemeni scepticism towards dance and physical expression. The dancer has been performing his morning gymnastic routine on the roof of his rented house in the Yemeni village. These 'täglichen Entspannungs- und Dehnungsübungen' have caused uproar among the village women, who see something 'zutiefst Heidnische[s] oder gar Obzöne[s]' in the 'seltsame[n] körperliche[n] Verrenkungen' (*NI*, p. 171) performed by the half-naked man. The incident is narrated in a report by Ahmed, who finds himself in the role of a cultural mediator, since he claims to understand both the Arab and Western mindsets, having lived for a while in England. Roes presents an unusually strong critique of elements of Yemeni mentality as the Arab admits that his people have a tendency towards narrow-mindedness and shallow judgementalism. After the incident Ahmed tells Jessy that appearances are what counts in Yemen: 'Hier unterscheiden die Menschen nicht zwischen tieferem Wesen und äußerem Schein. Hier wird der andere allein an dem gemessen, wie er sich verhält' (*NI*, p. 171). Yemen is portrayed as one that is at times unable to tolerate the Western Other, or indeed any alternative reality that threatens to question the Arab/Yemeni/Muslim world-view. The anthropologist Najwa Adra also notes this tendency and explains that 'rural Yemenis had very little reason to question the validity of their civilization'[75] because the northern Yemeni highlands were never colonized and were isolated from the influence of globalization for much of the twentieth century, a situation that has recently changed dramatically. This reluctance to examine their own belief systems limits the possibility of what the interested Western traveller would deem a successful interaction, what Roes terms the 'Dialog und eine Art Zusammenarbeit', since both sides must be actively involved in the exchange. As the narrator of *Leeres Viertel* asks himself at one point: 'Auch wenn ich sie [die Jemeniten] verstehen lernen könnte, wie sollte [*sic*] sie je mich verstehen können?' (*LV*, p. 147). For genuine intercultural understanding there must be willingness on both sides to listen, learn and understand. In this instance the lines of communication are closed due to the sensitivity of the Yemeni people to any transgression against their traditions and customs.

Dancing, it seems, is only partially successful as a means of communication between cultures since dance has different meanings and significances within different cultures. Whereas a Western character, especially one of an artistic, progressive bent, may expect dance to offer a point of contact with people of other cultures, this hope may be difficult to fulfil within a traditional Arab society. Pessimism and frustration regarding the possibility of connecting with people from other cultures is particularly prevalent in *Nah Inverness*, a fact that may well be accounted for by the numerous problems encountered by Roes while filming the 'real' *Someone is Sleeping in My Pain: Ein west-östlicher Macbeth* in Yemen in 2000 to 2001. In addition, Roes was writing the novel in the aftermath of the 9/11 terrorist attacks and the ensuing military campaigns in the Middle East, a period in which relations between the West and the Arab world were strained.

I now move on to examine another author, and to a novel which engages with German colonial history. Uwe Timm's *Morenga* (1978) features a scene in which dancing is portrayed as a stimulus to a potentially successful intercultural encounter, but one which likewise ultimately fails. Johannes Gottschalk is a military veterinarian stationed in German South-West Africa during the time of the Herero revolt between 1904 and 1908. He becomes increasingly sympathetic to the plight of the Africans under German colonial rule, and even considers going over to the other side to join the insurrectionists as a 'Zeichen [...] Ein Fanal'.[76] Gottschalk is eventually captured by Morenga, the leader of the uprising, and during Gottschalk's interrogation they form a

75 Adra, 'Dance and Glance', 65.

76 Uwe Timm, *Morenga* (Munich: DTV, 2000), p. 418.

certain bond. Gottschalk is permitted to take part in a celebration and, just like the narrator of *Leeres Viertel*, he is initially intoxicated by its naturalness: 'Er habe sich nie so fröhlich, so gelöst gefunden wie an diesem Abend, eine Fröhlichkeit, die aus allen kam, nicht allein durch Suff erzeugt, eine fröhliche Gelöstheit'.[77] However, when Gottschalk attempts to join in the dancing he fails miserably to abandon himself to the natural movements. Tellingly, he attempts, at first, to imitate Morenga, who dances more stiffly than usual due to injury. Gottschalk fails even in this and realizes that, were he to stay, 'er [...] anders [hätte] denken und fühlen lernen müssen. Radikal umdenken. Mit den Sinnen denken'.[78] Kora Baumbach argues that the reason for Gottschalk's failure to overcome the cultural differences lies not in matters of intellect or idealism – since he has already drawn near to the Nama culture on a moral and intellectual level after observing the cruel treatment meted out to them at the hands of the German army.[79] It is rather the sensual and physical dimensions of the intercultural contact that prevent him from 'going native'. The dance serves to demonstrate to him that there is a simplicity and naturalness to black African culture that he is unable to emulate, let alone embody. In his case dance reveals the distance that lies between their culture and his own, 'eine Ferne, die ihm nicht überbrückbar schien'.[80]

In this sense the protagonist of *Leeres Viertel* has a more successful intercultural encounter than Timm's Gottschalk. He is able to abandon himself to the dance, achieving a sense of union and brotherhood in the dancing. Both protagonists initially come nearer to the respective foreign cultures through a process of intellectual or moral understanding: in *Leeres Viertel* this process occurs as the anthropologist carries out his research of Yemeni culture, in *Morenga* it happens as Gottschalk observes the discrepancy between the German claim of having a 'civilizing mission' and the brutal reality of colonial politics. However, whereas Roes's protagonist is also able to connect with the Arab tribesmen on a physical and sensual level through the medium of dance, in Timm's novel the protagonist is unable to perform the dance that would symbolize his absorption into the Nama way of life. The anthropologist in *Leeres Viertel* has one distinct advantage in this respect: as he was researching the traditional games played by Yemeni children he was also observing, when such opportunities presented themselves, the dances performed by the tribesmen. This knowledge serves as a bridge between the intellectual challenge of understanding the foreign culture and the problem

77 Timm, *Morenga*, p. 419.

78 Timm, *Morenga*, p. 420.

79 Kora Baumbach, 'Verdrängte Kolonialgeschichte: Zu Uwe Timms Roman *Morenga*', *Monatshefte*, 97 (2005), 213–31 (pp. 223–24).

80 Timm, *Morenga*, p. 419.

of achieving a physical, sensual union with that culture; yet despite this, when the dancing comes to an end, the protagonist in Roes's novel is left with a similar paradox to that facing Gottschalk in *Morenga*: 'Diese Menschen waren ihm nah und doch zugleich so unendlich fern'.[81]

Gottschalk's lack of success in making contact through dancing can be accounted for in the fact that although the primary medium of dance is the body, the physical movements are conditioned by social and cultural forces.[82] Jane Desmond, a scholar of dance, states that:

> movement style is an important mode of distinction between social groups and is usually actively learned or passively absorbed in the home and community. [...] Its articulation signals group affiliation and group differences, whether consciously performed or not. Movement serves as a marker for the production of gender, racial, ethnic, class, and national identities.[83]

Thus although the body and physical sensations are universal, the way people use their bodies, in terms of movements, gait and posture, is subject to specific cultural conditioning. Moreover, movement, especially dance, can serve to display group belonging, be that distinction one of gender, nationality or class. In Timm's *Morenga*, dance and movement are exactly such indicators of belonging to, or conversely exclusion from, a specific group. For Gottschalk, the impossibility of joining the Nama becomes clear as he observes their sensual movements during the celebration. In *Leeres Viertel* the narrator is able to overcome this physical barrier and he dances the Yemeni dance without inhibitions, abandoning himself to the foreign culture. A problem remains for him, however: his weakened 'Western' body prevents him from being accepted fully into the tribe. All the tribesmen set off for war, leaving the narrator behind in the village. Despite having successfully danced the Yemeni war dance, he is not yet deemed by the tribesmen to be a real warrior ready for war. Despite his effort to connect, both intellectually and physically, he is left hanging in the liminal space between very different cultures.

Intertextuality in *Leeres Viertel*

Having examined the significance of play and dance for the staging of intercultural encounters in *Leeres Viertel*, I now explore how the novel's

81 Timm, *Morenga*, p. 420.

82 Jane C. Desmond, ed., *Meaning in Motion: New Cultural Studies of Dance* (Durham, NC: Duke University Press, 2006), 'Introduction', pp. 1–25 (p. 2).

83 Jane C. Desmond, 'Embodying Difference: Issues in Dance and Cultural Studies', in Jane C. Desmond, ed., *Meaning in Motion*, pp. 29-54 (p. 31).

engagement with its intertexts can be regarded as part of the intercultural exchange. *Leeres Viertel* is Michael Roes's most complex work in terms of its intertextual elements. At times, the reader may feel as if trapped in a Borgesian labyrinth, 'facing texts as mirrors, mirrors facing other text-mirrors, in a play of self-contained reflections in which the negotiator of the labyrinth may well lose himself'.[84] The remainder of this chapter is dedicated to finding a way through this intertextual 'labyrinth'.

The novel contains three interwoven levels of intertextuality. The first is the internal relationship that exists between the two narrative strands. The contemporary narrator is reading Schnittke's diary as he composes his own and the texts are interconnected. I will call this the contrapuntal level of *intra*textuality.[85] Secondly, both the Schnittke and contemporary strands contain allusions or references to various other external texts and writers. This second level is what is more commonly understood as intertexuality – those connections that exist, in various forms, between different texts. Examples from *Leeres Viertel* include references to Goethe, who is alluded to in both strands. The third level of intertextuality shows Roes at his most creative. The Schnittke strand, although largely a fiction created by Roes, actually includes numerous quotations from authentic travel accounts written by twelve European explorers to the Orient between 1774 and 1936. These are incorporated into the Schnittke diary as if they were his own. I will call this the playful level of intertextuality and will discuss it further in relation to Raymond Federman's concept of 'pla(y)giarism'. The following sections proceed to examine each of these three levels in more detail.

Contrapuntal Intratextuality

The term '*intra*textuality' has been defined variously as 'involving relations *within* the text'[86] and 'the relationship between different texts by the same author'.[87] In this analysis 'intratextuality' is understood as the former, and

84 Alan Thiher, *Words in Reflection: Modern Language Theory and Postmodern Fiction* (Chicago: University of Chicago Press, 1984), p. 165.

85 Another work of travel fiction that makes use of a similar contrapuntal intratextual construct is Christoph Ransmayr's *Die Schrecken des Eises und der Finsternis* (1984), whose first-person narrator is travelling in the footsteps of a (fictional) missing Italian explorer, who was in turn following the (authentic) diaries of the crew of the Payer and Weyprecht expedition to the Arctic (1872–74). Raoul Schrott's *Finis Terrae* (1995) also employs a comparable structure.

86 Daniel Chandler, *Semiotics: The Basics*, 2nd edn (Abingdon: Routledge, 2007), p. 251.

87 Daniela Caselli, *Beckett's Dantes: Intertextuality in the Fiction and Criticism* (Manchester: Manchester University Press, 2005), p. 57.

the term 'restricted intertextuality'[88] is used when referring to connections between works by the same author. My coinage 'contrapuntal intratextuality' refers specifically to the interplay between the two narrative strands in *Leeres Viertel*. Before venturing to examine the novel's relationship with external texts it is first necessary to consider these internal parallels. In the first strand, the contemporary anthropologist-narrator travelling in Yemen around the period of the outbreak of the Yemeni Civil War in 1994 has taken with him an incomplete copy of Alois Ferdinand Schnittke's diary, which records the journey the latter undertook around the beginning of the nineteenth century. As he travels, the narrator reads Schnittke's diary, which is the novel's second narrative strand. As he reads, we read with him. The anonymous contemporary reader-narrator is the 'Leserinstanz von Schnittke'[89] – everything we know about the Schnittke story is mediated by him. If he skips an episode in Schnittke's narrative, we miss out on it too. Since his copy of Schnittke's diary is in any case incomplete, its retelling in the novel is likewise fragmentary. This points towards the vagaries of historiography: we can only read what was recorded in the first place and has subsequently been passed down to us. Moreover, history, anthropology and travel writing all depend on texts but it takes a reader to bring them to life once more: this is literally what the 1994-narrator does. He re-lives, in a modern setting, the adventures of his predecessor and in the process restores the old text to life.

In addition to the disrupting element of incompleteness, the contrapuntal intratextual relationship, bound as it is within the covers of a novel, straddles the indeterminate border between fact and fiction since both strands are fusions of the real and the imagined. The 1994 narrator, a partly fictional construct based to an extent on the author, is referring to another fictional character's diary, which is a literary mosaic constructed partially from authentic travel accounts. Yet even within the narrative reality of the contemporary strand there is no confirmation that the Schnittke diary is 'authentic'. It must, nevertheless, be conceded that the suggestion made in the novel by the American Arabist Dick Barber that Schnittke's diary could be 'eine romantische fiktion, eine Insel Felsenburg oder dergleichen' (*LV*, p. 227) seems to be made in a spirit of antagonism rather than on the basis of academic expertise. The Schnittke diary is, of course, a fiction created by Roes, but at least within the construct of the novel it appears that its accuracy and ethnographic detail raise it above the level of a hoax.

88 Ann Jefferson, 'Autobiography as Intertext: Barthes, Sarraute, Robbe-Grillet', in *Intertextuality: Theories and Practices*, ed. by Michael Worton and Judith Still (Manchester: Manchester University Press, 1990), pp. 108–29 (p. 111).

89 Schmitt-Maaß, *Das gefährdete Subjekt*, p. 213.

By juxtaposing narratives from past and present, whether they are authentic, invented, or a mixture of the two, Roes accords his novel genuine historical depth. Schnittke's diary account is a supplement to the contemporary anthropologist's narration and provides a point of comparison that illustrates some of the social and technical developments that have come to pass since the 1800s. As the narrator sits on the plane during a stop-over at Cairo Airport, he comments: 'In so kurzer zeit reise ich von einem kontinent auf einen andern, dasz ich gerade einmal zeit finde, die aufzeichnungen Schnittkes über seine reise zu *lesen*. Um von Weimar nach Kairo zu gelangen, benötigt er sieben monate' (*LV*, p. 68). Travel has changed since Schnittke's era and journeys that used to take many months are now made in a matter of hours. Yet great technological advances, which in some ways make it easier to come into contact with other people and places, can put the whole intercultural project in jeopardy: 'Je schneller wir reisen, um so flüchtiger streifen wir orte, um so weniger *begegnen* wir' (*LV*, p. 691).[90] The dual-strand structure also calls attention to both historical constancies and discontinuities in Yemeni life. Both Schnittke (*LV*, p. 47) and the twentieth-century narrator (*LV*, pp. 718–19) take an anthropological interest in the Arabic names given to different types of camels, an interest that indicates the continued importance, both practical and symbolic, of those animals in that society. There are also, however, developments and changes. Many Yemenis now depend on off-road vehicles as a means of transport: 'Kamele seien unzeitgemäsz. Mit geländewagen komme man inzwischen selbst auf unwegsamen strecken schneller und bequemer voran' (*LV*, p. 523). The Yemeni hinterlands may, in some ways, have remained bound to ancient customs and ways of living, but to assume that the Arab world remains medieval is a gross underestimation of both the Arab countries and the penetrative power of modernization.

By including a historical strand, Roes depicts Yemen as a world doubly removed from that of the modern Western traveller: what Axel Dunker terms the 'doppelte Alterität' of both time and place.[91] However, in other ways, it appears that the experience of travelling in the interior of Yemen has remained constant over the centuries. The experiences of the two travellers

90 It is significant that the narrator makes this reference to the superficiality of encounters between human beings while waiting on a plane at an airport. In an influential study, Marc Augé defines as 'non-place' any 'space which cannot be defined as relational, or historical, or concerned with identity' and uses the airport as a prime example of this super-modern phenomenon (Marc Augé, *Non-places: Introduction to an Anthropology of Supermodernity*, trans. by John Howe (London: Verso, 1995), pp. 77–78). *Leeres Viertel* opens with a scene which draws attention to the airport's regularized functionality and arguably to its status as non-place: 'kühle chromglänzende kunststoffbestuhlte wartehalleatmosphäre: menschenumschlagplatz' (*LV*, p. 9).

91 Dunker, '"Als wisse ich endlich Alles"', p. 207.

are remarkably similar, with both enduring comparable difficulties including illnesses, intercultural misunderstandings and captivity. These similarities can be read as indicating a hypertextual relationship in Genette's sense since the contemporary strand evokes or mirrors its predecessor. We are also in the area of 'architextuality' here since both travellers write within the literary genre of the diary. Although the two accounts are normally narrated in clearly separated chapters, at one point (*LV*, p. 583) the two diaries mysteriously blend into each other. This is thematically appropriate at this point, a time when both diarists are despairing of their situation – alone, in captivity and considering taking action but unsure what steps to take. As the similarities between the two strands attest, the encounter with the alien environment and the people who live there remains a destabilizing experience that forces the traveller to draw upon all available resources, be they physical, intellectual or emotional. Dunker considers whether this may indicate that the novel uses the Arab setting purely as a stage for the protagonists' self-analysis and self-discovery but eventually dismisses this notion.[92] Robert Tobin, on the contrary, states that '[d]ie kritische Auseinandersetzung mit dem Fremden [...] hauptsächlich dazu dienen [soll], sich selbst zu erkennen'.[93] While it is undoubtedly true that engagement with the foreign people and cultures often affords insight into one's own culture, I would disagree with Tobin on this point. The focus of *Leeres Viertel* is overwhelmingly directed towards engagement with the Yemeni people. The consciously chosen, self-reflexive position adopted by Roes's two narrators, their inclusion of an inwardly directed gaze parallel to their anthropological observations, does not detract from their intercultural project. Rather, as the anthropological theorists analysed earlier in this chapter have argued, it enhances that research by providing the reader with the context in which their ethnography was produced.

The prominence of the dual-strand structure thematizes the complex relationship that exists between the two poles of real and reading experience. The contemporary narrator asks at one point: 'Kann es sein, dasz ich mitten in einem abenteuer bin, von dem ich früher voller sehnsucht gelesen habe?' (*LV*, p. 723). The answer to his question is, of course, yes. Schnittke's adventure is the 'pre-text' to his own. The unnamed narrator's experience of life in this most foreign of countries is influenced by a previously read text which functions as both a source and a mirror for his own. The intratextual level of *Leeres Viertel* (and this point will be even more apparent in connection to the playful mode of intertextuality) suggests that writing emerges from reading.

92 Dunker, '"Als wisse ich endlich Alles"', p. 212.

93 Robert Tobin, 'Postmoderne Männlichkeit: Michael Roes und Matthias Politycki', *Zeitschrift für Germanistik*, 12 (2002), 324–33 (p. 329).

As Christoph Schmitt-Maaß has shown,[94] the beginning of the novel is largely dominated by the Schnittke sections, with the contemporary narrator initially slow to find his voice. Over the course of the novel we read progressively less of Schnittke, while the contemporary narrator's writing flows with increasing force. It is therefore apparent that the modern-day narrator's diary emerges from his predecessor's, both from the words left behind by Schnittke and from the empty spaces that punctuate his fragmentary manuscript.

New texts are always to a certain extent amalgamations of previous works, whether or not authors are aware that they are reproducing material that they have read. This is a relevant problem for a traveller who intends to write. Previous reading can congest perception to such an extent that the traveller is unable to experience his new surroundings at first hand; the production of a new text about the place visited inevitably becomes an intertextual project. Even Schnittke expresses concern to this effect early in his journey: '[ich] weiss nicht mehr zu unterscheiden, was alleyne meinem Geiste entsprungen und was wirklich geschehen ist, erinnern wir uns doch nicht weniger lebendig an unsere abenteuerlichen Lectüren, Träume und Phantastereyen als an die wirklichen Abentheuer' (*LV*, p. 383). This is an important point in *Leeres Viertel* because Roes is drawing attention to the fact that his novel is a link in a chain of texts. For the well-read protagonists of *Leeres Viertel* it is possible at times that 'texts tend to prevail over the material world of real places, real people: past sight dominates present sight'.[95] The resulting effect is that the distinction between real experience and experiences mediated through text is obscured and reading adventures are perceived as more exciting than the real thing: 'Fremd, geheimnisvoll ist es nur zwischen den plastikverschweiszten leinenbänden der bibliothekausgabe' (*LV*, p. 723). Texts can prove to be misleading and the journey itself becomes a confusing disappointment as a result.

The contemporary narrator experiences two adventures: Schnittke's textualized adventure, which he reads from a page, and his own real-world adventure, which he perceives as a novel in which he is a character ('Nun bin ich inmitten dieses Romans' (*LV*, p. 723)). However, despite the perception that the adventure on the page is more exciting than the one he actually lives, he is uninterested in purely academic knowledge of Yemen and insists on the value of lived experience. He is not content to live his adventure through the pages of Schnittke's diary but has parallel, equally real experiences. He travels to Yemen after finding the Schnittke diary in a library in Weimar. The travel diary does not replace the journey; it appears, rather, to function as a catalyst,

94 Schmitt-Maaß, *Das gefährdete Subjekt*, p. 214.

95 Henderson, 'The Travel Writer and the Text', pp. 230–48 (pp. 230–31).

a reason to set off. The desire for personal experience is stronger than any satisfaction that can be obtained from reading about the experiences of others. He must travel so that he has his own, equally real, tales to tell. Despite the novel's intricate web of texts woven into and over each other, real experiences lie as a foundation for the work. After identifying the multiple textual layers, what lies at the core of the novel is a real experience mediated through words, which are, after all, the writer's only possible means of expression.

Intertextual Allusions

Schnittke's diary is not the only reading material taken by the narrator on his journey to Yemen. He also takes with him Marcus Aurelius's *Meditations* (161–180 AD) and Ludwig Wittgenstein's *Philosophische Untersuchungen* (published posthumously in 1953), works that fall into the second category of intertextual references in the novel's first strand. Despite their appearance as incongruous choices for a journey to the Middle East, they reveal much about the narrator's intellectual interests. The *Meditations* have been described as the 'Gerüst für Roes' eigenes subjektzentriertes Schreiben: Nicht die Geschichte des eigenen Lebens will er erzählen, sondern die Betrachtungen von Welt und Ich im anthropologischen Erkenntnisprozess zusammenschmelzen'.[96] Moreover, the engagement with Wittgenstein's concept of 'Sprachspiele' is pertinent to the anthropological research into games.[97] Wittgenstein's definition of 'Sprachspiel' includes any expression of language ranging from basic greetings to highly complex works of literature. He uses the analogy of play to signify that when language is used, the rules of grammar must be obeyed just as the rules of a game must be followed. The narrator of *Leeres Viertel* advances a 'metatextual' (Genette) critique of the concept, saying that Wittgenstein's definition is 'irreführend' (*LV*, p. 325), objecting to this use of the word 'Spiel':

> [es] fehlt der sprachwelt die sinn-losigkeit des spiels: Ein spiel, mittels welchem wir lernen, ist im wesentlichen kein spiel mehr, sondern lernhilfe, werkzeug [...]. Darin liegt ja gerade der reiz des spiels: Die auflösung dessen,

96 Schmitt-Maaß, *Das gefährdete Subjekt*, pp. 199–200.

97 In Section 66 of the *Philosophische Untersuchungen*, Wittgenstein provides less a definition of play than a method by which one can arrive at a definition: 'Sag nicht: "Es *muß* ihnen etwas gemeinsam sein, sonst hießen sie nicht 'Spiele'" – sondern *schau*, ob ihnen allen etwas gemeinsam ist. [...] denk nicht, sondern schau!' (Ludwig Wittgenstein, *Philosophische Untersuchungen / Philosophical Investigations* [Bilingual edition. English translation by G. E. M. Anscombe, P. M. S. Hacker and Joachim Schulte] (Chichester: Wiley-Blackwell, 2009), p. 36).

> was Wittgenstein "sprachspiel" nennt, das auf- oder auseinanderbrechen von sprache und gebrauch kennzeichnet das eigentliche sprachspiel (*LV*, p. 325).

Like Wittgenstein, the narrator is interested in the relationship between language and reality, between the world and the words we use to describe it. While the imprecise nature of language can lead to ambiguities and miscommunication, its limitations and imperfections can also be regarded as precisely what allow it to function as a system of communication:

> Ich rede von spiel, ohne die grenzen genau umreiszen zu können. Das bedeutet nicht, dasz ich die grenzen nicht kennte [*sic*]. Spiel ist in alltagserfahrung eingebettet. Hier, im alltäglichen leben, ist auch ein ungenauer begriff brauchbar. Im alltäglichen sprachgebrauch ist möglicherweise die ungenauigkeit eines begriffs ein kriterium seiner brauchbarkeit (*LV*, p. 445).

This section draws from research by Axel Dunker and Christoph Schmitt-Maaß, both of whom provide valuable analysis of the intertextual aspects of *Leeres Viertel*. The following section on 'playful intertextuality' then builds on that, taking the analysis in a new direction. Dunker and Schmitt-Maaß identify a range of intertextual references (apart from the 'plagiaristic' ones which will be discussed subsequently) that again illustrate the trans-historical range of Roes's intertextuality: references to Laurence Sterne; to scenes of animal suffering by George Orwell, Elias Canetti and Hubert Fichte; to Goethe; and lastly self-quotations of works by Roes. All of these references are related in that each communicates something about intercultural encounters or their literary representation. Their thematic relevance is fitting considering the scornful criticism voiced by Schnittke regarding the novels of his time: 'blättere ich in den grossen Romanen unserer Zeit, so scheint mir auch darin allenthalben ein beliebiges Zitat verwendet, welches in keinem erkennbaren Zusammenhange mit der übrigen Erzählung steht, sondern wohl alleyn die umfassende Gelehrtheit des Erzählers zu belegen hat' (*LV*, p. 550). Schnittke's own narration shows off his education but his references are at least connected to his theme. Take, for example, this utterance that reveals knowledge of Laurence Sterne's work:

> Der scharfsichtige Sterne theilt uns lose und ledige Personen, die wir unser Heim verlassen, in die Klassen jener ein, die wegen Gebrechlichkeiten des Körpers oder Schwächen des Geistes, die wegen Nothwendigkeiten der Seele oder des Gemüths oder aus irgendeinem anderen oder aus gar keinem Grunde reisen. Nun gehöre ich thatsächlich im strengsten Sterneschen Sinne zu allen diesen Klassen (*LV*, p. 11).

Schnittke is referring here to Sterne's *A Sentimental Journey* (1768) and to the list of reasons for travelling that that novel's narrator, Mr Yorick, compiles: 'Your idle people, that leave their native country and go abroad for some reason or reasons which may be derived from one of these general causes – Infirmity of body, Imbecility of mind, or Inevitable necessity'.[98] There follows a humorous list of traveller types identified by Yorick, ending with the newly coined category to which he feels he belongs himself: 'The Sentimental Traveller'.[99] Johann Joachim Christoph Bode's translation, *Yoricks empfindsame Reise durch Frankreich und Italien* (1769), became hugely influential in Germany and popularized the term 'Empfindsamkeit'.[100] By evoking Sterne's novel, Schnittke places himself in the tradition of sentimental travellers, at the centre of which stands 'der Reisende selbst und die Empfindungen seines Innenlebens'.[101]

Schnittke also indirectly but unmistakeably invokes his most famous fellow-resident of Weimar, Johann Wolfgang von Goethe. Notwithstanding the dispute between Schnittke and the 'Director des hiesigen Theaters' (*LV*, p. 11), there are echoes of Goethe's own *Italienische Reise* (1813–1817) to be heard in Schnittke's account of leaving Weimar:[102] 'Früh drei Uhr stahl ich mich aus Karlsbad, weil man mich sonst nicht fortgelassen hätte'.[103] Schnittke's illustrious contemporary left for Italy on 3 September 1786, desiring solitude and freedom, according to his biographer, from 'the burden of his literary reputation, [...] the attentions of the public he was gathering his courage to address once more, and [from] his noble rank and official status'.[104] Whereas Goethe 'steals away' owing to the pressures of success, the reasons for Schnittke's exit are less distinguished. Grieving after losing his wife and child to illness, and nursing wounded pride after professional rejection, he makes a decidedly misanthropic declaration: 'So reise ich vor allem aus Trotz' (*LV*, p. 11). Not only is Schnittke excluded from Weimar's cultural life by the 'Goethe-figure', he also functions to some extent as a negative counterfoil to Germany's national poet.

Goethe is, as the chronicler of the above-mentioned Italian journey, one of German literature's best known and most influential travel writers and cultural mediators. Moreover, his *West-östlicher Divan* (1819) is one of the founding texts of German engagement with Middle Eastern culture, despite

98 Laurence Sterne, *A Sentimental Journey* (Oxford: Oxford University Press, 1984), p. 10.

99 Sterne, *A Sentimental Journey*, p. 11.

100 Barbara Becker-Cantarino, 'Introduction: German Literature in the Era of Enlightenment and Sensibility', in *German Literature of the Eighteenth Century: The Enlightenment and Sensibility*, ed. by Barbara Becker-Cantarino (Rochester, NY: Camden House, 2005), pp. 1–32 (p. 11).

101 Dunker, '"Als wisse ich endlich Alles"', p. 208.

102 Schmitt-Maaß, '"mäandernd, ornamentalisch, ohne progression?"', 100.

103 Johann Wolfgang von Goethe, *Italienische Reise* (Frankfurt am Main: Fischer, 2009), p. 9.

104 Nicholas Boyle, *Goethe: The Poet and the Age*, 2 vols, I, *The Poetry of Desire* (Oxford: Oxford University Press, 1991), p. 394.

the fact that the poet never set foot on Middle Eastern soil. The contemporary strand in *Leeres Viertel* includes a chapter entitled 'West-östlicher Diwan', in which the divan referred to is not a volume of poetry, but rather the room in a house to which guests are invited. Roes's divan is the site of real-life interpersonal encounters, while Goethe's is an intercultural encounter of a purely literary kind. As discussed in the section on anthropological theory above, Roes's narrator feels that the divan symbolizes his partial acceptance into Arabic households: he is welcomed into the divan but is invited no further. His status as guest simultaneously marks him as a foreigner. Goethe, too, was 'aware of the limitations of the mediating role he adopted between East and West'[105] and states in his commentary 'zum besserem Verständnis des West-östlichen Divans': 'Man entschuldigt ihn [den Reisenden], wenn es ihm auch nur bis auf einen gewissen Grad gelingt, wenn er immer noch an einem eignen Akzent, an einer unbezwinglichen Unbiegsamkeit seiner Landsmannschaft als Fremdling kenntlich bleibt'.[106] Roes's ethnographic intercultural project thus parallels Goethe's poetic one in that both attempt to build bridges between cultures while simultaneously remaining aware of the limitations that such undertakings inevitably involve. Recent post-colonial re-evaluations of Goethe's *Divan* take this further, attempting 'not only to sketch out the "Grenzen der Dialogizität" exhibited by the work, but also to show how in formal terms the text strays into a realm of ambivalence (or "Zone der Ambivalenz") that cannot elude colonial discourse'.[107] Such re-evaluation demonstrates how respect for and admiration of foreign cultures are not always enough to aid even a writer as renowned as Goethe completely to escape and subvert the prevailing discourse of his age.[108]

Axel Dunker draws attention to the following passage in the contemporary narrator's diary and identifies a matrix of allusions to three authors:[109]

105 Yomb May, 'Goethe, Islam, and the Orient: The Impetus for and Mode of Intercultural Encounter in the *West-östlicher Divan*', in *Encounters with Islam in German Literature and Culture*, ed. by James Hodkinson and Jeffrey Morrison (Rochester: Camden House, 2009), pp. 89–107 (p. 97).

106 Johann Wolfgang von Goethe, *West-östlicher Divan* (Frankfurt am Main: Insel, 1974), p. 128.

107 May, 'Goethe, Islam, and the Orient', p. 92, referring to Anil Bhatti, '"zwischen zwei Welten schwebend" Zu Goethes Fremdheitsexperiment im *West-östlichen Divan*', in *Goethe: Neue Ansichten–Neue Einsichten*, ed. by Jans-Jörg Knoblock and Helmut Koopmann (Würzburg: Königshausen & Neumann, 2007), pp. 103–21 (p. 117).

108 'In the end Goethe's Orientalism too is a form of Western self-reflexion; the East is instrumentalised on behalf of the West's self-improvement' (Carl Niekerk, 'The Romantics and other cultures', in *The Cambridge Companion to German Romanticism*, ed. by Nicholas Saul (Cambridge: Cambridge University Press, 2009), pp. 147–61 (p. 153).

109 Dunker, '"Als wisse ich endlich Alles"', p. 216.

> Auf dem rückweg bleibe ich vor einem der hauseingänge stehen. Im niedrigen, fensterlosen souterrain dreht um eine staubverkrustete ölmühle ein geblendetes kamel seine engen runden. Gebannt starre ich auf das traurige tier mit seinen grotesken proportionen. All die kinder an den nähmaschinen oder hobelbänken berühren mich weniger als dieses blinde, eingeschirrte kamel (*LV*, p. 118).

The narrator's sympathy for the animal and his apparent disregard for the human element in the picture has an antecedent in George Orwell's essay 'Marrakech' (1939): 'There is no question that the donkeys are damnably treated. [...] This kind of thing makes one's blood boil, whereas – on the whole – the plight of the human beings does not'.[110] The primacy of animal suffering over that of humans in this piece is intended, paradoxically, to draw attention to the invisible suffering of the Moroccans. Orwell 'insists on the humanity of those who seem subhuman to the colonial eye. Whatever we may think of [the passage's] tone, it draws our attention to men, women, and beasts of burden alike'.[111]

Two major figures in German-language literature also comment on the plight of animals during visits to Marrakech. Elias Canetti, in *Die Stimmen von Marrakesch* (1967), observes a donkey being maltreated one evening: 'Der Esel war von allen armseligen Eseln dieser Stadt der ärmste'.[112] He is surprised to find the donkey still alive the following day, standing in the same place and looking even more miserable. Looking away for a moment, Canetti's gaze returns to the donkey to find the animal transformed:

> Er hatte sich nicht von der Stelle gerührt, aber es war nicht mehr derselbe Esel. Denn zwischen seinen Hinterbeinen, schräg nach vorn, hing ihm plötzlich ein ungeheures Glied herunter. Es war stärker als der Stock, mit dem man ihn nachts zuvor bedroht hatte. [...] dieses Wesen, weniger als nichts, ohne Fleisch, ohne Kraft, ohne rechtes Fell, hatte noch so viel Lust in sich, daß mich der bloße Anblick vom Eindruck seines Elends befreite. Ich denke oft an ihn. Ich sage mir, wie viel von ihm noch da war, als ich nichts mehr sah. Ich wünsche jedem Gepeinigten seine Lust im Elend.[113]

The above passage famously attracted Hubert Fichte's scathing criticism. Dunker identifies a short passage from Fichte's *Alte Welt* (published posthumously in

110 George Orwell, *The Collected Essays, Journalism and Letters of George Orwell*, I, *An Age Like This 1920–1940*, ed. by Sonia Orwell and Ian Angus (London: Secker & Warburg, 1968), p. 392.

111 Margaret Drabble, 'Of Beasts and Men: Orwell on Beastliness', in *On* Nineteen Eighty-Four: *Orwell and our Future*, ed. by Abbott Gleason, Jack Goldsmith and Martha C. Nussbaum (Princeton: Princeton University Press, 2005), pp. 38–48 (p. 46).

112 Elias Canetti, *Die Stimmen von Marrakesch: Aufzeichnungen nach einer Reise* (Frankfurt am Main: Fischer, 1980), p. 74.

113 Canetti, *Die Stimmen von Marrakesch*, pp. 75–76.

1992) in which he writes: 'Canetti: Die Stimmen von Marrakesch. Ungenauer, weinerlicher Käse. Empörend das Kapitel: Die Lust des Esels'.[114] Indeed, Fichte produces his own Marrakech-donkey scene in *Der Platz der Gehenkten* (1989) as a satirical response to Canetti:

> Der Esel bockt. Der Mann schlägt auf ihn ein. Der Esel rührt sich nicht. Der Mann schlägt weiter. Der Esel läßt einen riesigen violetten Dödel bis auf die Erde hängen. Und pißt. Der untersetzte Ausländer, mit einem Gesicht wie Strindberg, macht sich eine Notiz ins Lederbändchen. Der Eselstreiber springt auf den Rücken des Esels und zieht ihn am Schwanz. Der Esel legt sich hin. Der Eselstreiber schlägt weiter auf ihn ein.[115]

The thickset foreigner 'mit einem Gesicht wie Strindberg' is, of course, none other than a caricaturized Canetti, whose sense of wonder at the pitiful, lusty animal is mocked. It is likely that Roes is aware of these previous works and although his passage only indirectly evokes Canetti and Fichte's pre-texts, in doing so, he places his novel within a tradition of European writing about the Orient and indicates an awareness of Orientalist discourse.[116]

In addition to the numerous references to other authors, Roes includes quotations from his own poems and plays. These self-quotations constitute what Jean Ricardou has termed 'restricted intertextuality', defined as 'the reduplication of an item from another text [by the same author]'.[117] Towards the end of *Leeres Viertel* the narrator is told by the Bedouin Daūd that the recital of poetry is one of the means desert tribesmen use to express elevated states of feeling. There follows a collection of poems that evoke life in the desert, poems which were published again in the collection *Durus Arabij/Arabische Lektionen* (1997). Schnittke's diary also includes poems that later appear in *Arabische Lektionen*: the poem 'Achwar/Brüder' (*LV*, p. 739), for example, reappears in the later volume in revised form (*AL*, p. 81). *Leeres Viertel* also contains scenes from a play which depicts a story the narrator is told by local Yemenis (e.g. *LV*, p. 727). These scenes form part of a play called *Der Narr des Königs: Madschnun al-Malik*, published by Roes in 1997. Roes's anthropologist-narrator had, on arrival in Yemen, speculated that no theatrical tradition existed there. He later comes to realize 'dass nämlich in der arabischen Welt ein anderer Begriff von Theater existiert, der nicht weniger seine Berechtigung

114 Hubert Fichte, *Alte Welt* (Frankfurt am Main: Fischer, 1992), p. 564.

115 Hubert Fichte, *Der Platz der Gehenkten* (Frankfurt am Main: Fischer, 1989), p. 94.

116 Dunker, '"Als wisse ich endlich Alles"', pp. 217–18.

117 Jean Ricardou, 'Terrorisme, théorie', in *Robbe-Grillet: Colloque de Cerisy*, 2 vols, I, ed. by Jean Ricardou (Paris: Union générale des éditions, 1976), pp. 10-33 (p. 23), quoted (in Jefferson's translation) in Jefferson, 'Autobiography as Intertext', p. 111.

hat als der "westliche" Theaterbegriff'.[118] This anthropological discovery feeds into the textual composition of the novel as the anthropologist listens to his informant's narration of Madschnun al-Malik's story. Taken together, these poems and theatre pieces 'bilden einen Teil der Textcollage, die *Leeres Viertel* darstellt',[119] and represent a cultural collaboration between representatives of two different cultures. Like Goethe, Roes is seeking to be influenced by the cultural traditions of the Islamic world and channelling that influence into his creative work. These self-quotations also demonstrate how *Leeres Viertel* is interlinked with Roes's other literary projects. While his theme of intercultural encounters remains constant, he is flexible in terms of the genre in which he chooses to work. The novel has been and remains his principal medium of expression but he turns at times to poetry, plays, essays and films to reflect further on the themes that preoccupy him.

Playful Intertextuality

I now come to the final category of intertextual reference, those quotations from authentic travel accounts assimilated into the Schnittke diary. Some travel writers vehemently deny all influence from previous writers. They claim to forge their own paths, to break new ground; they are the first to experience the foreign country in the way they did. This is not surprising since the trailblazer enjoys elevated status: 'der in Spuren Reisende [steht] im Verdacht, dilettantischer Nachahmer zu sein'.[120] In such cases the notion of intertextuality in travel writing is problematic: reference to previous travellers would be an admission of belatedness that robs the journey of its uniqueness. Ulla Biernat argues that 'jeder Reisebericht [...] andere Texte auf vielfältige Weise [verarbeitet], auch wenn die Autoren den Rückgriff auf Prätexte häufig zu verschleiern versuchen'.[121] In *Leeres Viertel* Michael Roes makes no such attempt to conceal the texts of his predecessors. On the contrary, he displays the literary tradition in which he follows. He uses previous texts to forge a new one, thereby drawing attention to processes of textualization and intertextuality. The presence of intertextual elements indicates the falsity of the concept of the Western traveller as pioneering explorer. The historical strand in *Leeres Viertel*, by definition, reveals the idea of a traveller on paths never before trodden to be a conceit. The fact that the Schnittke diary is a

118 Schmitt-Maaß, *Das gefährdete Subjekt*, p. 234.
119 Schmitt-Maaß, *Das gefährdete Subjekt*, p. 216.
120 Ortrud Gutjahr, 'Der Entdeckungsbericht des Anderen: Erreiste Intertextualität in Felicitas Hoppes *Pigafetta*', in *Ins Fremde Schreiben*, ed. by Hamann and Honold, pp. 239–66 (p. 260).
121 Biernat, "*Ich bin nicht der erste Fremde hier*", p. 19.

compendium of twelve real-life Arabian journeys serves to reinforce this further. The presence of references to or quotations from other travel writing is an admission that the traveller was not the first to 'discover' a region or to 'conquer' a mountain. White spots on the map have long since disappeared and intertextual references are an indicator of this.[122]

Of the twelve sources listed in the postscript, Carsten Niebuhr's *Reisebeschreibung nach Arabien und andern umliegenden Ländern* (1774) is the one most heavily borrowed from. Carsten Niebuhr (1733–1815) was a German cartographer who took part in a Danish-funded expedition to the Orient in 1761, led by the philologist F. C. von Haven (1727–1763) and the scientist Petrus Forskål (1732–1763). The other members of the group were the doctor Christian C. Cramer (1732–1763), the artist G. W. Bauernfeld (1728–1763) and a dragoman called Berggren (?–1763). As the dates of death indicate, Niebuhr was the only member of the expedition to survive the journey. Schnittke's fictional expedition is loosely based on the Danish mission and his travelling companions also all meet their end on the journey. Schnittke's account of Doctor Schlichter's burial in Dschidda takes as its template Niebuhr's description of Forskål's burial. The similarities between the two passages are remarkable:

> Die nächste Schwierigkeit, die wir bey der Beerdigung unseres Freundes finden, ist die, dass wir keine Träger bekommen können, obgleich wir reichlich dafür zu bezahlen versprechen und es uns auch gefallen lassen wollen, dass man ihn des Nachts zu Grabe trage. Wir glauben, der Pflicht, welche wir unserem Reisegefährten schuldig sind, auch kein Genüge zu thun, wenn wir ihn nicht in einem Kasten begrüben. Wir würden aber besser gethan haben, wenn wir ihn bloss in schlechte Leinwand eingewickelt und so in die Erde gebettet hätten. Der Kasten giebt den arabischen Trägern Gelegenheit zu glauben, dass wir Europäer Schätze mit unseren Todten vergrüben. Es ward schon davon gesprochen als wir den Kasten machen liessen. – Nun kommen sie nicht eher des Morgens zwischen drey und vier Uhr, da Alles in tiefem Schlafe ist, und eilen so sehr, dass sie den Kasten zweymal auf den Boden stürzen lassen, wohl auch, um etwas über seinen Inhalt zu erfahren (*LV*, p. 200).

> Die größte Schwierigkeit, welche wir bei der Beerdigung unsers Freundes fanden, war die, daß wir keine Träger bekommen konnten, ob wir gleich reichlich dafür zu bezahlen versprachen und es uns gefallen lassen wollten,

122 Not to mention the fact that these 'white spots' were often only unknown empty spaces to Westerners. Local people were usually enlisted by white Western explorers to assist in their 'discovery'. Colonial travellers often attempted to aggrandize their discoveries in their writing by negating this local knowledge 'indem man entweder die Präsenz der Einheimischen so weit als möglich ausblendet oder sie von Subjekten zu Objekten des Wissens degradiert' (Bay, 'Going Native?', p. 122).

> daß sie ihn des Nachts zu Grabe trügen. Endlich erboten sich hierzu 6 Mann. Allein sie kamen nicht eher als (am 12ten Julius) des Morgens zwischen 3 und 4 Uhr, da alles im tiefem Schlaf war, und eileten so sehr, ihre Arbeit geschwinde und heimlich zu verrichten, daß wir bloß daraus schon schließen konnten, es werde für einen Mahommedaner nicht anständig gehalten, einen fremden Religionsverwandten zu tragen. [...] Wir glaubten, der Pflicht, welche wir unserm Reisegefährten schuldig waren, kein Genüge zu tun, wenn wir ihn nicht in einem Kasten begrüben. Wir würden aber besser getan haben, wenn wir ihn bloß in schlechter Leinwand eingewickelt und so in die Erde gelegt hätten. Der Kasten gab dem arabischen Pöbel Gelegenheit zu glauben, daß die Europäer Schätze mit ihren Toten vergrüben. Es ward schon davon gesprochen, als wir den Kasten machen ließen.[123]

Despite extensive textual appropriation (examined further below), significant differences also exist between Schnittke and his most important model:

> Niebuhr ist – obwohl mit den gleichen Aufgaben versehen wie Schnittke – sehr viel stringenter in der kartographischen und ethnologischen Erfassung der ihm fremden Welt. Demgegenüber scheint der Reiz des Schnittke-Tagebuchs in der wuchernden Selbstreflexivität zu liegen und in der Tatsache, dass er sein Wissen anekdotisch zu verpacken weiß.[124]

Christoph Schmitt-Maaß identifies passages taken from works by other historical explorers of the Orient, such as Johann Ludwig Burckhart's *Reisen in Arabien* (1830) and Eduard Glaser's *Reise nach Marib* (1913).[125] These historical travel accounts reveal a tendency by Roes to use the older accounts as a source for the beginning of Schnittke's diary, and to use the more recent ones towards the end. The result is that Roes 'nicht nur die Entwicklung eines kritischen Aufklärers zu einem einfühlenden Beobachter vollzieht, sondern dieser Vollzug parallel zur Geschichte der Orientreisebeschreibung abläuft'.[126] As a result, the seams of Schnittke's patchwork are revealed. At times a perfect example of Enlightenment tolerance (*LV*, p. 114), at other times consciously utilizing the Orientalist metaphors of his age,[127] Schnittke is a configuration

123 Niebuhr, *Reisebeschreibung nach Arabien*, pp. 401–02.

124 Schmitt-Maaß, '"mäandernd, ornamentalisch, ohne progression?"', 102.

125 Schmitt-Maaß, '"mäandernd, ornamentalisch, ohne progression?"', 101–04.

126 Schmitt-Maaß, '"mäandernd, ornamentalisch, ohne progression?"', 107.

127 'Als wir uns der Küste nähern, fühle ich mich wie ein orientalischer Bräutigam, der gerade den Schleier seiner Braut lüftet und zum ersten Male ihre Gesichtszüge sieht. Das mag klingen, als sey für den Abendländer, das Geschlechtliche, der Körper des Weibes oder Knaben, das Thor zum Orient. Doch welchem Menschen ist diese Sehnsucht fremd? Und gleicht die Lust zu Reisen nicht in der That der Lust, dem Schönen und Begehrenswerthen zu begegnen und sich mit ihnen zu vereinen?' (*LV*, p. 34).

of numerous separate figures. He is also in many ways ahead of his time and functions as a model for the contemporary anthropologist's 'postmodernen, aber aufklärerisch fundierten Forschung'.[128]

Having so far followed Schmitt-Maaß and Dunker's analysis of intertextuality in *Leeres Viertel*, this chapter now takes a new departure by introducing the concept of crimeless plagiarism that is played like a game. The quotations are unmarked in Schnittke's account. The pre-texts are passed off as Schnittke's own without signalling the borrowings in the body of the text itself. Despite this there can be no question of any intention to deceive. To accuse Roes of plagiarism would be to miss the point entirely. For one thing, he makes no attempt to conceal the 'theft'. On the contrary, the sources are revealed in the appendix as an invitation to further investigation. Within the body of Schnittke's text the perceived border dividing 'original' literary production on the one hand and quotation from external sources on the other has been completely dissolved. Peter Horst Neumann, articulating a theory of quotation, states that:

> Die Unterscheidungen zwischen Nähe und Ferne, Eigenem und Fremden sind fragwürdig geworden. Dadurch hat das Zitieren, wie mir scheint, eine historisch neue Qualität erhalten, eine, auf die sich der Begriff des *Plagiates* nur noch bedingt anwenden läßt. Immer häufiger tritt *unwillkürlich* das Fremde an die Stelle des Eigenen, und Eigenes erscheint immer öfter in verfremdender Gestaltung.[129]

With accusations of plagiarism misplaced and the question regarding ownership obsolete, Schnittke's diary bears all the hallmarks of a montage: the collective work of thirteen Western authors, each of which has travelled to and written about the Arab world.

The metaphor of play has often been applied to literature in a postmodern context, as indeed in many other cultural fields. Alan Thiher describes this playful element in literature in relation to post-structuralist theories of language, stating:

> Modern language theories agree in telling the storyteller that, whenever he tells a tale, he has already started to play. They are basically at one in telling the writer that to use the tribe's tongue is to undertake a ludic activity whose rule-bound forms are grounded only in themselves. Literature – inventing fictions, narrating tales, writing texts – would therefore be so many language games, play in language, to the second degree, or perhaps moves on the chess-board of being.[130]

128 Schmitt-Maaß, '"mäandernd, ornamentalisch, ohne progression?"', 107.

129 Peter Horst Neumann, 'Das Eigene und das Fremde: Über die Wünschbarkeit einer Theorie des Zitierens', *Akzente*, 4 (1980), 292–305 (p. 295).

130 Thiher, *Words in Reflection*, p. 156.

Intertextuality is often cited as one of the specifically playful practices available to an author. The vocabulary used by Peter Horst Neumann in an article on the desirability of theories of quotation reveals the applicability of the play metaphor when discussing intertextuality. He describes quotation using the following terms: 'Spielraum für Bezüge', 'Spiel zwischen Motto und eigenem Text', 'Kommunikationsspiel', 'Spielstruktur'.[131] Raymond Federman's writing on intertexuality is also of great relevance in this regard. In Federman's eyes all literature is inherently plagiaristic, not only works that highlight this by foregrounding their intertextual practices:

> creating a work of art, or in this case a literary text, is a mere process of displacing, of transposing language from one space into another. [...] creating, imagining, writing, is a simple act of quoting, of repeating the same old thing.[132]

With originality revealed to have been a myth, 'PLAGIARISM is not only admissible, it is also advisable'.[133] According to Federman, quotation contains immense ludic potential: 'For PLAGIARISM read also PLAYGIARISM'.[134] In this new postmodern context plagiarism has become a narrative game by means of which writers engage their readers in a more active process of reading. The reader brings to the new text his or her own reading experience and applies that knowledge in an effort to unlock the hidden meanings of the text.

The play metaphor has experienced a 'Hochkonjunktur' in the postmodern arts, to the point where it has at times been 'in geradezu inflationärer Häufigkeit verwendet'.[135] This prompts the question as to the extent to which the play metaphor is really applicable to Roes's intertextual process in *Leeres Viertel*. Roes's appropriation of passages from Niebuhr's *Reisebeschreibung* reveals a bias towards sections of particular ethnographic significance. Schnittke shares the contemporary narrator's interest in traditional Arab games and he quotes passages from Niebuhr's chapter on 'Leibesübungen und Zeitvertreib der Morgenländer bei müßigen Stunden' almost verbatim:

> Und wie die Spiele auf der ganzen Welt die selbigen zu seyn scheinen. Ich erinnere mich zum Beyspiel, Kinder an der Ilm in ähnlicher Weise mit kleinen Steinchen spielen gesehen zu haben wie jetzt hier die Kinder am Nil. Sie werfen einen Stein in die Höhe und fangen ihn wieder auf, wenn sie inzwischen einen,

131 Neumann, 'Das Eigene und das Fremde', 301–02.

132 Federman, 'Imagination as Plagiarism', 575–76.

133 Federman, 'Imagination as Plagiarism', 571.

134 Federman, 'Imagination as Plagiarism', 565.

135 Thomas Anz, 'Das Spiel ist aus? Zur Konjunktur und Verabschiedung des "postmodernen" Spielbegriffs', in *Postmoderne Literatur in deutscher Sprache: Eine Ästhetik des Widerstands?*, ed. by Henk Harbers (Amsterdam: Rodopi, 2000), pp. 15–34 (p. 22).

zwey, drey oder die vier Uebrigen von der Erde aufgenommen haben. Dies Spiel nennen die Egypter *Lakud* (*LV*, p. 96).

Die Spiele der Bauernkinder scheinen in der ganzen Welt dieselbigen zu sein. Ich erinnere mich zum Beispiel, die Kinder am Euphrat zwischen Basra und Helle mit fünf kleinen Steinen spielen gesehen zu haben, von welchen sie einen in die Höhe warfen und ihn wieder auffingen, wenn sie vorher einen, zwei, drei oder die vier übrigen von der Erde aufgenommen hatten. Dies Spiel nennen die Araber Lakud.[136]

Schnittke's diary continues with further descriptions of games taken from Niebuhr but sadly omits the remarkable drawings contained in Niebuhr's book. Schnittke also borrows Niebuhr's notes on other topics of anthropological interest, for example in the following sections: the description of the Monastery of Santa Katarina on the Sinai Peninsula: Schnittke (p. 63) corresponds to Niebuhr (pp. 253–54); descriptions of Cairo hospitals, mosques and baths: Schnittke (pp. 77–79) corresponds to Niebuhr (pp. 132–33); information on Arab music: Schnittke (p. 101) corresponds to Niebuhr (p. 191); mourning rituals: Schnittke (p. 108) corresponds to Niebuhr (p. 206); the acting profession in Egypt: Schnittke (p. 111) corresponds to Niebuhr (p. 207); burial scene of a colleague (quoted extensively above); descriptions of Sana'a: Schnittke (p. 385) corresponds to Niebuhr (p. 413). The intertextual borrowing here serves to provide accurate ethnographic information from a particular historical period in which the fictional Schnittke is travelling. Roes submitted his 'novel' as a *Habilitationsschrift* in the field of anthropology,[137] thus necessitating the absolute accuracy of the anthropological information, both contemporary and historical, in the novel. Since Roes's intertextual process is aiming here towards a specific end (anthropological knowledge), it is debatable whether it can be described as a 'game'. While the subject matter of the Schnittke plagiarism is focused on the anthropology of play, the process of borrowing cannot be described as purely playful or pla(y)giaristic.

Despite this, the play metaphor may prove to be useful in an analysis of the Schnittke 'plagiarism' in certain respects. Several signs suggest that Roes and Schnittke are indeed playfully conniving in this intertextual enterprise. In one instance Schnittke praises the accuracy of Carsten Niebuhr's maps and charts: 'Hiernach berechne ich die Länge des Weges in Schritten auf eine viertel Meile, und vergleiche Wegrichtung und zurückgelegte Strecke mit der von Carsten Niebuhr genauestens erstelleten Charte' (*LV*, p. 59). This remark is playful in a number of ways. First, it labels itself a non-quotation, or is at

136 Niebuhr, *Reisebeschreibung nach Arabien*, p. 185.
137 Schmitt-Maaß, *Das gefährdete Subjekt*, p. 219.

least not a quotation from Niebuhr. Second, it is highly ironic considering that, seen from a certain perspective, Schnittke *is* Niebuhr. Strictly speaking, the remark falls between our second and third categories of intertextuality. It is a reference to an external text (Niebuhr's charts), but it just so happens that that outsider is also one of the authors whose work is candidly plagiarized in other parts of the Schnittke strand of the narrative.

Another playful aspect to Roes's intertextuality is found in the amendments made in the process of assimilating a foreign text into Schnittke's account. One example is the appropriation from Ulrich Jasper Seetzen's *Reisen durch Syrien, Palästina, Phönicien, die Transjordan-Länder, Arabia Petraea und Unter-Aegypten* (1854). While in Jerusalem, Seetzen enlists a guide 'damit er mir alle merkwürdigen Gegenstände zeigen möchte'.[138] Schnittke, in contrast, had looked forward to a solitary walk to the Mount of Olives, 'doch bedrängt der Adjunet mich so sehr, ihn mitzunehmen, damit er mir alle Merckwürdigkeiten zeigen könne' (*LV*, p. 51). Schnittke's disinclination for company suggests a greater level of self-sufficiency and confidence than that possessed by his model. The idea of reluctance is developed and played with when the guide takes Schnittke to view the site of the stoning of the first martyr, Saint Stephen. Seetzen merely states that the guide 'mir die Stelle [zeigte], wo der heilige Stephan seinen Enthusiasmus mit dem Tode bezahlen musste'.[139] But Roes/Schnittke plays with the concept of martyrdom, exclaiming: 'Also lasse ich mir märtyrergleich den Grund zeigen, wo der Heilige Stephan seinen Enthusiasmus mit dem Tode bezahlen musste' (*LV*, p. 52). This unmistakably playful amendment to the appropriated text gives additional colour to an account that was originally primarily intended to be informative. In addition, Roes supplements the plagiarized passage with an additional intertextual allusion during the process of assimilation into Schnittke's text. Seetzen, in his original account, states: 'Mein Cicerone war sehr geschäftig, mich auf Alles aufmerksam zu machen, was einen frommen Pilger interessiren kann'.[140] By the time the passage has been embedded into Schnittke's diary an allusion to Cervantes's *Don Quixote* (1605–15) has been inserted, giving an additional layer to the intertextual fabric of the piece: 'Mein Sancho Pansa ist sehr beflissen, mich auf Alles aufmercksam zu machen, was einen frommen Pilgrim interessiren könnte' (*LV*, p. 52). This is one of numerous references to Cervantes's classic peppered throughout Roes's *oeuvre* and Schnittke will later describe Jaina, his Yemeni lover, as a 'Dulcinea des Leeren Viertels' (*LV*, p. 670).

138 Ulrich Jasper Seetzen, *Reisen durch Syrien, Palästina, Phönicien, die Transjordan-Länder, Arabia Petraea und Unter-Aegypten* (Berlin: Reimer, 1854), p. 26.

139 Seetzen, *Reisen durch Syrien*, p. 26.

140 Seetzen, *Reisen durch Syrien*, p. 26.

The huge extent of the passages borrowed from various authentic travel accounts prohibits their full exposition and explication here. The magnitude of the borrowing is also an indication of playful intent, with the plagiarism taking on the appearance of a game of 'dare'. How far dare an author go in his intertextual borrowing? How far can a writer venture before the new text is composed entirely of quotations? Examples exist in German literature in which authors take this game to extremes. Manfred Durzak's study of montage novels written in the late 1960s and early 1970s reveals a 'Hinwendung zur Zitation als sprachlichem Bauelement'. These novels are composed largely or exclusively of quotations and the montage technique is the 'Aufbauprinzip des Romans'.[141] Roes does not take his intertextual game as far as these earlier writers. Quotation remains a secondary element in his novel, an aspect that enriches the fabric of his text but only intermittently breaks the surface. Nevertheless, the audaciousness of the appropriation gives the novel the character of provocation and boldness infused with a distinctly playful tone.

It is also possible that Roes is playing a game at times with the reader, testing the latter's attention. Red herrings are a favourite manipulation technique of crime writers,[142] but at least one example can be found in *Leeres Viertel*. The appendix states that Schnittke's diary is partially composed of quotations from the aforementioned travel accounts, yet some of these accounts do not feed directly into Schnittke's diary. In the case of John Philby's *The Empty Quarter* (1933), they feed into the contemporary narrator's account instead.[143] Parting with some of his Arab fellow travellers, Philby remarks: 'The farewell of the Arab is manly indeed. With fair words on his lips he strides off into the desert and is gone. He never looks back'.[144] A similar feeling is evoked in the contemporary narrator's ending, notwithstanding his more taciturn Arab friends: 'Beim anbruch der dämmerung ist alles vorbei. Die männer klopfen sich den staub von den röcken, steigen mit knapper geste oder gruszlos in ihre geländewagen und fahren in ungeordnetem haufen und ohne licht in die wüste hinaus' (*LV*, p. 803). This falls short of being an actual quotation. Nevertheless, the powerful evocation of masculinity and the melancholy of

141 Manfred Durzak, 'Zitat und Montage im deutschen Roman der Gegenwart', in *Die deutsche Literatur der Gegenwart: Aspekte und Tendenzen*, ed. by Manfred Durzak (Stuttgart: Philipp Reclam, 1971), pp. 211–29 (p. 212). The examples used by Durzak are Oswald Wiener's *verbesserung von mitteleuropa* (1969), Peter Chotjewitz's *Vom Leben und Lernen* (1969) and Helmut Heißenbüttel's *D'Alemberts Ende* (1970).

142 Peter Hutchinson, *Games Authors Play* (London: Methuen, 1983), p. 111.

143 The closest correspondence between the Philby and Schnittke texts that I can identify is a shared fascination with the singing sands of the desert: *LV*, p. 592 and John Philby, *The Empty Quarter* (London: Century, 1986), p. 295 and p. 393.

144 Philby, *The Empty Quarter*, p. 299.

the farewell scene suggest that it is not only Schnittke who has been influenced by literary accounts of Orient expeditions from a previous age.

There is also a somewhat playful quality to the contrapunctal dual-stranded structure of the narrative.[145] The novel's subtitle 'Invention über das Spiel' suggests a musical counterpoint and music, while not a game as such, is nevertheless 'played'. The subtitle also suggests that elements of the narrative are inventions and that the borderline between fact and fiction is ambiguous. Such suggestions are signs for the reader to be prepared to engage more actively with the text, to be ready to play whatever game the author has in store. Such indications are important: the author's narrative game must somehow be signalled or the reader is liable to remain unaware that (s)he is 'being played'. Reading Schnittke's diary in the knowledge that it is a collage of other texts adds a dimension of playfulness. The reader can enter into the game of detecting and recognizing quotations and allusions, a test of knowledge and learning which functions as a source of both pleasure and pride: '[D]as Entdecken solcher Anspielungen [kann] zu einem lustvollen Spiel werden, bei dem [der Leser] seine Wissenskompetenz auf die Probe stellt und im Falle des Erfolgs genießt'.[146]

Play, the anthropological subject matter, is linked to the formal structure and intertextual constitution of the novel. Not only do both narrators share an ethnographic interest, they also share parallel fates. This parallelism is in itself a narrative game, a playful technique that illuminates our understanding of the characters and their journeys. The incorporation of stolen passages from old travel accounts constitutes another layer of depth to this connection between play, anthropology and intertextuality. On the one hand, the passages are stolen precisely for this anthropological reason: to ensure that Schnittke's fictional world is infused with historically accurate descriptions of the country in which he is travelling. While the borrowing is not inherently playful in this regard, it is thematically related to play. On the other hand, there is a distinctly playful aspect to Roes's intertextual ingenuity. As he plagiarizes his forebears' texts, he is also self-consciously playing an intricate textual game. This takes on, at various times, the aspect of a jigsaw puzzle, a game of hide-and-seek, of dare, or of role-playing. Following Federman, it appears that in *Leeres Viertel* plagiarism is 'playgiarism'. Not only is play the novel's anthropological subject, it is also a motif found at the core of Roes's conception of intercultural encounters. However, play also forms part of Roes's approach to intertextuality in the novel

145 Peter Hutchinson touches on the counterpoint technique as a game in literature (*Games Authors Play*, pp. 29–30), referring to its use in Aldous Huxley's *Point Counter Point* (1928), Andre Gide's *The Counterfeiters* (1925) and Thomas Mann's *Doktor Faustus* (1947).

146 Anz, 'Das Spiel ist aus?', p. 30.

and he thereby establishes a complex link between the anthropological, the intercultural and the intertextual elements of the work.

CHAPTER 2

Engaging the American Literary Canon in *Haut des Südens*

Literary accounts of journeys to America have a tendency to be heavily intertextual. Travellers to the USA will inevitably have been exposed to countless images of that nation and its culture before setting off on their voyage. Preconceived ideas about America gleaned from films, television programmes, photographic images and literary works fire up the imagination and inspire journeys, which can in turn be photographed, filmed or textualized. According to Oliver Simons, '[s]cenes of arrival in America begin quite frequently with second-hand descriptions, with a quotation of another travelogue, with images seen long ago. [...] America is a textual construction, a topos whose history is first and foremost literary in nature'.[1] Wolfgang Koeppen, on his arrival in New York, quotes from Herman Melville and Franz Kafka in his *Amerikafahrt* (1959). He also writes of 'die irren Lichter O'Neills, die Durchleuchtungen Tennessee Williams', Faulkners Genie'.[2] Koeppen views America through the lens of previously read books and searches for 'das Amerika meiner Erwartung'.[3] In Peter Handke's American novel, *Der kurze Brief zum langen Abschied* (1972), the narrator evokes Schiller's *Don Carlos*, F. Scott Fitzgerald's *The Great Gatsby*, and Raymond Chandler's *The Long Goodbye*, all 'in an effort to underscore the story of his conversion to a community-orientated point of view'.[4] It appears that the real America, if it exists at all, is obscured behind a mass of texts and images.

Such foregrounding of other texts can also be observed in Michael Roes's *Haut des Südens*, published in 2000, a novel in which a German traveller (who in a number of ways resembles the author) journeys along the Mississippi river. The novel opens with a passage from Mark Twain's memoir *Life on the Mississippi* (1883); other texts read before setting out on the journey also play a

1 Oliver Simons, '"Amerika gibt es nicht": On the Semiotics of Literary America in the Twentieth Century', *German Quarterly*, 82 (2009), 196–211 (p. 196).

2 Wolfgang Koeppen, *Amerikafahrt* (Frankfurt am Main: Fischer, 1962), p. 6.

3 Koeppen, *Amerikafahrt*, p. 12.

4 Kurt Fickert, 'The Myth of America in Peter Handke's *Der kurze Brief zum langen Abschied*', *German Studies Review*, 21 (1998), 27–40 (p. 36).

central role in illuminating the traveller-narrator's understanding of the Deep South and its racial divisions. He engages with works by Herman Melville (1819–1891), Mark Twain (1835–1910), William Faulkner (1897–1962), Ernest Hemingway (1899–1961) and Martin Luther King Jr (1929–1968) to reveal the history of race relations in the Southern States. In addition, the narrator's encounters with people reveal how communities in the present-day South still struggle to come to terms with a past that includes the horrors of slavery, the American Civil War (1861–1865), which formally ended slavery, and segregation, which continued for another hundred years afterwards, leaving the problems of racism and divided communities still unresolved.

The plot of *Haut des Südens* is easily summarized. An anonymous German traveller arrives in Hannibal, Missouri, on a pilgrimage to Mark Twain's childhood home. Quoted newspaper extracts from 1998 suggest that the journey was undertaken in that year. From Hannibal, the narrator proceeds to St Louis, Memphis, Oxford (Mississippi) and New Orleans, seeking to learn more about American attitudes towards race during the nineteenth and twentieth centuries. The journey exhibits the narrator concurrently as anthropologist, sociologist and literary historian. At an exhibition of African artworks in St Louis he befriends Daniel, a Nigerian from Lagos, who accompanies him for the duration of the novel. The pair attempt unsuccessfully to gain employment as sailors on a Mississippi freighter, and proceed to Memphis where they witness the macabre execution of a dog at the hands of its psychopathic owner. The narrator experiences the stay in Memphis as a fantastical synthesis of two different times; and he reports the 1968 sanitation workers' strike and Martin Luther King's assassination as if they were events he witnesses at first-hand. Impelled to move on to Oxford due to the increasingly malodorous state of affairs in Memphis, the narrator meets 'ganz normale Rassisten' (*HS*, p. 165) and attends a lecture by the Civil Rights campaigner James Meredith. New Orleans, the last station on the journey, introduces another fantastical turn as the pair escape the impending hurricane (of the sort that would inundate the city in 2005 when Hurricane Katrina took 1,800 lives) by heading for the open waters of the Atlantic on their home-made raft.

Over the course of five chapters, each written in a distinctive style that in some way represents five different authors or genres, the narrator experiments with form and presents a multitude of voices. *Haut des Südens* is a polyphony in that it is both an autobiographical travelogue and a fictional novel, both a literary essay and a compendium of other people's stories. Private lives and political history intertwine. Quotations abound: not only from classic novels but also from legal documents, private correspondence, newspaper articles and even instructions on how to survive a hurricane. The chapter dealing with the traveller's stay in Oxford, Mississippi (William Faulkner's hometown) is written loosely in the form of a film script – a nod towards the work Faulkner did for Hollywood studios.[5] The third chapter, which deals primarily with Martin Luther King and the Civil Rights Movement, is written in the form of an epic in verse, or, as one critic has suggested, a Gospel hymn.[6] It also includes quotations from Paul Celan's poem 'Der Gast'. The final chapter contains numerous religious references, in particular to the story of Noah and the Great Flood. Each sentence is numbered in a structure reminiscent of the books and verses of the Bible. The novel ends, as the two friends begin their Atlantic crossing, with a parody of Ishmael's statement in Herman Melville's *Moby Dick* (1851). Daniel sets course for home: '"Heim nach Rokovoko." – "Rokovoko?" – "Such dieses Land auf keiner Karte. Wirkliche Orte stehen nie darauf"' (*HS*, p. 260).[7]

This fusion of styles and voices divided critics upon the novel's publication. Julia Kospach in *Der Bund* admired the 'bewundernswert kunstvoll gewobenes Textmosaik',[8] while Herbert Wiesner in the *Süddeutsche Zeitung* regarded it as 'ein reizvolles, nicht in jedem Fall gelungenes Experiment',[9] and Gennaro Ghirardelli in the *Frankfurter Allgemeine Zeitung* saw the regular changes in form and style as pretentious.[10] A review in *Neues Deutschland*, formerly the official paper of the ruling party of the GDR, not only seeks to address this balance with a positive review, but also attempts to explain the sometimes brutal criticism that Roes is dealt by Feuilleton reviewers:

5 Faulkner initially adapted his own story 'Turn About' (1932) for the director Howard Hawks, the result of which was a film called *Today We Live* (1933). He was credited as a scriptwriter on five other films, including the screen adaptations of Ernest Hemingway's *To Have and Have Not* (book 1937; film 1944), and Raymond Chandler's novel, *The Big Sleep* (book 1939; film 1946). He did not, however, work on the 1959 screenplay of his own novel, *The Sound and the Fury* (1929); cf. John B. Padgett, 'William Faulkner as Screenwriter', in William Faulkner and Motion Pictures, www.mcsr.olemiss.edu/~egjbp/faulkner/mph.html [accessed 13 August 2012]. The latter film is widely regarded to be a 'dilution of one of his darkest, most uncompromising works' (Gene D. Phillips, *Fiction, Film, and Faulkner: The Art of Adaptation* (Knoxville: University of Tennessee Press, 1988), p. 163).

6 Cf. Rytz, 'Die Metaphorik der Haut', p. 59.

7 In *Moby Dick* Ishmael states that 'Queequeg was a native of Kokovoko, an island far away to the West and South. It is not down on any map; true places never are' (Herman Melville, *Moby Dick* (London: Penguin, 1994), p. 70). The variation in the island's name is due to a discrepancy between the initial English and American editions of the novel.

8 Julia Kospach, 'Schwarz und weiss: *Haut des Südens* von Michael Roes', *Der Bund*, 10 February 2001, p. 2.

9 Herbert Wiesner, 'Immer bleiben Narben: Die hautnah erfahrbare Mississippi-Reise des Michael Roes', *Süddeutsche Zeitung*, 6 December 2000, Section B, p. 7.

10 Gennaro Ghirardelli, 'Pustelkuchen: Michael Roes am Mississippi', *Frankfurter Allgemeine Zeitung*, 21 October 2000, p. V.

> Bei ihm [Roes] gibt es weder Salonbanalitäten noch Sozialkitsch, er ist in den Formen experimentierfreudig und dennoch unterhaltsam. Dass ihn das Feuilleton teilweise nicht mag, dürfte genau daran liegen: Roes ist mehr als eine junge Erscheinung, er watscht keine 68er ab, wie das die Neu-Yuppies tun, die sich damit von jedem kritischen Verständnis emanzipieren, er verbindet Literatur und Erkenntnis, und bei Roes lieben sich Männer, ohne dass es deswegen ums Schwulsein ginge. Offensichtlich ertragen manche Feuilletonisten so viel selbstverständliche In-Frage-Stellung nicht.[11]

The most critical of all the media voices was Uwe Wittstock in *Die Welt*, who disliked the 'intellektuelle[s] Imponiergehabe' he perceived in the novel and the feeling that Roes was attempting to impart a 'Gefühl moralischer Überlegenheit' to his liberal readers.[12]

Wittstock also put forward the charge of unsound anthropology with regard to a passage on nomadism and settlement in which Roes's narrator states: '[...] der Preis unserer Seßhaftigkeit ist das Eingemauertsein, Haut ist ersetzt durch Stein, Frauen sind die Besitzer der Zelte, Männer Eigentümer der Häuser' (*HS*, p. 79). The dichotomy between *Haut* (or *Zelt*) and *Haus* reflects two different modes of living, two ways of life. Roes regards nomadism, as represented by the tent, as an earlier, more natural way of life: 'atmend, zusammenfaltbar, beweglich' (*HS*, p. 79). Houses, in contrast, represent a patriarchal mode of living: solid, inflexible and constricting. As Julianne Rytz observes:

> Die Argumentation von Roes unterstellt also, dass die Alliteration Haut – Haus auf zwei völlig entgegengesetzte Konzepte verweist. In einer Vorgehensweise, die seinen gesamten Roman kennzeichnet, verkehrt er binäre Oppositionen, nicht nur indem er diese in ihrer Funktion als Wahrnehmungskonstrukte zeigt, sondern auch die den Oppositionspaaren immer inhärente Hierarchie in ihr Gegenteil verkehrt.[13]

Wittstock, however, regards this 'Ethno-Ode ohnegleichen' as exoticizing kitsch and suggests that ownership of nomad tents varies from tribe to tribe. This issue is in many ways reminiscent of Bruce Chatwin, who was obsessed throughout his writing career with the subject of nomadism and humankind's urge to wander. Both authors, Chatwin and Roes, formulate anthropological theories relating to nomadism, express them in literary form, and are criticized for allegedly erroneous or defective anthropology. After failing in his attempt to write a study of nomadism, Chatwin included some of his notes on the topic as part of his novel about the Australian Aborigines, *The Songlines* (1987).

11 Raul Zelik, 'Fremde Haut: Michael Roes auf Spurensuche in den USA', *Neues Deutschland*, 12 January 2001, p. 10.

12 Uwe Wittstock, 'Was Wale wirklich wollen', *Die Welt*, 25 November 2000, p. 7.

13 Rytz, 'Die Metaphorik der Haut', p. 64.

The anthropological theories put forward in that literary work have been described at worst as 'profoundly flawed and inadequate',[14] at best as 'wont to oversimplification and overgeneralization, but not seriously misleading'.[15] Roes remarked in an interview that he, too, has reservations with regard to Chatwin's anthropology, but admires his 'Kunst, seine eigenen Erfahrungen zu versprachlichen und mit dem Leser in einen Dialog zu treten'.[16]

As the selection of media responses noted above suggest, *Haut des Südens* was not universally applauded upon its publication. It is nevertheless a rich work that reveals the extent and scope of the author's literary and intellectual interests. It is a provocative look at the question of race, not only in a literary-historical context as the references to American writers suggest, but also with an eye on contemporary social problems. Although Roes's works may appear postmodern in their experimentation with form, he attempts, as he states in one interview, 'gegen die postmodernen Unterstellungen anzuschreiben, es gebe kein Gut und Böse mehr, es gebe keine Werte zu vermitteln'.[17] Roes was castigated by Wittstock on the grounds that it takes very little courage or originality for an author to take a position against slavery and racism at the end of the twentieth century. This is a fair point, but as Ilija Trojanow, another contemporary German writer engaged with multiculturalism, states in reference to G. E. Lessing's *Nathan der Weise* (1779), 'das gute alte Lied muß halt immer wieder mit frischen Stimmen gesungen, die zentralen Fundamente einer zivilisierten Gesellschaft in jeder Generation zu neuer Selbstverständlichkeit gebracht werden'.[18] Yet Roes's programme goes well beyond a traditional anti-racist stance. His novel's utilization of the metaphor of skin undermines the concept of race altogether and reveals it to be a social construct.[19] Roes's analysis of literary forebears also forms part of this effort to reveal the dubitability of race as a concept. This chapter will proceed to analyse Roes's use of and interaction with those predecessors, many of whom also attempted to challenge racial prejudice. As will become clear, they did so with varying degrees of success.

14 Thompson, *Travel Writing*, p. 91.

15 Howard Morphy, 'Proximity and Distance: Representations of Aboriginal Society in the Writings of Bill Harney and Bruce Chatwin', in *Popularizing Anthropology*, ed. by Jeremy MacClancy and Chris McDonaugh (London: Routledge, 1996), pp. 157–179 (p. 174).

16 Roes in interview with Schmitt-Maaß, *Das gefährdete Subjekt*, p. 285.

17 Roes in interview with Raul Zelik. See Raul Zelik, 'Der Phallus ist Kultur', *Der Freitag*, 1 December 2000, www.freitag.de/autoren/der-freitag/der-phallus-ist-kultur, quoted in Rytz, p. 58.

18 Ilija Trojanow, 'Weltbürgertum heute: Rede zu einer kosmopolitischen Kultur', in *Ilija Trojanow*, ed. by Julian Preece (Bern: Lang, 2013), pp. 15–45 (p. 20).

19 For a history of the development of the cultural concept of race, see Brian Niro, *Race* (Basingstoke: Palgrave Macmillan, 2003).

Following in Huck's Footsteps?

The narrator arrives in Hannibal, Missouri, at 4.30 on a clear night. The Greyhound bus sets him down at a motorway service station located three miles outside the town; and after an early morning walk to the centre it is all he can do to set himself down in a shop-doorway and fall asleep. The traveller, insofar as he is willing to sleep freely under the stars and in shop-doorways, resembles the hero of Mark Twain's *The Adventures of Huckleberry Finn* (1884), a novel which will come under intense scrutiny over the course of the traveller's stay in Hannibal. The doorway he has chosen is that of the 'Tante-Polly-Buchladen', Aunt Polly being Tom Sawyer's naïve but loving aunt. It is one of numerous shops and attractions in Hannibal that depend on the tourist trade associated with Samuel Langhorne Clemens, better known to the world's readers as Mark Twain. The space traversed by the traveller is in itself a literary reference: the streets he walks, the buildings he enters, his whole surroundings are a living museum of Twain's life. Roes quotes extensively from Twain's memoir *Life on the Mississippi* (1883), evoking a historical sense of place and contributing to the intertextual setting. Certain quotations function as a mirror to the narrator's movements around Hannibal and along the Mississippi, reinforcing the idea of a traveller following in a forerunner's footsteps. For example, the novel opens with a quotation from *Life on the Mississippi* (in German translation) in which Twain arrives in Hannibal early one morning after many years' absence (*HS*, p. 9). Shortly thereafter the novel describes how the German narrator arrives in the town, which is likewise deserted on account of the early hour. Twain goes on: 'It was Sunday morning, and everyone was abed yet. So I passed through the vacant streets, still seeing the town as it was, and not as it is'.[20] One of the criticisms of Twain that comes to light in *Haut des Südens* is that he fails to write about 'die Wirklichkeit, wie er sie vorfand' (*HS*, p. 35), choosing instead to make comic what was in fact a very grim and brutal reality.

Roes is hardly the first literary tourist on the Twain trail. A literary pilgrimage ordinarily involves a degree of admiration for the author whose footsteps are being followed. Jonathan Raban's travelogue *Old Glory: An American Voyage* (1981) is more aligned with such a tradition of homage. Raban's journey down the Mississippi in a small boat is inspired by ideas of the river that he accepted readily as a child reading *The Adventures of Huckleberry Finn*. Raban, however, in an accidental but symbolic move, leaves his copy of Twain's novel in his hotel on the first day of his river journey and soon learns that the only way to travel down the treacherous Mississippi is to forget romantic ideas gleaned

20 Mark Twain, *Life on the Mississippi* (London: Penguin, 1984), p. 371.

from literature. As Roger George explains, 'To be more like Twain on Twain's river, Raban learns, he has to *forget*, at least during the journey, all the Twain he has ever read and pay intense attention to the river at his bow'.[21]

Like the other travellers and tourists, the German narrator is in Hannibal because of the celebrated author, but his journey differs from more conventional literary pilgrimages. To borrow terms and categories of intertextuality from Manfred Pfister (who, in turn, draws on Mikhail Bakhtin's terminology), the references to Twain, far from developing into a 'huldigende' form,[22] take on a 'dialogische' nature, revealing an antagonistic and polemic stance towards the pre-texts in question.[23] Roes's narrator examines Twain's hometown, its history and its present inhabitants, attempting to gain an insight into the racial attitudes of the town's most famous son. The historical account given of Hannibal's origins suggests the stance that Roes will take with regard to Mark Twain. The first reference made to the Clemens family firmly suggests an association between them and the racism prevalent in an age when chattel slavery was still a reality:

> Bis zur Übersiedlung von Mark Twains Vater, John Marshall Clemens, und seiner Familie im Jahr 1844 ist die Bevölkerung immerhin auf tausendvierunddreißig Einwohner angewachsen, der Anteil der Afro-Amerikaner nicht mitgerechnet. Sie tauchen in den Grund- und Personenstandregistern der Stadt nicht auf (*HS*, p. 15).

By juxtaposing the arrival of the Clemens family in Hannibal and the growth in the town's population with the unsavoury facts regarding the absence of black people from the official statistics, the narrator is already preparing the ground for his argument that conventional nineteenth-century racial attitudes are ingrained in Twain's literary work.

The Adventures of Huckleberry Finn was banned from many public libraries upon its first publication because it was judged to contain 'but little humour, and that of a very coarse type'. The *Boston Transcript* of 17 March 1885 proceeds to state:

> The library and the other members of the committee entertain similar views, characterizing it as rough, coarse, and inelegant, dealing with a series of experiences not elevating, the whole book being more suited to the slums than to intelligent, respectable people'.[24]

21 Roger George, 'A Boat Swamped with Abstractions: Reading Raban's River', in *Temperamental Journeys*, ed. by Kowalewski, pp. 249–63 (p. 260).

22 Manfred Pfister, 'Intertextuelles Reisen', p. 120.

23 Manfred Pfister, 'Intertextuelles Reisen', p. 126.

24 Quoted in James S. Leonard and Thomas A. Tenney, 'Introduction: The Controversy over *Huckleberry Finn*', in *Satire or Evasion?: Black Perspectives on* Huckleberry Finn, ed. by James

These criticisms were levelled at Twain's novel largely due to his innovative utilization of an uneducated child as the narrator. As Shelley Fisher Fishkin states:

> What was so offensive about *Huckleberry Finn*, and what helped destine it to outdistance all of the productions of his peers and precursors in the immorality sweepstakes, were one and the same thing: by making Huck the 'author' of his own book, Twain validated the authority of vernacular culture more boldly than any book that had gone before.[25]

Roes, as an author who often experiments with narrative perspectives and with narrators who are outsiders, might be expected to have admired the audacity of giving an uneducated child narrative authority. According to one character in *Haut des Südens*, however, Twain chooses an outsider to narrate his novel, '[n]ur, um auch diese Figur letztendlich zu verraten, indem er sie zu Geld kommen und in die kleinbürgerliche Klasse wechseln läßt' (*HS*, p. 35). Precisely what others admire in Twain and what made his novel daring in its day, Roes turns against him, arguing that the American writer belongs firmly in the tradition of the white middle class into which he was born.

Roes's main criticisms of *Huckleberry Finn* centre on the portrayal of Jim, the black slave, whom Huck assists in his escape down the Mississippi river. These criticisms are discussed most fully during an exchange between the German traveller-narrator and Hank Sweet, the curator of Hannibal's Mark Twain Museum. Despite its status as fiction, the passage also contains elements of the literary essay and resembles in many ways a transcribed panel discussion. This scene highlights the tension inherent in the novel's representation of reality: the border dividing fact and fiction is made indistinct.[26] So, too, is the boundary between author, narrator and character, as the discussion on literary opinions presented below will reveal. Surprisingly, it is the museum curator, Hank Sweet, who disapproves of Twain's novel, while the traveller (who otherwise resembles Michael Roes) offers points in its defence. The discussion touches upon the deep divisions that separate Twain scholars on the issue of race. Some have argued that *Huckleberry Finn* is 'the most grotesque example

---

S. Leonard, Thomas A. Tenney and Thadious M. Davis (Durham, NC: Duke University Press, 1992), pp. 1–11 (p. 2).

25 Shelley Fisher Fishkin, *Was Huck Black?: Mark Twain and African American Voices* (New York; Oxford: Oxford University Press, 1993), p. 116.

26 It is, of course, impossible to tell from the novel how true to reality the account is. It is, however, possible that Roes, during his stay in Hannibal, really did have a conversation with the curator of the Mark Twain Museum, whose name is Henry Sweets (not Hank Sweet as it is in the novel). Whether a curator of a museum dedicated to Mark Twain really holds such antagonistic attitudes toward the author whose memory he is responsible for celebrating is more difficult to believe.

of racist trash ever written',[27] while others see in the novel an 'explicitly antiracist stance'.[28] Each time the narrator of *Haut des Südens* praises Twain's novel, the curator presents a counter-argument that reveals Twain to be racist. This approach, somewhat disingenuously, allows Roes to utilize the museum curator – a figure of austere authority – as a mouthpiece for his own opinion of *Huckleberry Finn*. Confirmation that Roes's stance towards Mark Twain is represented in *Haut des Südens* by Hank Sweet's statements is to be found in the essay 'Prometheus am Mississippi', in which Roes uses material from his novel to explain his position: the curator's opinions are presented as Roes's own.[29] In addition to his power and capacity as museum curator, Hank Sweet's status as a local man is emphasized. He is therefore to be regarded as having a deeper understanding of the specific nature of the American South, thus sealing the argument over the validity of his literary interpretation. He tells the visitor: 'Sie haben viel gelesen über Mark Twain und den Süden, doch muß man schon eine Weile hier gelebt haben, um die wahre Ironie Mark Twains zu verstehen' (*HS*, p. 38). The outsider's interpretation of *Huckleberry Finn* is rendered invalid by the expertise of the local specialist – even though, in fact, Roes's real stance on Mark Twain is that which is articulated by the curator. Ironically, Roes is both insider and outsider as he utilizes the character of the curator, a local man, to expound his opinions on Twain – and has that local character invalidate other, more approving interpretations, stating that an outsider cannot possibly comprehend the true nature of the Southern mind.

It has been argued in the postmodern context that 'beinahe alles zum Essay [wird], [...] Dokumentarfilme werden zu Filmessays, es entsteht der Essayroman und der Romanessay [...]. Heute kann man den Eindruck gewinnen, daß der Essay allgegenwärtig ist'.[30] *Haut des Südens* fuses the genres of novel and essay and is a striking example of the *Essayroman*. The narrative context within a novel, however, alters the status of the essayistic element contained within it. In an essay no distinction is made between author and narrator. Whereas the essay reader may justifiably assume that the opinions aired are those of the person under whose name the piece is published, it is generally accepted that a novel's narrator should never be confused with the author who pens the work. The essay 'Prometheus am Mississippi' can be taken as Roes's considered opinion. The status of opinions, arguments and

27 John H. Wallace, 'The Case Against *Huck Finn*', in *Satire or Evasion?*, pp. 16–24 (p. 16).

28 David L. Smith, 'Huck, Jim, and American Racial Discourse', in *Satire or Evasion?*, pp. 103–20 (p. 104).

29 'Prometheus am Mississippi' was first published in *Krieg und Tanz* in 2007, but originally delivered as a lecture by Roes in the Goethe Institute, Barcelona, in March 1999.

30 Christian Schärf, *Geschichte des Essays: Von Montaigne bis Adorno* (Göttingen: Vandenhoeck & Ruprecht, 1999), p. 7.

essays contained within *Haut des Südens* are potentially more complex. The novel contains an essay entitled 'Namen' which analyses the main characters of *Moby Dick* (*HS*, pp. 107–11). This essay could justifiably be attributed to the anonymous German narrator, although the opinions therein appear to reflect Roes's own. In the first chapter of *Haut des Südens*, opinions on Twain are presented largely through conversations and debates between characters. The conversation between Hank Sweet and the narrator described above includes arguments both pro and contra the author, but the reader becomes aware of Roes's distaste for Twain without reverting to extra-textual means (such as turning to 'Prometheus am Mississippi') due to the dominance of the critical voices. This feeling is shared by placing critical opinions in the mouths of locals who are presented as experts: Hank Sweet, the curator (*HS*, pp. 29–41); and the Halfgoods, compilers of an electronic encyclopaedia on Mark Twain (*HS*, pp. 51–63).

This aspect of intertextuality in *Haut des Südens* accords relatively clearly with the sub-category Gérard Genette termed 'metatextuality'. This he defined as 'the relationship most often labelled "commentary." It unites a given text to another, of which it speaks without necessarily citing it (without summoning it), in fact sometimes without even naming it. [...] This is the *critical* relationship par excellence'.[31] Genette does not develop his ideas on metatextuality further than to state that works of literary criticism are always metatextual, and that metatextuality 'never pertains, in principle at least, to narrative or dramatic fiction, [...] the metatext is by essence nonfictional'.[32] Despite the (semi-)fictional status of *Haut des Südens*, the novel's transtextual method is obviously and predominantly metatextual. Its relationship to the intertexts is that of a critical commentary, with the elements of criticism presented in essay form, as fictional narrative, and as a combination of both. The similarity of the essay 'Prometheus am Mississippi' to *Haut des Südens* supports this argument. However, the metatextual argument advanced in the novel is supported by the presence of extensive quotations, which come into Genette's category of 'intertextuality'. This indicates that more than one mode of transtextuality is in operation. Later in this chapter, I also demonstrate how the friendship between Daniel and the narrator of *Haut des Südens* evinces a 'hypertextual' relationship with Melville's *Moby Dick*.

What exactly are Roes's complaints about *Huckleberry Finn*? The analysis of Twain's novel presented in *Haut des Südens* centres on concerns regarding the lack of individuality accorded to Jim, the runaway slave. Hank Sweet hones in on Jim's introduction:

31 Genette, *Palimpsests*, p. 4.

32 Genette, *Palimpsests*, p. 397.

> Die Art und Weise, wie Mark Twain Jim in den Roman einführt, ist bezeichnend für die gesamte Darstellung Jims: *Miss Watson's big nigger, named Jim, was sitting in the kitchen door; we could see him pretty clear, because there was a light behind him.* – Ein Licht in seinem Rücken! Das, was Huck und Tom und letztlich auch die Leser so klar erkennen, ist nicht Jim, sondern nur seine Silhouette. Jims Gesicht ist in Dunkelheit gehüllt. Die Identität des bisher Unbekannten bleibt auch weiterhin hinter einer Maske der Schwärze verborgen (*HS*, p. 36).

Hank Sweet's (or Roes's) argument about the white narrator's (and author's) failure to recognize Jim's individual identity due to his all-pervading blackness is borrowed from an essay on the subject by Mary Kemp Davis. She writes:

> What Huck and Tom Sawyer see is not Jim at all but his silhouette; Jim is enveloped in darkness, his hulking frame thrown into relief by the light at his back. This seemingly naturalistic detail foreshadows Huck's later association with Jim when he slowly discovers that much of Jim's identity is concealed behind a mask of blackness.[33]

Although the casual reader may not be aware of the fact, the passage shows that Roes's intertextual borrowing extends further than the field of literature to include academic literary criticism.[34] On the one hand, Roes's passage is a quotation without quotation marks, suggesting that the borrowing is knowingly concealed. On the other hand, Roes's quotation is, in fact, quoting a quotation (by quoting Davies's quotation from Twain). This is a particular example of a postmodern intertextual device known as 'raising a quotation to the second power', which 'in itself foregrounds intertextuality and substantiates the poststructuralist view, according to which each text refers to pretexts and those in turn refer to others, and so on *ad infinitum*'.[35] Roes may paradoxically be indicating the diverse processes of referencing and borrowing that he is employing. Read in this way, the passage can be regarded as testing the limits of intertextual borrowing, with the author probing the boundaries of acceptability in terms of textual appropriation.

In an instance discussed below, Roes favourably compares Herman Melville's literary treatment of race and colour with Twain's. Roes could also have pitted the two authors against each other over the issue of 'silhouette scenes' by referring to Melville's first novel *Typee* (1846), thus advancing further his argument regarding the differences between the two writers.

33 Mary Kemp Davis, 'The Veil Rent in Twain: Degradation and Revelation in *Adventures of Huckleberry Finn*', in *Satire or Evasion?*, pp. 77–90 (p. 77).

34 See Davis. The volume also includes an essay by Julius Lester which is quoted with an acknowledgement in *Haut des Südens*.

35 Pfister, 'How Postmodern is Intertextuality?', p. 217.

Tommo, the narrator of *Typee*, and his companion Toby are guests of the eponymous South Sea tribe after having escaped from a tyrannically ruled whaling ship. Suspecting that the tribesmen are vicious cannibals, the two guests are unable to enjoy their stay in paradise as they suspect that they are being fattened for slaughter. They are awakened one night by an unidentified noise: '"There! I told you so! they are coming for us!" exclaimed my companion the next moment, as the forms of four of the islanders were seen in bold relief against the illuminated background'.[36] The narrator robs his subject of human qualities. All he perceives is the silhouettes of the islanders, illuminated (as is Jim in *Huckleberry Finn*) from behind. Fear of cannibalism is projected onto the black surface of the silhouettes, replacing any sign of individual characteristics. As Claudia Benthien remarks with regard to such a narrative standpoint:

> Da die dunkle Haut (aus "weißer" Perspektive) als undurchdringlich interpretiert wird, sich weniger sichtbar verändert und dadurch auch nicht semiotisierbar ist, wird sie oftmals als verhüllend gedeutet – sie wird zur *hide* (dem anderen englischen Wort für Haut) im wörtlichen Sinn.[37]

Melville, however, reveals that his narrator's fears and preconceptions were misplaced:

> Suddenly the silence was broken by the well-remembered tones of Mehevi, and at the kindly accents of his voice my fears were immediately dissipated. "Tommo, Toby, ki ki!" (eat). – He had waited to address us until he had assured himself that we were both awake.[38]

In one short moment the anonymous, black, threatening figure is replaced by a named individual of a caring and considerate nature. Mehevi's voice is particularly emphasized, praised as it is for its soothing qualities. The narrator's depiction of the silhouetted islander is thus shown to have been an unwarranted representation of the Other; and the silhouette motif reveals more about the visitor's fears and prejudices than it does about the people of the Marquesas Islands. Melville's utilization of the silhouette motif is a critique of the mode of representation used by his narrator, one which would later be used by Mark Twain.

Another major concern expressed in *Haut des Südens* is the lack of intellectual capacity granted to Jim. Roes criticizes Twain for the unrealistic plot in which Jim escapes by travelling down the Mississippi rather than

36 Herman Melville, *Typee & Billy Budd* (London: Dent, 1958), p. 92.

37 Claudia Benthien, *Haut: Literaturgeschichte – Körperbilder – Grenzdiskurse* (Reinbeck bei Hamburg: Rowohlt, 1999), pp. 209–10.

38 Melville, *Typee & Billy Budd*, p. 93.

simply crossing the river to the free state of Illinois. In *Haut des Südens* it is Bruce Hermann, the narrator's host in Hannibal, who points out this weakness in Twain's novel, and he does so spontaneously after hearing the narrator's synopsis of the plot. That Bruce is able to produce such an insight into a novel he has never read reinforces the impression that the plotting of *Huckleberry Finn* is transparently weak. Roes expands on this critique in the essay 'Prometheus am Mississippi', stating that 'Der "Realismus" Mark Twains endet bereits mit dem Plot. [...] Offenbar sind Mark Twain die humoristischen Einfälle wichtiger als die Glaubwürdigkeit seiner Geschichte' (*KT*, p. 76). Although the novel includes both sides of the debate concerning Twain's racial views, Roes overwhelmingly stacks the weight of the argument against the American writer. Roes takes a particularly strong stance, giving his novel a strong message and bias. However, a more balanced and lengthier assessment of Twain, his work and its historical context could have been presented. For example, Jim's baffling decision to go downstream can be explained without reverting to the argument that Twain denies his black character any intelligence.

Roes provides the first key to an alternative interpretation of Jim's actions in *Haut des Südens* but fails to explicate the matter to its conclusion. Bruce Hermann, an activist with the Republican party, notes with satisfaction that even the citizens of free states 'uns in der Regel gut nachbarschaftlich das entlaufene Eigentum zurückgebracht [haben]' (*HS*, p. 22). Were Jim to reach Illinois he would still be in danger of being caught by bounty hunters and returned to his owner in Missouri. In addition to this danger, Jim is suspected of having killed Huck (who disappeared from St Petersburg at about the same time) and can expect only brutal treatment if he is caught. The citizens of Illinois, despite the fact that slavery had been outlawed, were on the whole hostile to African Americans; indeed, they were 'racist to the core'.[39] Going downriver, far from demonstrating astonishing dullness of mind, may actually have been a counter-instinctive but astute move: 'By going downriver to Cairo and then northeast up the Ohio, Jim might also have been safer because Ohio had a far more extensive Underground Railroad than any other state'.[40] The Underground Railroad was a network of abolitionists who secretly assisted fugitive slaves to make their way north to Canada. There is a section in *Haut des Südens* in which Bruce Hermann recounts their exploits (and not without

39 Stephen B. Oates, *Our Fiery Trial: Abraham Lincoln, John Brown, and the Civil War* (Amherst: University of Massachusetts Press, 1979), p. 66, quoted in James Tackach, 'Why Jim Does Not Escape to Illinois in Mark Twain's *Adventures of Huckleberry Finn*', *Journal of the Illinois State Historical Society*, 97 (2004), 216–25 (p. 218).

40 Thomas Cooley, ed., *Adventures of Huckleberry Finn*, 3rd edn (New York: Norton, 1999), p. 56, quoted in Tackach, 'Why Jim Does Not Escape to Illinois', p. 217.

a certain sympathy for the 'enorme[n] materielle[n] Schaden' [*HS*, p. 68] suffered by the owners of escaped slaves). This information throws new light upon Jim's decision to head south and, crucially, opens the door to a more ambiguous interpretation of the plot of *Huckleberry Finn* than is put forward by Roes.

The black dialect spoken by Jim is also a matter of some controversy. Hank Sweet accuses Twain of endowing Jim and other black characters with:

> eine extreme Form verrotteter Umgangssprache, die absolut nichts mit den spezifischen Dialekten der Afro-Amerikaner jener Zeit zu tun hat, sondern eine Erfindung Mark Twains zur Charakterisierung seiner Romanfiguren darstellt. Die Wirkung ist fatal: Im Unterschied zu den Weißen kennzeichnet die Schwarzen bereits ihre inkompetente Redeweise als intellektuell minderwertig (*HS*, p. 36).

Twain, in contrast, claims in an explanatory note that precedes his novel that the various dialects which appear within it 'have not been done in a haphazard fashion, or by guess-work; but painstakingly, and with the trustworthy guidance and support of personal familiarity with these several forms of speech'.[41] How accurately he was able to transfer those black voices onto the pages of his novel is fiercely debated. A number of positions can be assumed with regard to this issue and Roes's critical stance is by no means the only viable one. Fishkin writes that Twain had a 'special talent for creating characters who, while true to their vernacular roots, also managed to "speak like a man" in a way that creates, attributes, and commands human dignity',[42] but she notes that 'Jim's voice is, ultimately, a diminished voice, a voice cramped with boundaries as confining as his prison-shack on the Phelps Plantation'.[43]

It is now clear that in *Haut des Südens* Roes takes an antithetical stance towards his intertext. He disapproves of Twain's representation of black characters, and believes Twain's work to be deeply embedded in nineteenth-century racial politics of the South. This is, however, not the whole story and a number of ambiguities exist in his life and work. As a thirty-two-year-old, Twain revised his attitude to race, turning his back on the overt racism that had characterized his youth.[44] However, he was never able to renounce the fascination that the 'minstrel darky' shows held for him.[45] Twain's work can be regarded as an unsuccessful attempt to challenge the racism prevalent in his time. His literary output, at times, holds a critical light to racist attitudes,

41 Mark Twain, *The Adventures of Huckleberry Finn* (London: Penguin, 1994), p. 6.
42 Fishkin, *Was Huck Black?*, p. 105.
43 Fishkin, *Was Huck Black?*, p. 107.
44 Fishkin, *Was Huck Black?*, p. 80.
45 Fishkin, *Was Huck Black?*, p. 82.

revealing them to be loathsome and misguided, for example Pap Finn's tirade against the 'free nigger' from Ohio.[46] However, a number of cultural stereotypes of blackness remain. As Fishkin puts it:

> In *Huckleberry Finn* and throughout his life and work, Mark Twain interrogated his culture's categories and conventions of what it meant to be 'black' or 'white.' This is not to say that he did so consistently or consciously, or that he invariably succeeded in transcending those categories and conventions. On the contrary, it can be argued that, in a number of key ways, he left them in place. Rather, Twain wove back and forth between challenge and affirmation, rejection and assent, as regards his culture's norms of 'blackness' and 'whiteness.'[47]

Roes interprets this ambiguity as failure and condemns Twain outright. As a result, the Mark Twain that Roes presents in *Haut des Südens* can be read as a literary construct. Twain is the villain in a cast of heroes and bigots. He functions as one point in a triangular argument, with Herman Melville taking the role of a positive counterfoil (see below), and Faulkner posited as a genuinely ambiguous figure somewhere in the middle.

Mark Twain was an assumed name, indicating Samuel Clemens's desire to take shelter behind an alternative persona. Twain explains the acquisition of the pseudonym in *Life on the Mississippi*:

> The old gentleman [Captain Isaiah Sellers] was not of literary turn or capacity, but he used to jot down brief paragraphs of plain practical information about the river, and sign them 'MARK TWAIN,' and give them to the *New Orleans Picayune*. They related to the stage and condition of the river, and were accurate and valuable [...]. [...] At the time that the telegraph brought news of his death, I was on the Pacific coast. I was a fresh new journalist, and needed a *nom de guerre*; so I confiscated the ancient mariner's discarded one, and have done my best to make it remain what it was in his hands – a sign and symbol and warrant that whatever is found in its company may be gambled on as being the petrified truth.[48]

Despite this claim to truth, the name 'Mark Twain' suggests duality or duplicity: he is creating a second identity ('marking' himself as 'two') under which he publishes his literary work. In addition to the clear 'fascination with alternate selves in his writing: [...] Samuel Clemens himself invents a persona that not only becomes a second self but after a time enslaves the first, so that the twin Twain eclipses Clemens.'[49] Mark Twain is a literary construct created by Samuel

46 Twain, *The Adventures of Huckleberry Finn*, pp. 34–35.
47 Fishkin, *Was Huck Black?*, p. 79.
48 Twain, *Life on the Mississippi*, pp. 351–52.
49 Susan Gillman, *Dark Twins: Imposture and Identity in Mark Twain's America* (Chicago: University of Chicago Press, 1989), p. 1.

Clemens as a means of concealing elements of his real self and projecting an alternative identity. Roes takes this duality a stage further and creates another Twain figure, one which he uses to his own end: as a representative of bigoted, literary America in the period following the Civil War. Twain's attempt to undermine categorizations of black and white is regarded as deficient and Roes must look elsewhere for a writer who was able to subvert racial stereotypes in the nineteenth century.

'Das Ungeheuer "Weißheit"': Herman Melville and *Moby Dick*

The metatextual critique of American literary classics in *Haut des Südens* continues with an investigation of Herman Melville's *Moby Dick*. Unlike Mark Twain (and William Faulkner), Melville was not a native of the Deep South. He was born in New York City in 1819 and died there in 1891. During his lifetime he took to the sea more than once, crossing the Atlantic to Liverpool in 1839, travelling on various vessels in the Pacific between 1841 and 1844, and venturing in 1856 to the Mediterranean and the Middle East. Melville is included in Roes's novel by virtue of his Mississippi novel *The Confidence Man* (1857), as well as by virtue of the engagement with intercultural and racial themes that characterizes his work. This section of the chapter offers a critical analysis of Roes's comprehensive approval of Melville's writing on race, and examines what attraction Melville's conception of the intercultural encounter holds for Roes. *Haut des Südens* contains references to a number of Melville's works but this study will focus primarily on *Moby Dick* as a representative text that illustrates most clearly Roes's opinion of the nineteenth-century writer. Two aspects of Melville's *Moby Dick* earn Roes's particular attention: first, Melville's deconstruction of the black-white dichotomy; and, second, the implications of this for Melville's representation of intercultural friendship.

Quotations that demonstrate Roes's (or his narrator's) admiration for Melville are many. On Melville's representation of the Other he writes:

> Der Fremde bekommt individuelle Züge ('Ich brannte vor Begierde, sein Gesicht zu sehen.'), einen Namen, einen Körper, Sprache, Scham und Würde. Ohne die Fremdheit des anderen zu leugnen, erscheint sie doch nicht unüberbrückbar. [...] Der Wilde darf hier ein unversehrter Mann bleiben, ja bekommt darüber hinaus noch besonders virile Attribute wie die Harpune und den Tomahawk zugeordnet (*HS*, p. 87).

On Melville's challenge to the black-white dichotomy he observes:

> Melville deckt auf, daß das, was Margaret Mead für universale Wahrnehmungen hält, vor allem kulturelle Metaphern sind. Die Obsession, der in Melvilles *Moby*

> *Dick* nachgejagt wird, und der schließlich alle, bis auf den Ich-Erzähler, zum Opfer fallen, ist nicht das Schwarze Herz der Finsternis, sondern ein *weißer* Leviathan, das Ungeheuer 'Weißheit' (*HS*, p. 95).

On Melville's aesthetic accomplishment he comments:

> Die Subversion setzt sich fort in der Vielsprachigkeit des Romans. Parodie, Hymnus, Predigt, Spekulation, wissenschaftliche Fakten – scheinbar unvereinbare Stimmen und Gattungen koexistieren nebeneinander, ohne daß der Text auseinanderfällt. Im Gegenteil, charakteristisch für die Kunst Melvilles ist, die heterogenen Sprachebenen zusammenzuführen wie die einander fremden Protagonisten des Geschehens, eine Hochzeit der Gegensätze. Das, was als sperrige Textcollage wirkt, ist im höchsten Maße aus der Kongruenz von Sprache und Idee gewirkt: Die Sprache drückt die Ideen nicht einfach aus, sie verkörpert die Ideen (*HS*, p. 124).

In the essay 'Prometheus am Mississippi', Roes elaborates on many of the themes that occupy him in *Haut des Südens*. The narrative context is very different (located within an essay rather than a novel) but the underlying argument is identical:

> Und nun kommt ein junger euro-amerikanischer Schriftsteller daher und macht die Farbe *Weiß* zum Symbol alles Unheimlichen und Bösen! Kein amerikanischer Autor ist bedeutender in der Analyse des euro-amerikanischen Rassismus als Herman Melville. Der Wahn, dem in seinem Roman *Moby Dick* nachgejagt wird, ist 'Weißheit'. Und bezeichnenderweise wird der Erzähler, Ishmael mit Namen, vor dem Untergang durch seinen dunkelhäutigen Busenfreund Queequeg gerettet. Während Bilder von der Macht, der Überlegenheit und Unantastbarkeit von Weißheit, gerade im Zusammenhang mit Repräsentanten von Dunkelheit oder Farbigkeit, die ganze amerikanische Literatur durchziehen, wobei in der Regel schwarz für Minderwertigkeit, Abhängigkeit und Tod steht, bricht Melville diese Farbsymbolik auf. Ihm ist bewußt, daß nicht allein die Behauptung genügt, alle Menschen seien gleich oder, in den Worten Ishmaels, ein Weißer sei nichts Großartigeres als ein weißgetünchter Neger. Zu tief ist der Schwarz-Weiß-Gegensatz im Denken der westlichen Kultur verankert, so daß jede Umwertung tiefer gehen muß als die Haut: Es geht um eine Frage von Gut und Böse. Und Melville führt in seinem grandiosen Roman vor, daß das Gute sehr wohl von dunkler Farbe und das absolute Böse weiß sein kann (*KT*, pp. 80–81).

The intertextual relationship between *Haut des Südens* and Melville typifies (reverting again to Pfister's terminology) a specific kind of 'huldigende Intertextualität'.[50] Although not a pilgrimage in a literal sense, since the

50 Pfister, 'How Postmodern is Intertextuality?', p. 120.

landscapes and cityscapes through which the narrator travels are not always concrete reminders of Melville's life and work, *Haut des Südens* offers a journey through Melville's *oeuvre* that functions metaphorically as a literary pilgrimage. In his chapter on Twain, Roes disguises the literary interpretation by depicting fictional characters discussing *Huckleberry Finn*. His engagement with Melville's novels is more akin to a traditional essay of literary criticism, with the narrative of Roes's novel interrupted at times by passages of literary essay (see, for example, *HS*, pp. 107–11).

Roes's narrator extols Melville's attitude to race relations, while remaining deeply suspicious of the racial politics that lies behind Twain's novels. Melville and Twain are placed at opposite ends of the spectrum in terms of aesthetic value and the subversion of racial stereotypes. Nonetheless, as was the case with Twain, critics are divided over Melville's attitude to race, some 'seeing [him] as antiblack, some as problack'.[51] Although the case for and against each of these two authors may not be as unequivocal as Roes makes it out to be, the contrast achieved provides an antithetical framework within which both writers can be understood. As a result, Roes's Herman Melville, as he is represented in the novel, can be regarded as a literary construct in the same way as Mark Twain can.

Roes insists that literature must challenge racial stereotypes and refutes the Western identification of blackness with badness. He finds his ideal in *Moby Dick* and quotes from the chapter entitled 'The Whiteness of the Whale' to illustrate his point (quoted in German in *HS*, p. 95):

> Aside from those more obvious considerations touching Moby Dick, which could not but occasionally awaken in any man's soul some alarm, there was another thought, or rather vague, nameless horror concerning him, which at times by its intensity completely overpowered all the rest; and yet so mystical and well nigh ineffable was it, that I almost despair of putting it in a comprehensible form. It was the whiteness of the whale that above all things appalled me.[52]

The whale represents nature – it is neutral, impartial, focused only on survival. This neutrality is ideally suited for human projections to be thrust upon it. It is 'paradoxically benign and malevolent, nourishing and destructive. It is massive, brutal, monolithic, but at the same time protean, erotically beautiful, infinitely variable'.[53] To Ishmael, and the other whalers, it is also terrifying – not

51 Edward S. Grejda, *The Common Continent of Men: Racial Equality in the Writings of Herman Melville* (Port Washington: Kennikat, 1974), p. 8.

52 Melville, *Moby Dick*, p. 189.

53 Richard Chase, 'Melville and *Moby Dick*', in *Melville: A Collection of Critical Essays*, ed. by Richard Chase (Englewood Cliffs: Prentice-Hall, 1962), pp. 49–61 (p. 60).

only due to its power and size but due to its whiteness. By ascribing such a value to the colour white, Melville is subverting the conventions of his time, according to which black was the colour to be feared, controlled or ruled over. Whiteness functions in *Moby Dick* as a '*tabula rasa* which may be imaginatively endowed with significance according to the desire or obsession of him who beholds it'.[54] As other writers, and society in general, had previously endowed blackness with largely negative significance, now Melville attributes unfavourable characteristics to whiteness.

Roes, too, attempts to demonstrate the cultural relativity of colour significance. He compiles a long list of mainly negatively laden German and English terms that contain the word black or *schwarz*:

> schwarz sehen, schwarz hören, schwarz malen, schwarz fahren, Schwarze Messe, Schwarze Magie, schwarzes Schaf, schwarzer Tag, schwarzer Passagier, schwarze Liste, schwarzes Loch [...]. In den meisten Kulturen des Orients wiederum gilt als Farbe der Tugend Schwarz und Weiß als Farbe der Trauer (*HS*, pp. 93–94).

Roes draws attention to the blind spots of Western culture and reveals how the metaphorical language of the everyday expresses the idea that blackness corresponds to the abhorrent. The fascination of *Moby Dick* lies for Roes in its reversal of these unconscious metaphors.

Like the whale he seeks to destroy, Ahab is associated with whiteness.[55] The obsessive captain, intent on gaining revenge on the beast that took away his leg on a previous voyage, 'als Personifikation des unheimlichen Weiß' gibt alle menschlichen Züge im Kampf um Moby Dick auf' (*HS*, p. 109). Whereas in Twain's novel it was the black slave who was robbed of his individuality and humanity, in *Moby Dick* it is Ahab with his '"leichenfahlen" Gesichtsnarbe' and the 'künstliche[n] weiße[n] Bein aus Walknochen' who is devoid of humanity. Both Ahab and the focus of his hatred are, according to Roes, representatives of an abominable whiteness. This interpretation takes a 'queer' turn as Roes presents Ahab's pursuit of the whale as a homosexual 'Haßliebe' (*HS*, p. 109): 'In der Beziehung zwischen Ahab und Moby Dick dient das sexuelle Begehren allein dem Streben nach Vorherrschaft, während ihm in der Freundschaft

54 Chase, 'Melville and *Moby Dick*', p. 60.

55 Roes regards Melville's representation of malevolent whiteness as a feature that lifts him above Twain. He could, however, have drawn comparisons between the whiteness of Ahab and that of Huck's father in Twain's novel. Pap Finn's abhorrent whiteness serves to reveal the ludicrousness of his racist rant. Pap is described as follows: 'There weren't no colour in his face, where his face showed; it was white; not like another man's white, but a white to make a body sick, a white to make a body's flesh crawl – a tree-toad white, a fish-belly white' (Twain, *The Adventures of Huckleberry Finn*, p. 27).

zwischen Queequeg und Ishmael eine katalysierende Kraft zuwächst' (*HS*, p. 110). The friendship between Queequeg and Ishmael is for Roes an ideal that is not only a counterfoil to the hate-love that drives Ahab, but the utopia of a friendship between men, based upon equality, that challenges sexual and gender conventions.

Roes reads Ishmael as a feminine man: he is 'melancholisch, *mädchenhaft*, passiv' (*HS*, p. 108). He is an observer, a thinker and writer. In contrast Queequeg, the Other, is a man of action and is the epitome of masculinity. He is associated with symbols that point towards heightened vigour and virility such as his harpoon and his tomahawk. What particularly interests Roes is that this friendship, while not necessarily overtly homosexual, is characterized by affection and 'eine erotische Zuneigung' (*HS*, p. 87). The famous scene in which Ishmael shares a bed with Queequeg at The Spouter Inn illustrates the ambiguous gender and sexual dynamics of Melville's novel. The passages are laden with matrimonial language, with Ishmael at one point stating that he and his friend 'in our hearts' honeymoon, lay [...] a cosy, loving pair'.[56] For Roes, Melville's genius lies in the way he challenges two major taboos of his age. 'Der Leser ist sich nicht sicher, welcher Affront schwerer wiegt: Die Hochzeitsnacht zweier Männer oder die Blutsbrüderschaft eines "Weißen" mit einem dunkelhäutigen "Wilden"' (*HS*, p. 88). In Roes's novel, and indeed in his work as a whole, there exists a link between the two issues of men loving men, and interculturality. The following section examines these issues first in relation to *Moby Dick* and second by seeking for evidence of similar ideas in *Haut des Südens*.

Intercultural Friendship

Part of Roes's interest in *Huckleberry Finn* derives from the novel's representation of a friendship that transcended the racial divisions of the period in which it is set. The same is true of Herman Melville's *Moby Dick* and William Faulkner's *Intruder in the Dust* (discussed below). In *Moby Dick*, the 'wedding' of Queequeg and Ishmael is symbolic of an alternative way of life that can be achieved only through a process of transformation. According to Roes: 'Das gemeinsame Rauchen aus Queequegs Tomahawk-Pfeife symbolisiert diesen alchimistischen Akt' (*HS*, p. 125). Not only does smoking the tomahawk seal the friendship, it transforms the smokers and makes them open to a different kind of interaction. Ishmael overcomes his fear of the 'cannibalistic' harpooner, and his emotional state is transformed

56 Melville, *Moby Dick*, p. 68.

by Queequeg's warmth and brightness: 'I felt a melting in me', he states, 'No more my splintered heart and maddened hand were turned against the wolfish world. This soothing savage had redeemed it'.[57] The healing provided by Queequeg derives directly from his foreignness. As Edward S. Grejda remarks, 'Queequeg's spontaneous "flame of friendship" glows in warm contrast to the cold isolation of the civilized world'.[58] Foreign influences bring new ways of seeing the world and Queequeg brings innocence and spirit to warm the 'damp, drizzly November in [Ishmael's] soul'.[59]

Of greater interest for Roes is the way the two men are able to form a warm friendship that has erotic undertones. It seems that the intercultural friendship between Ishmael and Queequeg exists outside the jurisdiction of social conventions regarding sexual and gender dynamics. Existing as it does on the border between two cultures, the friendship appears to be free of the limitations imposed by either of those two cultural frameworks. Ishmael suggests that there exists a possibility for greater freedom for men to express affection and that this results directly from the cultural division that exists between the two. Friendships between two 'civilized' Westerners have proved unsatisfying and so a friendship with a foreigner is to be desired: 'I'll try a pagan friend, thought I, since Christian kindness has proved but hollow courtesy'.[60] Rather than being a hindrance to the process of communication and friendship formation, having vastly different cultural backgrounds and different colour skin gives the two the liberty to redefine the boundaries of the acceptable and the desirable. In such a friendship the usual constrictions of social etiquette are forgotten: 'In a countryman, this sudden flame of friendship would have seemed far too premature, a thing to be much distrusted; but in this simple savage those old rules would not apply'.[61]

In *Haut des Südens*, the German narrator's friendship with the Nigerian student Daniel mirrors closely the friendship between Ishmael and Queequeg. They, too, enjoy the broader space and the liberating potential that exists in an intercultural friendship. Like his counterpart in Melville's novel, Roes's narrator must stay in communal accommodation due to limited funds: 'Eigentlich zu alt für die Jugendherberge, das Schlafen in einer Gemeinschaftsunterkunft, das Duschen in Gesellschaft und das Scheißen unter Aufsicht. Doch finde ich in St. Louis keine meinem Geldbeutel angemessene Alternative' (*HS*, pp. 73–74). Having formed a friendship with Daniel, they shower together in the youth hostel: 'Die übrigen Herbergsgäste schenken unserer wachsenden Vertrautheit

57 Melville, *Moby Dick*, p. 66.
58 Grejda, *The Common Continent of Men*, p. 93.
59 Melville, *Moby Dick*, p. 21.
60 Melville, *Moby Dick*, p. 66.
61 Melville, *Moby Dick*, p. 67.

keinerlei Beachtung' (*HS*, p. 104). The youth hostel, as a resting place for travellers and open minds, is a space in which the freedom of intercultural friendship can be exploited. Later the two friends lie in bed together in a scene that mimics Ishmael and Queequeg's matrimonial bed ceremony:

> Solcherart liegen wir im Bette, bald schwatzend, bald schlafend, und mein Gefährte legt ab und zu vertraulich seine braunen tätowierten Beine über meine wildentzündeten, so völlig ungezwungen betragen wir uns. Nun seht, wie geschmeidig unsere starrsten Vorurteile werden, wenn die Liebe sie beugt! (*HS*, p. 126).

In Chapter 11 of *Moby Dick* Ishmael states:

> We had lain thus in bed, chatting and napping at short intervals, and Queequeg now and then affectionately throwing his brown tattooed legs over mine, and then drawing them back; so entirely sociable and free and easy were we; [...] yet see how elastic our stiff prejudices grow when love once comes to bend them.[62]

The friendships in the two novels are represented as being so similar that Roes is justified in describing his own narrator's friendship with Daniel by using a minimally adapted quotation from *Moby Dick*. Such playful imitation of an admired literary work accords with Genette's definition of pastiche, a sub-category of what he terms hypertextuality.[63] The reference to the narrator's badly inflamed skin is the only indication that this paragraph refers to the friendship between Daniel and the narrator. This hypertextual relation is an indication of Roes's admiration for Melville's novel. Whereas in *Haut des Südens* the transtextual method in relation to Twain remains on the metatextual level of commentary, *Moby Dick* has had a more profound effect on Roes's text, with the hypertextual relation between them evincing a deeper level of engagement and approbation.

Roes's exploration of the topos of intercultural friendship begins with *Haut des Südens* but continues in other works. In *Nah Inverness* (2004), *Die Fünf Farben Schwarz* (2009) and *Geschichte der Freundschaft* (2010), there is a recurring pattern in which Westerners enter into erotically charged friendships with foreigners. The combination of friendship, homo-eroticism and cultural divisions are regarded by Roes as fertile ground with unlimited potential to establish new forms of friendships. That the focus of so much of Roes's work on relationships between men is directed towards exploring the dynamics of intercultural friendship rather than friendship between Germans suggests that he, like Melville and his narrator Ishmael, sees more potential for a progressive

62 Melville, *Moby Dick*, pp. 68–69.
63 Cf. Genette, *Palimpsests*, p. 28.

and liberal friendship to develop if the two men entering a friendship do so from two opposing cultural poles. This is not to say that Roes is oblivious to the potential difficulties inherent in a cross-cultural friendship. *Geschichte der Freundschaft* in particular shows that such friendships can contain the seeds for personal crisis and catastrophe. In *Haut des Südens*, however, the cultural division seems to assist in the quest to establish a new, liberal foundation for friendship. Spatial distance from home, liberty from pressures to conform, and exposure to alternative modes of interacting all serve to increase the sense of freedom that exists between the two protagonists.

There are numerous ways in which one could read Roes's interest in erotically-charged friendships with foreigners: as a form of sexual tourism, as an idealization and exoticization of the Other, or as a subconscious attempt to reinforce Western dominance over the East/Third World. Yet the predominant characteristic of Roes's interaction with other countries and cultures is the search for mutual understanding and common ground. Roes holds an ideal vision of a relationship in which both parties are fundamentally equal. He regards this as a necessity for any thriving relationship, leaving no room for protracted power struggles. The key to understanding Roes's fascination with homo-erotic, intercultural friendships lies in a quotation which Roes includes in *Geschichte der Freundschaft* (discussed more fully in the final chapter). In the first of many quotations in that novel, Roes draws from Michel Foucault's multi-volume *History of Sexuality* (1976–1984), paying particular attention to Foucault's argument that intense friendships between men came into disrepute around the seventeenth century when the category 'homosexuality' came into existence and 'zu einem sozialen, politischen und medizinischen Problem erklärt wurde' (*GF*, p. 7). The move from homosexual acts to the new category of homosexual identity changed the dynamics of emotional and physical relations between men. Such a change did not come about to the same extent in the Middle East. Brian Whitaker writes:

> Arabs who engage in same-sex activities do not necessarily regard themselves as gay, lesbian, bisexual etc. Some do, but many (probably the vast majority) do not. This is partly because the boundaries of sexuality are less clearly defined than in the West but also because Arab society is more concerned with sexual acts than sexual orientations or identities.[64]

These less rigid forms of sexual identity and the resistance to applied labels clearly appeal to Roes; and his interest in friendships with men from culturally different backgrounds can be interpreted as a search for male-male friendship

64 Brian Whitaker, *Unspeakable Love: Gay and Lesbian Life in the Middle East* (London: Saqi, 2006), p. 10.

as it existed in Europe in the sixteenth century before homosexuality became a 'problem'.

The whaling ship on which Ishmael sails, the *Pequod*, is the ultimate homosocial environment. Although the narrator of *Haut des Südens* claims that the ship 'einen beispielhaften Mikrokosmos der amerikanischen Gesellschaft [...] dar[stellt]' (*HS*, p. 110), half of that American society (women) are not represented on board. The whaler, with its crew taken from all strata of society and with all 'races' represented, is, however, a symbol of the potential for a multicultural society as envisioned by Melville midway through the nineteenth century. In Melville, the multicultural experiment fails: that failure is symbolized by the sinking of the ship and the drowning of all but one of its crew. Roes, however, resurrects the multicultural, multiracial nautical experiment. At the end of *Haut des Südens*, in what can only be described as a bizarre, fantastical twist, Daniel builds a raft upon which he and the narrator escape from the flooded city of New Orleans. They are blown eastwards towards the African coast, protected from the sun by the leaves of a 'Pisakko-Bonsai' (*HS*, p. 260), a tree native to Senegal, which also provides thirst-quenching nourishment. The raft mirrors the *Pequod* and represents the ideal of multicultural harmony. After a long journey through the American South, with its lengthy and continuing history of racial discord, the narrator and Daniel sail away in a spirit of transcultural affinity. Roes's portrayal of this kind of friendship testifies to the possibility, indeed the necessity, of forming bonds between nations, 'races' and cultures. At the same time it is suggested that the space that exists in such a friendship leaves open the possibility to explore alternative gender and sexual identity, something that remains more difficult to achieve in a friendship between two Western men in a European setting. As this study has shown, the intertextual relationship between *Haut des Südens* and *Moby Dick* plays a central role in Roes's engagement with this theme.

A Postmodern Intertextuality?

Having analysed two of the main intertexts that feature in *Haut des Südens*, comments regarding the modes of intertextuality employed in the novel will now be noted. Intertextuality has 'become the very trademark of postmodernism'[65] and it is useful to establish whether and how Roes can be regarded as a postmodern intertextualist, and to what extent he resists such categorization. That will shed further light on Roes's use of intertextual references, on his world-view and his aesthetic principles. How does Roes use

65 Pfister, 'How Postmodern is Intertextuality?', p. 209.

other texts? What function do these other texts have within Roes's text? Are they used to assist in the search for meaning (the modernist approach)? Are they to be regarded as part of a postmodern aesthetic game where 'there is no message, only messengers, and that is the message'?[66] Is the distinction between high and low culture maintained, as in modernist culture, or destroyed, as in postmodernism?

The sheer number of intertexts alluded to in *Haut des Südens* (at least 57 individual works,[67] counting the various biblical references as one) inevitably foregrounds the practice of intertextuality in the novel and marks the work as a commentary on other texts and on the creative process. Such auto-reflection has been described as a trait of postmodern literature. Manfred Pfister states: 'The ideal-type postmodernist text is [...] a "meta-text", that is, a text about other texts or textuality, an auto-reflective and auto-referential text, which thematizes its own textual status and the devices on which it is based'.[68] At first glance, Roes's novel may appear to be exactly such a postmodern meta-text. An example of this is the foregrounding of the post-structuralist concept that it is impossible to refer to another text without opening a Pandora's Box of further chains of references. *Haut des Südens* could be read as a concrete manifestation of the post-structuralist theory that every text exists

66 Raymond Federman, 'What are Experimental Novels and Why Are There So Many Left Unread?', *Critifiction* (Albany: State University of New York Press, 1993), pp. 65–75 (p. 68), quoted in Pfister, 1991, p. 219.

67 These intertexts are: the novel's epigraph by Paul Valery (p. 7); definitions from a dermatological dictionary (p. 9); Mark Twain's *Life on the Mississippi* (p. 9), *The Adventures of Tom Sawyer* (p. 16), and *The Adventures of Huckleberry Finn* (p. 20); an aphorism by Georg Christoph Lichtenberg (p. 13); literary criticism by Mary Kemp Davis (p. 36) and Julius Lester (p. 64); The American Declaration of Independence (p. 46); quotations from various newspapers (p. 60, p. 117, p. 119, p. 123, p. 127, p. 187, p. 203); Herman Melville's *The Confidence Man* (p. 73), *Typee* (p. 78), *Billy Budd* (p. 78), and *Moby Dick* (p. 79); Gandhi's writings (p. 83); Rabindranath Tagore's poetry (p. 83); Daniel Defoe's *Robinson Crusoe* (p. 87); medication usage instruction (p. 93); Margaret Mead's interview with James Baldwin (p. 94); the personal stories of Roger Casement (p. 100), Dred Scott (p. 112), and James Meredith (p. 188); Aeschylus's *Oresteia* (p. 104); various legal decrees (p. 121, p. 190, p. 194); Paul Celan's poem 'Der Gast' (p. 133); Harriet Martineau's *Retrospect of Western Travel* (p. 133); Martin Luther King's 'I Have a Dream' speech (p. 157); Michael Roes's own *Leeres Viertel* (p. 162); William Faulkner's novel *Intruder in the Dust* and the film version (both p. 175), Faulkner's *Light in August* (p. 178), *Flags in the Dust* (p. 183), *Soldiers' Pay* (p. 183), *Absalom, Absalom!* (p. 184) and *New Orleans Sketches* (p. 212); Margaret Mitchell's *Gone with the Wind* (p. 182); personal letters (p. 191, p. 220); Ernest Hemingway's *To Have and Have Not* (p. 216); Ralph Ellison (p. 216); The Bible (p. 218); the New Orleans authorities' instructions for hurricane survival (p. 239); Tennessee Williams's *A Streetcar Named Desire* (p. 248); and the films *One Flew Over the Cuckoo's Nest* (p. 86), *Psycho* (p. 104), *The Heart of Dixie* (p. 163), *The Gun in Betty Lou's Handbag* (p. 163), *Roads and Bridges* (p. 163), and *Easy Rider* (p. 245).

68 Pfister, 'How Postmodern is Intertextuality?', p. 215.

in a universe of previously uttered words and phrases, and that each literary work is a collage of citations taken from other works. The novel could also be regarded as a link in a long chain of textual references – it refers to *Moby Dick*, which refers to the Bible, to Shakespeare and, in the chapter entitled 'Extracts', to a large number of cultural and scientific works on whales. Another highly postmodern intertextual method that appears in the novel is the raising of quotations to the second degree, or quoting a quotation (see above discussion on the borrowing from Mary Kemp Davis's essay).

Nevertheless, significant elements of Roes's novel prevent it from being labelled a postmodern novel. Intertextual references generally play an exegetic role in *Haut des Südens*. A critical explanation or interpretation of other texts is given (Genette's metatextuality), with those texts regarded as signifying broader historical and social developments. Roes engages with the racial politics of Twain's novel and with the social implications of Melville's depiction of intercultural friendship. That Roes seeks out the meaning of other texts and engages critically with them is suggestive of a more modernist approach to intertextuality. Peter V. Zima writes:

> In der Postmoderne verdrängt das intertextuelle Spiel mit historischen und zeitgenössischen Sprachformen die intertextuelle Suche der Moderne: die Suche nach Wahrheit, Wertsetzung, Subjektivität und Identität sowie das Streben nach Utopie. Die Gesellschaftskritik ist im postmodernen Kontext durchaus präsent: Das zeigen die Werke von Fowles, Becker und Pynchon, in denen literarische Formen parodistisch hinterfragt, Ideologien ironisch relativiert werden. Aber sie mündet nicht mehr in eine Suche nach Alternativen.[69]

Roes is still looking for alternatives and has not given up hope that the aspects of society he finds repulsive, dysfunctional or unjust can be transformed. *Haut des Südens* is not only a sustained work of social criticism, it also offers the reader glimpses of a utopia – most concisely symbolized in one particular intertextual reference. The matrimonial bed at The Spouter Inn (*Moby Dick*) functions in *Haut des Südens* as a symbol for the possibility of human relations that are characterized by equality, respect and truth. Roes seeks alternative lifestyles characterized by an authenticity that goes against social conventions: loving relations that blur the boundary between friendship and homosexuality and communication across cultural and racial boundaries. Roes's vision of a reformed world, presented partly by means of the intertextual reference, suggests that his novel cannot be read as postmodern since the search for truth and meaning, the 'Streben nach Utopie', continues.

69 Peter V. Zima, *Das literarische Subjekt: Zwischen Spätmoderne und Postmoderne* (Tübingen: Francke, 2001), p. 195.

The type of material quoted is of great importance with regard to the question of (post-)modernity. Roes quotes from works that could be regarded as high-, mid- and low-culture. Canonical American literature is placed side by side with broadsheet newspapers and hurricane survival instructions. In *Geschichte der Freundschaft* a similar range of pre-texts are quoted: Foucault and Derrida are placed next to Batman and Robin. The important question is whether all sources are considered to be of equal value. The answer is surely 'no'. Roes considers some sources to be of greater value than others – a fact revealed clearly in his critical stance towards Twain's *Huckleberry Finn*. Whereas an avowed postmodernist such as Raymond Federman refrains from disclosing his sources 'because there are no sacred sources for thinking and writing',[70] Roes almost always indicates references or quotations by name or title, suggesting that the source must be evaluated for relevance and reputability.

Perhaps the most important consequence of the intertextuality in *Haut des Südens* is the resulting polyphony. Quotations and references can be read as the author-narrator's attempt to open his or her text to other voices. Quoting other people's words inevitably allows their opinions a presence in the new text. By quoting, so the theory goes, the author-narrator is opening the text democratically, working 'to "decentre" the narratorial self'.[71] Incorporating quotations and utilizing other voices in a multivocal narrative allows an author to minimize his or her authority over the text. In a novel that engages with multiculturalism and racial politics, the narrator's act of self-decentring allows a multitude of other people to voice opinions and to express their cultural identity. Nevertheless, the ultimate control of the author is not necessarily undermined by such an approach. The author still wields the power to choose which literary forebears to quote, which historical figures are worthy of mention, and which characters met on the journey are given a voice. As James Clifford writes in an ethnographic context, '[q]uotations are always staged by the quoter', the final output, irrespective of the number of different voices contained within, can be read as a 'virtuoso orchestration by a single author of all the discourses in his or her text'.[72] It is fruitful, in a reading of *Haut des Südens* and its intertextual and polyphonic aspects, to question to what extent Roes succeeds in his attempt to dislodge his (or his narrator's) authority over the text; and to ask whether he truly achieves a multivocal and democratic narrative.

Haut des Südens gives voice to a number of historical black figures, allowing their personal stories to be told. The story of Dred Scott, a slave who

70 Federman, 'Imagination as Plagiarism', 566.

71 Thompson, *Travel Writing*, p. 127.

72 James Clifford, 'On Ethnographic Authority', *Representations*, 2 (1983), 118–46 (p. 139).

underwent a ten-year legal battle to secure his freedom, is narrated from a first-person perspective. James Meredith's story is told, complete with quotations from letters and legal statements, as he battles to be the first black man to be admitted to the University of Mississippi in 1962. The narrator is also present as an elderly Meredith addresses a church congregation on the issue of black identity in the present. By giving prominence to these voices Roes's narrator takes a step back, allowing their voices to reveal the history of discrimination and oppression that has been a characteristic of life in the American South for centuries. The vocabulary used in this paragraph ('gives voice', 'allowing other voices') suggests that the narrator remains powerful but that he willingly yields (at least partially) this position of control.

Quotations from literary works function slightly differently. The position of the author-narrator as an all-powerful figure is not in doubt. More important than 'what' is quoted, is 'how' the chosen texts are presented, juxtaposed and interpreted. The literary texts are not quoted from in a neutral manner – they are commented upon by the narrator and judged for their merit and their deficiencies. Far from being a postmodern text whose author – *pace* Barthes – is 'dead', the intertextuality of *Haut des Südens* reveals it to be a 'tissue of citations' which have behind them an author whose subjectivity is alive and well. This is not intended as a criticism of the novel. Roes's project is clearly driven by a set of values – both ethical and aesthetic – which can only be upheld from a position of uncompromising judgment. An example of this aesthetic judgement is Roes's rejection of the postmodern insistence on breaking down the traditional distinction between high and low culture. Although he briefly quotes from more banal sources, he has chosen to focus his attention on novels that belong to the (white) American canon. Within that canon he establishes a further hierarchy, a moral one, within which he places Melville above Twain. The intertextual encounter staged in *Haut des Südens* therefore resists the postmodern abandonment of values. Roes seeks instead to challenge social and racial inequality where he finds it to have existed, and where he finds it exists still.

William Faulkner: Fear and Lynching in Yoknapatawpha

As when he arrived in Hannibal, the narrator disembarks from the Greyhound bus in Oxford, Mississippi, early one morning, some distance out of town. Preceding this scene is a fictionalized account of the arrival of the Faulkner family in Oxford ninety-six years previously: 'Nun machen sie sich auf den Weg zu ihrem neuen Zuhause, über den Hauptplatz des Städtchens, um ein imposantes Gerichtsgebäude mit weißen Säulen herum [...] . Der Junge staunt' (*HS*, p. 161). The boy is William Faulkner and those white pillars of the courthouse will later appear in his novels, with Oxford thinly disguised as the fictionalized town of Jackson, Yoknapatawpha County. Faulkner's writing career is often divided into three periods. Following an early 'apprenticeship' comes the 'major' period between 1929 and 1942 during which he wrote such classics as *The Sound and the Fury* (1929) and *As I Lay Dying* (1930). The work that Faulkner produced after 1942 is often regarded as evidence of 'declining powers'.[73] Considering that this later work is often ignored, it is perhaps surprising that Roes uses *Intruder in the Dust* (1948) as one of two main intertexts in the Faulkner chapter of *Haut des Südens* (the second being *Light in August*, published in 1932).

Despite the novel's relatively low reputation among critics, Roes's interest in *Intruder in the Dust* is understandable due to Faulkner's 'concern about race as a political problem, his increasingly rich and fully dimensional portrait of black people, and his abiding concern for the debts that white people owe to blacks'.[74] Central to Roes's interest in the novel is Faulkner's representation of the friendship between Lucas Beauchamp, a black man wrongly accused of murdering a white man, and the young Charles 'Chick' Mallison, who comes to his rescue (with the aid of another black friend, Aleck Sander). It is clear that the thread that links all three of Roes's main intertexts in *Haut des Südens* (*Huckleberry Finn*, *Moby Dick* and *Intruder in the Dust*) is the representation of interracial or intercultural friendships.

In the first chapter of *Haut des Südens*, the curator of the Mark Twain Museum suggests that the friendship between Huck and Jim is represented as a friendship between two children. A black man becomes a sidekick to a twelve-year-old white boy and demeans himself in the process. The curator points his visitor in the direction of another Southern novel to find a more acceptable representation of such a friendship:

> In Faulkners *Intruder in the Dust* gibt es eine ähnliche Beziehung, die zwischen Lucas Beauchamp und dem sechzehnjährigen Chick Mallison. Während in Faulkners Roman Lucas Beauchamp den Abstand und die Würde eines Erwachsenen wahrt, begegnen Huck und Jim einander als Gleichaltrige, das heißt als Kinder (*HS*, p. 35).

Although Faulkner is praised here for his portrayal of interracial relations, Roes's treatment of Faulkner is generally far more ambiguous than it was of

73 Theresa M. Towner, *Faulkner on the Color Line: The Later Novels* (Jackson: University Press of Mississippi, 2000), p. 6.

74 Joseph Romance, 'Patriots and Philosophers: The Idea of Obligation and Race in William Faulkner's *Intruder in the Dust*', in *Democracy's Literature: Politics and Fiction in America*, ed. by Patrick J. Deneen and Joseph Romance (Lanham: Rowman & Littlefield, 2005), pp. 79–96 (p. 80).

Twain, who was criticized, or Melville, who was praised. While Faulkner's novels are admired for their modernist aesthetics, Faulkner the man and his racial politics are shown to be complex. On the one hand, he is criticized by many whites in Oxford as 'Jammernder Willie, der Niggerfreund' (*HS*, p. 203). On the other hand, in February 1956 he delivers a drunken outburst with racist undertones during an interview with the New York correspondent of the *Sunday Times*. One of the voices included in *Haut des Südens*, and quoting from *Intruder in the Dust*, captures this ambiguity well:

> Natürlich ist er [Faulkner] zu klug, die Sklaverei als eine zwar monströse Idee, aber im großen und ganzen humane Praxis zu verharmlosen. Und trotzdem finde ich bei ihm dieselben Verbindungen von dunkler Haut und animalischem Charakter wie bei Margaret Mitchell: *Ein Geruch, den er zeit seines Lebens* [...] *ganz selbstverständlich als den Geruch von Orten hingenommen hat, an denen Menschen mit auch nur einer Spur von Negerblut hausten* (*HS*, p. 182).

Although Faulkner was genuinely interested in the race issue, he was of the opinion that blacks and whites would never be able to integrate, largely because they did not want to. The narrator concludes that Faulkner's arguments '[...] also auf einen Status quo ante hinaus [laufen]: auf die Südstaatendoktrin "getrennt, aber gleich"' (*HS*, p. 204), a doctrine which elsewhere in the novel is regarded as a paradox since segregation is inherently unequal.

The friendship between Chick and Lucas features very little affection and is very different from that between Queequeg and Ishmael, or between Huck and Jim. It is, therefore, no surprise that the Chick/Lucas friendship is not mimicked by Daniel and the narrator in the way they mimicked Queeqeg and Ishmael. Lucas is a proud man who maintains a cautious distance from Chick from the very beginning. Having fallen into a frozen creek, a twelve-year-old Chick sets eyes upon Lucas for the first time:

> [G]asping, shaking and only now feeling the shock of the cold water, he looked up at the face which was just watching him without pity commiseration or anything else, not even surprise: just watching him, whose owner had made no effort whatever to help him out of the creek, had in fact ordered Aleck Sander to desist with the pole which had been the one token toward help that anyone had made – a face which in his estimation might have been under fifty or even forty except for the hat and the eyes, [...] what looked out of it had no pigment at all, not even the white man's lack of it, not arrogant, not even scornful: just intractable and composed.[75]

The unorthodox friendship is based on a sense of obligation. Chick is anxious to repay Lucas for the meal he is given following his rescue from the creek. Lucas

75 William Faulkner, *Intruder in the Dust* (London: Vintage, 1996), pp. 6–7.

refuses payment, judging that the favour cannot be repaid in monetary terms. Chick feels enslaved by this debt.[76] The black man has reversed the customary dynamics of the South, thereby gaining a position of social superiority. Indeed, Lucas's determining characteristic in the novel is his refusal to 'be a nigger'.[77] He refuses to perform acts of submissive deference to whites and to conform to white expectations of how a black man should behave. His rare visits to town are made, not on Saturdays like the other blacks and the white workers, but on weekdays, 'as if he refused, declined to accept even that little of the pattern not only of Negro but of country Negro behavior'.[78] Grandfatherly imagery supports this representation of Lucas as a dignified man who refuses to be downtrodden. While Twain's Jim, as Roes's narrator states, becomes a child, Faulkner's Lucas takes on the magisterial air of a wise elder.

The second of Faulkner's novels from which Roes quotes extensively is *Light in August*, which likewise features a white murder victim and a 'black' suspect. Joe Christmas, the suspect, has been told ever since childhood that he has some 'black blood', even though he has the appearance of a white man. The novel shows how the confusion regarding his racial identity ultimately destroys him. He stands, according to Towner:

> perhaps as Faulkner's greatest example of the constructedness of racial categories and their relationship to individual identity [...], [he] who murders and is murdered because of the American color line, yet who never knows where he stands in relation to it'.[79]

Christmas's white mother died during childbirth; his father is said to be a Mexican, although that is never conclusively established. He is called a 'nigger' by the other children in school; and at various times in his life he lives and works in black communities. By creating a character whose racial identity is never conclusively determined, Faulkner undermines what were and still are seen as obvious racial lines of demarcation. Faulkner was, in many ways, a writer before his time: 'No writer knew better than Faulkner what critics have only recently begun to explore so provocatively: that "race" itself is a linguistic and cultural construction; that this construction both shapes and reflects, is mold and mirror both'.[80]

Roes, too, is interested in the linguistic and cultural constructedness of race, an issue he explores by means of the most recognizable motif in the novel – skin. In the oppressive heat and humidity of the South, the narrator

76 Cf. Romance, 'Patriots and Philosophers', p. 86.

77 Faulkner, *Intruder in the Dust*, p. 18.

78 *Intruder in the Dust*, p. 24.

79 Towner, *Faulkner on the Color Line*, p. 21.

80 Towner, *Faulkner on the Color Line*, p. 30.

of *Haut des Südens* encounters many characters whose physical condition is in a deteriorated state. The narrator, too, suffers in the foreign climate. Able to muster up a suitable literary reference in every situation, he reads from Georg Christoph Lichtenberg's aphorisms and discovers an adage concerning the insights one gains as one ages into the 'Fehlerhaftigkeit unseres Organismus' (*HS*, p. 13), before using the book as a fan to gain some respite from the overwhelming heat. His skin is blighted by an unsightly condition that attracts much attention during his journey. The narrator's unusual skin affliction functions as a symbol that illuminates further Roes's philosophy of race. As was the case with the list of words and sayings that revealed the linguistic manifestation of race, the narrator's skin is a device that Roes uses to reveal race to be a cultural construct. Skin is not only a point of contact between the self and the outside world,[81] but also a canvas upon which others project their ideas, interpretations and fears. While a healthy white male may not have had to experience this phenomenon of projection, the narrator's skin, blighted as it is by vasculitis, becomes a target: '[A]lle werden ihre geheimsten Ängste in die Verunstaltung hineinprojizieren' (*HS*, p. 22).

As a result, the narrator's cutaneous vasculitis functions as a device that allows him to experience a variation on the prejudice faced by black people. As Julianne Rytz states: 'Durch die Erkrankung, als Stigma verstanden, wird er – als weißer, westlicher Mann eigentlich dem normativen Ideal entsprechend – selbst zum Anderen. Sein Stigma ist insofern als Identifikation mit seinem Untersuchungsgegenstand zu verstehen'.[82] Just as Daniel, the Nigerian friend, is liable to suffer discrimination on the grounds of his black skin, the narrator's skin condition makes him distinctive and liable to be judged on his appearance. He states: 'Wir Hautkranken wissen es besser: Allein die Oberfläche macht uns zu einem abgegrenzten, identifizierbaren Wesen' (*HS*, p. 24). The 'wir' here signifies that a process of identity-formation has already begun (mirroring perhaps a black identity), even if that identity is bound to such a peculiar classification or subculture as 'Hautkranken'. The parallels between the two friends' skin 'afflictions' is ironically commented upon when the two are disturbed in their shared hotel room and Daniel gets out of bed to answer the door. Medical experts have arrived in response to a reported outbreak of leprosy. Daniel responds: 'Wenn er mich damit gemeint haben sollte, so kann ich Ihnen versichern, daß die möglicherweise wie Aussatz erscheinende

81 The point is often made in critical literature that '[d]ie Haut [...] seit dem Beginn der Neuzeit zunehmend als Grenze erfahren [wurde] und [...] als solche bedeutsam für moderne Identitätskonstruktionen [ist] (Rytz, 'Die Metaphorik der Haut', p. 63). The body had previously been regarded as a 'poröse[n], offene[n] und zugleich grotesk mit der Welt verwobene[n] Leib' (Benthien, *Haut*, p. 49).

82 Rytz, 'Die Metaphorik der Haut', p. 61.

Farbe meiner Haut allein auf einen angeborenen Pigmentschaden zurückgeht und weder abfärbt noch sonst irgendwie übertragbar ist' (*HS*, p. 141). The exchange is a bitter, ironic reference to racist discourses that talk of blackness as a dye or dirt that can be washed away. For example, during the nineteenth and early twentieth centuries products were available that were expressly designed for use by blacks who wanted to wash away the black pigment in their skin.[83] In another passage Daniel describes himself as a 'waschechter Schwarz-Afrikaner' (*HS*, p. 99), where Roes exploits the double meaning, which can be understood as a 'genuine' black Nigerian, or as one that will not fade in the wash.

The narrator's skin affliction is described as being particularly conspicuous and uncomfortable, but neither life-threatening nor infectious. Any meaning attributed to it is inevitably a projection by the observer and liable to be inaccurate. The unusual appearance of the skin is described in varying terms. Metaphors of religious architecture are used, foreshadowing perhaps the status he will acquire as a holy man. The narrator speaks of 'blauglasierten Kuppeln, roten Zwiebeltürmen und eitergelben Minaretten auf der Haut' (*HS*, p. 143). Comparisons are drawn between the skin and the litter-infested streets of Memphis ('die schorfige Stadt', *HS*, p. 155), where sanitation workers are on strike. The discrepancy between the two images highlights the arbitrariness of attributing meaning to a visual, surface phenomenon. The narrator's experience of being Othered as a result of these manifestations on his skin is radically different to the Othering experienced by black people in the United States. The negative reactions are outnumbered by unexpectedly warm, inquisitive or reverent responses:

> Würde der tägliche Blick in den Spiegel mir nicht versichern, daß ich derzeit so anziehend wie ein ausgestopftes Warzenschwein bin, könnte der Blick der anderen mich glauben lassen, Balggeschwulst, Grützbeutel und bröckelnder Hautgrieß seien in Wirklichkeit rosa Gladiolen, blaue Winden und Anemonen in den Gärten des Vatikans (*HS*, p. 225).

The novel repeatedly turns normative dichotomies and hierarchies on their heads: for example, Daniel advises the narrator that if he had more, rather than fewer, boils and pustules this would lead people to regard and admire them as an individualistic 'Körperzier' (*HS*, p. 143) rather than an unwanted affliction. When the narrator comes to be revered as a holy man in New Orleans, his skin affliction functions as a metaphor which reveals the limitations of racial binaries. Parallels can be drawn between the absurdity of calling a person holy due to a skin affliction and calling someone inferior due to skin pigmentation.

83 Cf. Benthien, *Haut*, p. 208.

Just as his 'leprous' skin can be re-evaluated and regarded as a positive trait associated with holiness, so can any arbitrary meaning be attributed to white, black or any other skin colour. The skin motif is used to similar ends as the analysis of canonized literary texts by Melville, Twain and Faulkner: to deconstruct race and challenge the validity of the beliefs associated with blackness and whiteness. Those beliefs are revealed to be cultural constructs that are conceived, propagated and reflected in language, literature and cultural life.

The analysis presented in this chapter has revealed Roes's intertextual process in *Haut des Südens* to be very different from that in *Leeres Viertel*. In both, the intertexts themselves are usually of an intercultural nature, be they travelogues, travel novels or novels about intercultural friendships. However, apart from the pastiche of the friendship between Ishmael and Queequeg in *Haut des Südens*, the playfulness that characterizes the intertextual appropriation in *Leeres Viertel* is largely absent from *Haut des Südens*. Roes's later novel takes an almost academic approach to analysing his intertexts and the authors behind them; and the intertextuality takes on a predominantly 'metatextual' quality. The two novels we have looked at so far share a reliance upon quotation, whether signalled or not, as a means of incorporating the pre-texts into the new work. The following chapter proceeds to analyse a novel in which very few quotations appear. Instead, the intertextual relationship is founded on shared plot structure, thematic commonalities and hypertextual links that take us back to the ancient world.

CHAPTER 3

Bloodless Retribution: *Weg nach Timimoun* as a Modern-day *Oresteia*

Ezra Pound tells poets: 'Be influenced by as many great artists as you can, but have the decency either to acknowledge the debt outright, or [...] try to conceal it'.[1] In his novel *Weg nach Timimoun*, Michael Roes follows Pound's advice to the letter – the first edition of the novel proudly includes a synopsis of the Orestes myth, which serves as Roes's template, on the back cover. Unlike the two novels discussed in previous chapters, quotation plays only a minor role in *Weg nach Timimoun* and the Greek tragedy is not literally present in Roes's novel. Rather, the relationship between *Weg nach Timimoun* and its main intertext is 'hypertextual' (Genette), with shared elements of plot, character correlation and mutual thematic concerns. However, this chapter argues that instances of deviation from the main pre-text are even more significant for Roes's thematic approach than occasions where he remains faithful to his source.

Roes joins a long list of writers who have drawn on the material of the Orestes myth in their work. The earliest surviving reference to Orestes is to be found in Homer's *Odyssey*, which dates back to the eighth century BC. Aeschylus, Euripides and Sophocles all wrote plays based on the Orestes material in the fifth century BC. According to Greek sources, Orestes is the son of King Agamemnon of Mycenae, commander of the Greek army during the Trojan War, and his queen, Clytemnestra. In preparation for war Agamemnon sacrifices his daughter Iphigenia in return for favourable winds for his fleet of ships. Ten years later, when he returns victorious with his concubine Cassandra at his side, he is murdered by his wife and her lover, Aegisthus, because of the sacrifice. Orestes then returns home, at the behest of his sister Electra, to avenge their father. After killing Clytemnestra and Aegisthus, Orestes is hounded by the Furies, female gods of vengeance, until he is cleared of any misdeed by the judgement of Athene's court. Even in this classical period great variations are to be found in the portrayal of Orestes' character.

1 Ezra Pound, 'A Retrospect', in *Poetry in Theory: An Anthology 1900–2000*, ed. by Jon Cook (Oxford: Blackwell, 2004), pp. 83–90 (p. 85).

As Simon Goldhill notes, 'Orestes in Homer was exemplary; in Aeschylus, an example of the tragic double bind; in Sophocles, unjudged, but also unpraised; in Euripides, he is said by the god simply to have done wrong in killing his mother'.[2]

More recently the material has been reworked by Eugene O'Neill in the play *Mourning Becomes Electra* (1931), in which the action is moved from Ancient Greece to the United States in the period following the Civil War. T. S. Eliot's play *The Family Reunion* (1939) and Jean-Paul Sartre's *Les Mouches* (1943) both use elements of the Greek story. There have been numerous adaptations of the Greek source in German, including Goethe's *Iphigenia auf Tauris* (1779), Hugo von Hofmannsthal's *Elektra* (1904) and Gerhard Hauptmann's *Atriden-Tetralogie* (1940–1944). Since the 1980s there has been renewed interest on the part of German-language writers in the classical world.[3] Elfriede Jelinek's *Das Lebewohl* (2000) draws on elements of the Orestes story in her treatment of Jörg Haider's resignation from his position as leader of the Freiheitliche Partei Österreichs. Other recent German works which engage with classical literature, history and myth include Christa Wolf's novels *Kassandra* (1983) and *Medea. Stimmen* (1996), Christoph Ransmayr's *Die letzte Welt* (1988) and Raoul Schrott's *Finis Terrae* (1995). Furthermore, Roes has published two other novels that draw on Greek mythology: *Ich weiß nicht mehr die Nacht* (2008), a modern rendering of the Phaedra myth located in Bocholt; and *Die Laute* (2012), in which Asis, a young Yemeni composer, is working on an opera that tells the story of Apollo's skinning of the satyr Marsyas. Putting Roes's *Weg nach Timimoun* in this context leads the reader to the realization that reworking classical sources is nothing new. It also raises questions about the author's intention in revisiting older texts. References to classical works can function as homage to their continuing relevance, but they can also serve to challenge their canonical status. The following discussion not only attempts to answer the question of how Roes adapts and assimilates his Greek source, but also seeks to establish the author's intention in doing so, and to determine what principles or concepts lie behind the intertextual borrowing.

The Orestes figure in *Weg nach Timimoun* is Laid, a pensive young man who runs a photography studio in modern-day Bejaia, a seaside town in northern Algeria. He is summoned home by his sister, Assia, who demands that he avenge their father's death. Ibrahim, the father, has been killed by the mother during a domestic argument following his return from fighting in

2 Simon Goldhill, *Aeschylus: The Oresteia* (Cambridge: Cambridge University Press, 1992), p. 95.

3 Cf. Kathleen L. Komar, *Reclaiming Klytemnestra: Revenge or Reconciliation* (Chicago: University of Illinois Press, 2003), p. 151.

the Algerian Civil War. Laid's other sister, Laila, serves as the Iphigenia figure in the novel. In a variation on Agamemnon's sacrifice of Iphigenia, Ibrahim had given his young daughter away in marriage to a fellow soldier against the mother's wishes. In a later flashback Laila's mutilated body is returned to her parents' house after she is killed in an attack on her new husband's compound. The novel opens with a scene showing the two friends, Laid and Nadir (a modern-day version of Orestes' confidante Pylades), discussing Assia's summons. Nadir offers to accompany Laid and they set out together on the 1,300-kilometre journey.

The novel is in seven chapters, each one titled after the name of a station on the way. The pair encounter numerous problems on their journey. Laid's wallet is stolen even before they have bought their first bus ticket. The loss of Laid's identity papers is a hindrance throughout their expedition, especially during encounters with unhelpful policemen and hoteliers. In one dramatic incident the pair narrowly avoid being murdered at a terrorist group's roadside checkpoint; and they receive a very cold welcome in Beni Isguen, a holy town with whose customs they are reluctant to conform. The narration of the journey's events moves fluidly between Laid's first-person perspective and an unspecified third-person stance. In addition there are flashbacks to Laid's formative years in which the events surrounding his father's death are revealed. The narration also features flash-forwards to a hypothetical future in which Laid visualizes his return to Timimoun to kill his mother. Whereas the journey itself is often slow and wearisome, there is a considerable degree of fluidity and dynamism in the narrative, which is in a state of constant flux between past, present and an imagined future.

Roes has made adjustments to important elements in his source material, over and above its relocation to contemporary Algeria. In Aeschylus's trilogy Orestes' journey home is omitted, falling between the first and second plays (*Agamemnon* and *The Libation Bearers* respectively). In Roes's novel, the journey is the main focus. Another significant difference between the two works lies in the motivation of the protagonists. In Aeschylus's play, Orestes faces the tragic dilemma: he is torn between a desire to avenge his father and knowing at the same time that in doing so he would grievously wrong his mother. Laid feels no such urge for vengeance and is only reluctantly making the journey to his past, driven by a sense of obligation and fear. He admits to himself 'daß ich vor allem aus Feigheit aufgebrochen bin. Aus Furcht, für feige gehalten zu werden. Der Erwartung zu gehorchen, braucht es keinen Mut' (*WT*, p. 123). Roes draws clear parallels between Classical Greece and contemporary Algeria – in both, the family's honour must be retained at any cost and life must be paid for with life. Laid ultimately decides not to fulfil his traditional duty and refuses to kill his mother. The novel closes with Laid and Nadir riding down the sand dunes outside Timimoun on inflated tyre tubes: 'Ich springe auf meinen Reifen und schlittere [Nadir] hinterher, bäuchlings den steilen Hang hinab. Habe ich damit nicht meine Menschenpflicht erfüllt und wenigstens einen Augenblick meines Lebens in ungetrübter Freude verbracht?' (*WT*, p. 175). The novel thus concludes with a return to childhood as it should or can be, not as these two experienced it. They abandon themselves to a spontaneity and playfulness that are the antithesis of the angst and abuse that defined their childhoods. This instinctive reaching back to childhood signifies a longing to return to a state or a time when both mother and father were alive, and to a time when the child was not expected to make such weighty decisions about matters of life and death. By sledging down sand dunes the two men become symbols of innocence, simplicity and clear conscience. They present an alternative to the traditional 'Menschenpflicht' of insisting on the preservation of honour at any cost, and another ideal, that of human happiness, is advanced in its stead.

The novel is written both within and against the generic conventions of the road movie and the road novel. In some ways *Weg nach Timimoun* conforms to the expectations of the genre (compare, for instance, Jack Kerouac's *On the Road* (1951) and the film *Easy Rider* (1969)): two friends, a long journey, and characters who occupy the fringes of society. Reflecting the outsider status of its protagonists, the preferred topography of the genre includes deserts, wilderness and empty wastelands, whether the novels are set in the USA or in Algeria. The beaten track is avoided, 'die Fahrt findet statt in totaler Ortlosigkeit'.[4] In other ways, however, Roes is writing against the genre. It has been said that the classic road novel 'erst mit dem Zusammenbruch klassischer Familienstrukturen möglich [wird]'.[5] In *Weg nach Timimoun* the journey does not become possible due to a breakdown in conventional family structures, it is the very breakdown of those structures that makes Laid's journey home necessary in the first place. He is required to travel home so that he can repair the damage done to his family's honour. Whereas the hero of the road novel is usually free to roam due to the absence of family ties, Laid sets off unwillingly to satisfy familial obligations that he would rather leave unfulfilled; and the novel's ending refuses to comply with the expectations not only of the reader familiar with Greek tragedy, but also of the reader of road novels. While the road novel often ends with a pointless death, *Weg nach Timimoun* closes with an assertion of hope that the conventions which required the journey to be made may be abolished, making scenes of violent oblivion unnecessary.

4 Wieland Freund, '"Eine Generation von Wallfahrern": Roadnovels – sehr europäische "Amerikanische Reisen"', in *Der deutsche Roman der Gegenwart*, ed. by Wieland Freund and Winifried Freund (Munich: Fink, 2001), pp. 45–52 (p. 49).

5 Freund, '"Eine Generation von Wallfahrern"', p. 48.

Friedmar Apel, in his review for the *Frankfurter Allgemeine Zeitung*, reads the novel as 'ein poetisches Plädoyer für die Selbstbestimmung des Individuums'.[6] He cautiously adds that this could appear as a 'politisch ziemlich unkorrekter Traum', considering Algeria's recent history, but he sees this 'Traum der Emanzipation' as a welcome respite from the pessimistically pragmatic statements of other experts, 'die in den Krisenzonen nur die Auswegslosigkeit wahrnehmen'. That Roes, as an outsider, presumes to offer, through the pages of a novel, solutions to the problem of violence that perpetuated itself in Algeria during the 1990s may raise a few eyebrows. That the solution offered is an optimistic, perhaps didactic, affirmation of emancipatory ideals and a rejection of traditional conventions and codes of honour could also potentially be read as problematic. Roes is presenting an ethical position here that is critical of the Algerian patriarchy and its cult of repression and violence. This stance is essentially a rejection of cultural relativism in its most passive and permissive form: the cultural norms of a given country are not simply accepted as different but equally valid to those of any other. As Evanoff explains: 'The ultimate effect of cultural relativism is to cut off debate both within and between cultures as to whether or not the norms actually adopted by a particular culture are worth endorsing'.[7] Roes resists this and bravely enters the debate on the social and familial dynamics of the patriarchy in Algeria.[8]

The narrative perspective of the novel is an important aspect in the way this critique is presented. The protagonist of *Weg nach Timimoun*, unlike the other three novels discussed in this book, is not a German intellectual but a young Algerian man from a small oasis town in the desert. There is clearly a considerable degree of separation between Roes and his protagonist-narrator in terms of nationality, culture and education. Roes overcomes this distance to some degree by using Laid's voice to narrate the novel from a first-person perspective, but also allows the standpoint to move to that of a third-person narrator. As Steffen Richter astutely puts it: 'So entgeht Roes der Anmaßung, die in der reinen Mimesis an die algerische Sicht liegen würde. Gleichzeitig

6 Friedmar Apel, 'Sein Algerien', *Frankfurter Allgemeine Zeitung*, 3 July 2006, p. 38.

7 Richard J. Evanoff, 'Universalist, relativist, and constructivist approaches to intercultural ethics', *International Journal of Intercultural Relations*, 28 (2004), 439–58 (p. 447).

8 'Natürlich gerate ich immer wieder in das Dilemma, daß mein Respekt vor dem Fremden in Widerspruch zu meinem Gerechtigkeitssinn gerät. Wie oft habe ich auch in der muslimischen Welt über die Ungleichbehandlung der Frauen oder, noch drastischer, die Ächtung von Schwulen diskutiert! Für dieses Dilemma gibt es keine grundsätzliche Lösung, sondern letztlich nur das: die Diskussion, das Gespräch, die Offenlegung des Dilemmas, die Hoffnung auf Einsicht oder Verständnis oder zumindest denselben Respekt für das Eigene, den man dem Fremden entgegenbringt' (*KT*, p. 103).

aber hütet er sich vor einem homogenen, auktorialen Deutungsdiskurs'.[9] This dual perspective obscures the distinction between the voices of outsider and insider, and presents an Algerian point of view while also incorporating the external perspective of a foreigner. Embedding the fictional experience of an individual Algerian within a more distanced, international perspective creates a space in which the social and political context of this experience can be reassessed and critiqued.

On the Road to Timimoun

Laid and Nadir's journey from Bejaia to Timimoun is presented as both a geographical odyssey through the landscape of the Sahara desert and as a passage through time. The city of Bejaia represents modernity while Timimoun stands as a symbol of the 'Mittelalter' (*WT*, p. 8, p. 125) that has persisted into the present. Beni Isguen, a holy town located at the mid-point of their journey, is likewise described in these terms: '[...] in dieser Hölle der Heiligen kennt man ohnehin nur eine einzige Zeit, die Vergangenheit, die erstarrten Augen der Toten, die nicht vergessen können' (*WT*, p. 119).[10] The geographical journey is also a temporal journey in that Laid experiences a number of flashbacks in which scenes from his childhood and teenage years come to mind. The memories recalled are largely of difficult situations within the family – moments of sexual awakening (*WT*, p. 27, p. 45), domestic violence (*WT*, p. 72), and a failed rite of passage as a hunter (*WT*, p. 61). These flashbacks intrude upon the narrative at certain 'flashpoints' in the literal sense – when Laid takes a photograph (*WT*, p. 27, p. 44), during a roadside massacre (*WT*, p. 85), or when Laid loses the light of consciousness after a fall (*WT*, p. 127).

Laid's return home is depicted as a regression, a return to a tradition which values notions of honour and faith. Laid departs on his journey reluctantly: '[...] ich will nicht zurück in diese sepiafarbene Vergangenheit. Doch habe ich die Wahl?' (*WT*, p. 9). This question is fundamental to the novel's plot. It suggests that a link exists between the dichotomy of tradition/modernity and the question concerning the nature of fate and free will. Classical Greek

9 Steffen Richter 'Rache sei dein Weg: Michael Roes reist mit der Orestie nach Algerien', *Der Tagesspiegel*, 15 March 2006, p. 32.

10 Bernd Schirmer, a GDR writer, similarly describes the area in which Beni Isguen is located in these terms: 'Es surren leise die Motoren. Ansonsten hat sich, scheint es, wenig verändert in den Jahrhunderten. Die Zeit ist stehengeblieben. Die Sitten sind die alten, die Dogmen, die Bräuche, die Muster auf den Teppichen' (Bernd Schirmer, *Die Hand der Fatima auf meiner Schulter: Algerische Reisebilder* (Leipzig: Mitteldeutscher Verlag, 1984), p. 103).

and contemporary but traditionally-minded Arab societies are portrayed as having a number of things in common. Emphasis is put on fate and the limited choices available to man. Outside forces – the gods, fate, traditions – are believed to play an important role and the individual is subject to the will of the gods and also to the expectations imposed upon him or her by society. In contrast, modern society is associated in the novel with free will and the power to determine one's own destiny. Although Laid's journey seems at first to represent a return to traditional places and to traditional values, at the close of the novel he is portrayed rejecting the traditionalist stance and applying his own will in defiance of expectations.

The geographical landscape through which the protagonists travel is described in more detail than is normally the case in Roes's novels. It becomes clear that these topographical descriptions do not simply describe a landscape, but that they also function as a representation of the psychological landscape of Algeria. An example of this double function occurs towards the beginning of the bus journey:

> Dann biegt die abschüssige Küstenstraße in das schroffe, aber dicht begrünte Gebirge und windet sich zu den hochgelegenen Pässen hinauf. Im Norden das Massiv von Ait Djenat, ein unüberwindlicher Wall zwischen der Wüste und dem Meer, im Süden die noch abweisendere Djurdjura, eine wilde unwirtliche Welt. Wie ein gestürzter Titan liegt das Gebirge da, mit aschfarbenen Flanken und wolkenverhüllten Gipfeln. Winzige Dörfer klammern sich an die steilen Hänge oder hocken auf den kahlen Bergsätteln, verängstigten Menschen gleich, die vor einem allzu strengen Gott in die Knie gehen. Die Winter hier sind hart, die Verbindungswege zwischen den Siedlungen rar und schwierig (*WT*, p. 23).

The simile of the fallen Titan emphasizes the enormity and the wildness of the landscape, an immensity that is contrasted with the minuteness of human presence within it. The villages are described in anthropomorphic terms, they are endowed with human personalities, complete with fears and insecurities. Those fears are of a religious nature, anxiety is suffered in the face of an authoritarian God. Villages thus function as a reflection of the situation in which the young men of Algeria, not least Laid, find themselves. Their weakness in relation to their omnipotent fathers is perceived as being comparable to a fearful supplicant's approach to an all-powerful God. By thus describing the mountain ranges and villages, Roes conveys the character of both the region and its people, and combines descriptions of landscape with the development of one of the main themes in the novel.

The descriptions of the landscape reveal the psychology of its inhabitants and the protagonist's reaction to that landscape reveals something of his own psychology. As he sits in the bus watching the desert roll by, Laid is described in the third person: 'Sein Herz schlägt ruhig und kalt, als sähe er einen Kinofilm, der ihn unberührt läßt. Der Blick aus den staubverklebten Busfenstern sucht vergeblich nach Abwechslung und richtet sich nun auf den zerschlissenen Innenraum' (*WT*, p. 23). The journey is monotonous and Laid reacts to it as he would to a tedious film.[11] Seated in the bus, he is detached from the landscape. To observe anything of interest he must redirect his gaze to the interior of the bus. This adjustment in focus allows Laid to examine the dynamics that play out between the other passengers. Seeing the families seated in the bus, the men separate from the women and children, leads Laid to consider his own situation once more. At this point the third-person narrative assumes Laid's perspective, conveying his thoughts in free indirect speech. Once more parallels are drawn between topographical features and psychological states but this time the psychology under discussion is Laid's own (note the movement in the narrative perspective):

> Sein Kopf ist nicht anders als das Dorf, aus dem er stammt. Es gibt darin verschlossene Kammern, in denen er Schreckliches ahnt, aber nichts davon dringt hinaus, in den offenen Raum. Manchmal glaube ich, ein Wimmern zu hören, oder auch Schreie, Hilferufe, doch alles von dicken Lehmwänden gedämpft und dem Lärm auf den Gassen übertönt. Ich darf nicht hören, was ich höre, nicht erkennen, was ich sehe, vor allem darf ich nicht darüber reden! (*WT*, p. 24).

The narrative context suggests that the first two sentences are in the free indirect style or 'erlebte Rede'. The content of the second sentence originates, ironically, from the very head that is being discussed. The third sentence of the quotation then slips into Laid's first-person narration, which is naturally similar to the previous sentences in terms of narrative consciousness. The imagery of the metaphor (village/buildings) is used throughout, providing the reader with a framework within which Laid's frustration can be understood. As the narrative assumes the first-person form it becomes more desperate and frenzied, even as it maintains the imagery of the 'village as mind' that was provided by the free indirect voice. The quality of free indirect speech and

11 Roes's original conception of the Timimoun project was as a film, for which he wrote a screenplay. After facing difficulties attracting the funds to realize this project he rewrote the material as a novel. Roes eventually directed a film version on a no-budget basis entitled *Timimoun* which was given a commercial release by Salzberger & Co. on DVD in 2010. Traces of the novel's origin in a film script can still be detected, not least in the opening scene in which, as the reviewer in the *Süddeutsche Zeitung* states, 'der Erzähler sich [den Charakteren] nähert in einer Weise, die an den Wechsel von Einstellungsgrößen erinnert' (Christoph Haas, 'Die Menschenpflicht der Freude', *Süddeutsche Zeitung*, 3 August 2006, p. 14).

its 'dual-voiced'[12] essence subtly asserts itself in the narrative and contributes to the multi-voiced nature of Roes's novel. The impersonal third-person narrator not only concedes authorial dominion to Laid during the first-person passages, but also assumes Laid's perspective at certain points of the third-person passages as well. Flaubert famously used free indirect style to 'transport himself into his characters'.[13] In *Weg nach Timimoun* Roes has seemingly set that as his task as well. Through the use of such a technique, something is revealed which cannot normally be made known in Algerian society – the despondency of the youths and the pressure that accumulates as a result of their not having an outlet for their desperation.

Laid may have been disconnected from the landscape while he was sitting on the bus at the start of his journey but he and Nadir soon have the opportunity to experience the desert up close. Following an argument with the bus driver over their right to play Kabyle love-songs on the bus stereo (*WT*, p. 55) they are ejected and forced to find alternative transportation to their next destination. They are left to face the extreme conditions of the desert alone: 'Wüste. Hitze. Ein feindseliger Wind. Herausforderung zum Überleben. – Er hat Mühe, mit Nadirs athletischem Ausschreiten Schritt zu halten. Kriegerische Monotonie. Land ohne Frauenantlitz. Er denkt es ohne Groll' (*WT*, pp. 57–58). The desert remains exactly as it was before; now Laid is forced to react to it. Although his emotional reaction to the situation is at first measured, it becomes clear that he is eventually overwhelmed by the landscape:

> Alles wird vom blendenden Licht zersetzt. Die Oberfläche der Dinge löst sich auf, große Flächen von Weiß, barbarisch einfach und unverbunden, schwindelerregende Orientierungslosigkeit, das Weiß fängt mich, füllt mich, ich und das Weiß sind eins in der weiten bodenlosen Landschaft (*WT*, p. 58).

It is a vision that is at once terrifying and illuminating – in the literal sense. The superficial is dissolved, leaving only the substantial, the real, the truthful. Faced with this dizzying whiteness the mind gives up the attempt at orientation and abandons itself to a greater force. In this experience of dissolution the Self becomes one with its surroundings as everything is penetrated by the white light of the desert sun.

Their arrival in Timimoun marks the end of their journey, but instead of rediscovering the community in which he spent his childhood, and thus risking a violent encounter, Laid chooses to escape from the oasis town and leads Nadir up the sand dunes nearby: 'Als [Nadir] ein wenig atemlos neben Laid steht, ist er stumm vor Erstaunen. Vor ihnen liegt das endlose gelbe

12 Cf. Roy Pascal, *The Dual Voice* (Manchester: Manchester University Press, 1977).

13 Pascal, *The Dual Voice*, p. 98.

Sandmeer des Grand Erg Occidental' (*WT*, p. 175). A sea of sand devoid of villages and roads, the Grand Erg Occidental is the epitome of a desert landscape. As one traveller notes:

> The experience of it [the Erg] will be from the fringe, most of the time from a distance, other times it will be feasible to make long enough walks into it to really get [a] feeling of solitude and inferiority compared to the powers of nature.[14]

Laid's journey ends on the fringe of human civilization, the wild frontier, the edge. According to Ulla Biernat, it has become increasingly common since the 1990s for German travel writers of both fiction and non-fiction to travel to and write about such 'Grenzgebiete, das Ende der Welt: Ultima Thule, Land's End, Terra Incognita'.[15] By choosing the empty expanse of the desert over the 'verschachtelte[n] Ksar mit seinen zugemauerten Wasserschöpfstellen' (*WT*, p. 173), Laid is symbolically repudiating the narrow world of his upbringing with its traditional notions of patriarchy and is rejecting the obligations of the 'Gesetz des Blutes. Das Gesetz der Sohnespflicht' (*WT*, p. 124). In their stead he claims for himself a space in which it is possible to interpret his existence anew. The virgin landscape of the desert serves as a *tabula rasa* on which he is free to project his own values and principles, and to impose a template for living that radically breaks away from the life he has rejected.

In addition to the geographical and psychological landscapes encountered during the course of the journey, Laid is confronted by Algeria's political landscape. The backdrop to the action of the novel, as was the case in *Leeres Viertel*, is civil war. Roes is once again creating a fictional world by using historical events. The Algerian Civil War was triggered by the military intervention of January 1992 in which the elections won by the FIS (Islamic Salvation Front) were annulled and the Islamist party banned. For the following ten years Algeria was plagued by terrorist attacks in which politicians, civil servants, civilians and foreigners were brutally killed, leaving a total of over 150,000 dead. Through these violent means the MIA (Islamic Armed Movement), the GIA (Armed Islamic Group), and later the AIS (Islamic Salvation Army), attempted to put pressure on the political and military elite in order to lift the ban and allow the Islamists a part to play in governing the country. The situation was made more complex by suspicions that the government was also involved in some of the massacres:

14 Tore Kjeilen, 'Grand Erg Occidental: The Endless Dunes', http://lexicorient.com/algeria/g_erg_oc.htm [accessed 18 August 2011].

15 Biernat, "*Ich bin nicht der erste Fremde hier*", p. 185.

> There is much anecdotal evidence suggesting that undercover SM [Sécurité Militaire] agents linked to the regime's 'eradicator' trend directed GIA cells, on occasion selecting high-profile targets for assassination. Their objective would have been to carry out terrorist atrocities to reclaim public opinion for the regime.[16]

After Abdelaziz Bouteflika's appointment as President in 1999 the violence declined in intensity, and over the next two years what was left of the GIA was destroyed by government forces. Despite the relatively peaceful situation in recent times, the state of emergency announced at the outbreak of violence in 1992 was not lifted until February 2011.

During the course of their fictional journey, Laid and Nadir narrowly escape falling victim to a terrorist massacre. As they travel by night in a taxi-bus toward Berriane they are stopped at a road block and hustled out of the bus. Lined up on the roadside, faced with a militia of armed men, their situation seems ominous. When a mother and daughter try to escape into the darkness of the desert the militia open fire and Nadir, ever alert, takes advantage of the chaos and leads his friend behind an embankment. The barrage of gunfire and explosions, much as the flash of Laid's camera in other instances, leads the narrative into a flashback section – a section which ends with the death of Ibrahim at the hands of Zarouia. Laid then awakes from that violent dream of the past to an even more gruesome scene in the present:

> Die in der Nacht zum Anhalten gezwungenen Wagen stehen noch dort, doch die Landrover sind verschwunden. Statt dessen blockieren mehrere Polizeifahrzeuge und Krankenwagen die Straße. Uniformierte laufen herum, fotografieren, suchen die Straße ab, rollen Meßbänder aus und malen Kreidezeichen auf den Asphalt. Vor und zwischen den leeren Wagen regungslose Körper, zum größten Teil mit weißen Laken oder Planen bedeckt (*WT*, p. 94).

The novel points towards the complexity of the Algerian political landscape during this tumultuous period. Laid suspects that the militia leader of the previous night is one and the same man as the police chief who investigates the murders on the following morning. It is only after the police depart that the pair feel safe to leave their hiding place. They then see clearly the literal impact that the political situation has on the landscape: 'schwarzbraune[e] Flecken' (*WT*, p. 95) in the earth, an image which brings to mind the prayer of the Furies in *The Oresteia* 'that the good Greek soil never drinks the blood of Greeks'.[17] In this case the Algerian soil drinks Algerian blood, and the Algerian landscape is forced to cannibalize its own people.

16 Martin Stone, *The Agony of Algeria* (London: Hurst, 1997), pp. 187–88.

17 Aeschylus, *The Oresteia*, trans. by Robert Fagles (London: Penguin, 1979), p. 274.

In these landscapes – geographical, psychological and political – the two travellers come face to face with Algeria's multiple identities. They come to know their own country as an enigmatic land and they encounter their fellow countrymen as Other. Nadir is led to remark: 'Nun habe ich mein ganzes Leben in diesem Land verbracht und weiß so gut wie gar nichts von ihm' (*WT*, p. 125). Travel is not only an encounter with the unknown, it is also a means of encountering the Self, and allowing the Other to encounter the Self. Roes, as ever, suggests that travel entails making oneself vulnerable, opening up and letting go of self-protective mechanisms: 'zu entdecken heißt ja immer auch, selber entdeckt zu werden' (*WT*, p. 173). The long journey, the shared experiences and the distance from home bring the two friends closer and at the end of the novel Nadir discusses personal matters with Laid for the first time: '[...] zu Hause, in Bejaia, würde er es wohl auch nicht getan haben' (*WT*, p. 172). The journey not only leads Laid and Nadir to discover their own country, but also teaches them to reveal much about themselves that had remained locked behind the closed doors and the 'dicke[n] Lehmwände[n]' (*WT*, p. 24) of their minds. Laid's journey is a journey home in two senses: on the one hand, it is Laid's journey back to his childhood home, back to his family, and back to the traditional way of life which he had left behind. On the other hand, it is a journey that leads him back to himself, to recognize the values by which he wishes to live. To quote Albert Camus: 'Le voyage, qui est comme une plus grande et plus grave science, nous y ramène' [Das Reisen, das gleichsam eine höhere und ernstere Wissenschaft ist, führt uns zu uns zurück].[18]

Ancient Greece in Modern Algeria

At one point during Laid's southward journey he reads a newspaper story about a terrorist attack: twenty people, most from the same family, have been killed in their homes. After their names have been listed in full, the narrative states coldly: 'Allen Opfern wurde die Kehle durchgeschnitten' (*WT*, p. 54). Nadir's response to this news, regarded in the context of the novel's intertextuality, is ironic: 'Klingt wie eine griechische Tragödie [...]. Als habe ein göttlicher Fluch die ganze Familie ausgelöscht' (*WT*, p. 54). This statement establishes a link between contemporary Algeria and ancient Greece and explains Roes's decision to relocate the action to the North African country. Ironically, however, the fictional characters are naturally unaware that they are

18 Albert Camus, *Carnets: mai 1935 – février 1942* (Paris: Gallimard, 1962), p. 26. Quoted in German in Schirmer, *Die Hand der Fatima*, p. 57.

featuring in a novel based on one of the most canonical of all Greek tragedies, thus creating a sense of metafictional dramatic irony.

Revenge is a central and recurring theme in Aeschylus's tragic play and Roes's novel, as a hypertext of that play, reflects this thematic interest. However, although Roes uses Aeschylus as a starting point for his treatment of the theme of revenge, his novel takes a fundamental turn away from the vengeful patterns that play out in the Greek model. The 'prefiguration' that is, according to John J. White, inherent to novels based on mythology is not followed to its conclusion.[19] This chapter proceeds to argue that the intertextuality of Roes's novel advocates a process of 'demythologizing' and a turn towards reason. In the case of *Weg nach Timimoun* and the *Oresteia*, where the applicability of the pre-text rests upon parallels between two cultures of honour and revenge, it appears that the time has come to seek new archetypal patterns.

The *Oresteia* features a pattern of 'revenge and reversal', whereby 'he who acts is acted upon' or 'the doer suffers'.[20] Transgression, revenge and wrongdoing have hung over the House of Atreus like a curse ever since Atreus, Agamemnon's father, on discovering that his wife had committed adultery with his twin brother Thyestes, had killed Thyestes' sons, cooked them and fed them to their father. In the *Oresteia* Aegisthus, Clytemnestra's lover and another of Thyestes' sons, claims Agamemnon's death as revenge for this misdeed. Vengeance permeates life in the House of Atreus and each violent act in the play is a link in a long chain of killings, committed in the hope of reaching an end point at which justice is restored. However, as Crotty notes, 'revenge is a highly inefficient mode of keeping the peace, for the costs it exacts threaten to outweigh the benefits it provides'.[21] The repercussions of taking vengeance are uncontrollable even when they are predictable: 'Revenge can foment intergenerational conflicts; it does not point to any sure closure'.[22] As is clear in Orestes' tragic dilemma, righting his father's murder is to wrong his mother; and taking revenge 'reverses' his position from that of the wronged to that of the wrongdoer. To claim vengeance is thus to perpetuate a never-ending cycle of bloody intrafamilial strife.

Goldhill notes that this 'seemingly endless pattern of revenge and reversal [...] is also a pattern of male-female opposition'.[23] Each link in the chain of revenge is committed by one gender against the other. Even the

19 Cf. John J. White, *Mythology in the Modern Novel: A Study of Prefigurative Techniques* (Princeton: Princeton University Press, 1971).

20 Goldhill, *Aeschylus*, p. 27.

21 Kevin M. Crotty, *Law's Interior: Legal and Literary Constructions of the Self* (Ithaca: Cornell University Press, 2000), p. 43.

22 Crotty, *Law's Interior*, p. 44.

23 Goldhill, *Aeschylus*, p. 42.

gods are gendered and stand in opposition to each other, as is the case when Apollo opposes the Furies. It is up to Athene, who represents a 'diffusion of the rigid and sharply focused opposition of male and female',[24] to lead to reconciliation. In his study on Aeschylus, R. P. Winnington-Ingram claims that 'the relationship of the sexes in society' is one of the principle themes of *The Oresteia*.[25] He describes Clytemnestra as a 'woman with the will and mind of a man, resentful of male domination' and he consequently reads Orestes' act of vengeance as a restoration 'of male domination, playing the return match in the struggle between the sexes'.[26] In *Weg nach Timimoun* Zarouia, Laid's mother, by killing her husband, challenges the power of an abusive patriarchy in an act that is legitimized in the novel by the negative portrayal of adult male figures. Consequently Laid's refusal to 'restore male domination', his unwillingness to perpetuate the cycle of violence by killing his mother, mark a significant break from the traditional patriarchal order. His refusal to exact revenge for the father can be read as a means of avenging himself upon the father – a bloodless retribution to right the wrongs inflicted upon him by a harsh and domineering patriarch. Roes's re-interpretation can also be read as a feminist deconstruction of the myth in which he re-examines the motivation of the Clytemnestra figure, exploring the motives of a woman who kills her husband.

The murder of the husband, and the son's refusal to avenge him, is partly justified in Roes's novel by the consistently negative portrayal of Arab fathers. The negative portrayals of fathers in *Weg nach Timimoun*, as well as in other works, constitute a sustained critique of Algeria's patriarchal culture. Two father figures appear in *Weg nach Timimoun*. Laid's father, Ibrahim, was a military commander in the Algerian Civil War. He is abusive, domineering and irresponsible towards his family. Despite the characterization of Ibrahim as a brutal man, or perhaps because of it, he is revered in the community as a strong leader and warrior. This discrepancy emphasizes the sharp distinction between the private and public spheres of Algerian society, in which the shameful secrets of the home must never be revealed. The local community is complicit in this concealment and is blind to their war hero's weaknesses of character. Nadir's father, who does not appear in the novel, is initially described as well-meaning but weak. Laid speculates that Nadir likes his father, 'auch wenn der es nie über Hilfsarbeiterjobs hinausgebracht hat und vor allem von dem lebt, was Nadir heimbringt' (*WT*, p. 14). Nadir's father is a

24 Goldhill, *Aeschylus*, p. 44.

25 R. P. Winnington-Ingram, *Studies in Aeschylus* (Cambridge: Cambridge University Press, 1983), p. 96.

26 Winnington-Ingram, *Studies in Aeschylus*, p. 76.

figure who represents failure. He falls short of what is expected of him in his role as provider for the family.

Violent fathers are an even greater problem. Laid reflects on the situation he and his generation face:

> Die anderen tun so, als gäbe es aus ihrer Kindheit nichts Bemerkenswertes zu berichten. Alle tun so, selbst du, Nadir. Also bleibt jeder mit seinen Verletzungen allein. Jeder glaubt, nur in seiner Familie habe es diese Gewalttätigkeit des Vaters und diese Ohnmacht der Frauen und Kinder gegeben, diese Racheschwüre und Mordphantasien. Irgendwann werden wir groß und stark sein, haben wir uns vorgestellt, und uns schützend vor die Mutter werfen und dem Vater zurufen: Keinen Schritt weiter, Alter, oder du wirst es bereuen! (*WT*, p. 26)

Towards the end of the novel Nadir reveals that his father, too, participated in the violence that here characterizes family life in Algeria. The complexity of the situation becomes clear as Nadir tells how his father sobs when confronted by his son about the abuse his mother suffers at his hands: 'Und mir wird klar, es ist nicht seine Schuld. Aber wessen Schuld dann?' (*WT*, p. 173). The psychological damage inflicted is highlighted by the fact that the fathers are ever-present, even when they are dead or hundreds of kilometres away. Laid is haunted by memories of his father, which are manifested in the text as flashbacks. The father-son relationship is depicted by the absence of love and affection. And in Timimoun, Nadir sighs at the thought of his father: 'Ich weiß nicht, was mich daran hindert weiterzureden. Es ist, als stünde mein Vater hinter mir und hielte mir den Mund zu' (*WT*, p. 172). In contrast, Assia (who occupies the role of the brooding, vengeful Electra) carefully tends the precious memories of her beloved father: '[Sie] hütet die ersten dilettantischen Schnappschüsse von ihm wie Ikonen. [...] neben anderen Erinnerungsstücken wie den hartledrigen Fußballschuhen meines Vaters oder seiner schwarzen Sonnenbrille mit den zersprungenen Gläsern' (*WT*, p. 19). In Assia's case fond memories are deliberately preserved, mementos treasured, and vengeance plotted for the perceived injustice. The reasons behind this bond between father and daughter are explored later in this chapter. The young men, in contrast to Assia, would rather leave behind memories of their fathers. The presence of the father, however, lingers on well after he is gone – crippling and haunting a generation of Algerian men who struggle to come to terms with the injustice they faced at their fathers' hands.[27]

27 *Weg nach Timimoun* represents a continuation of Roes's engagement with this theme, but the novel also contains a variation on it. In Laila's case the reader is presented with a daughter who suffers due to her father's ruthlessness. Iphigenia's fate in the *Oresteia* is even more explicit as a representation of a daughter sacrificed by her father.

The final chapter of this book examines the novel *Geschichte der Freundschaft* (2010), in which the reader is presented with a further example of a hateful Algerian father figure who beats his wife, keeps his daughter under close confinement, and orders his eldest son to carry out a fratricidal honour killing. Roes's depiction of the abusiveness of the Algerian father focuses not only on the fathers themselves, but also on the suffering that the sons endure as a result. Matthias, the German narrator of *Geschichte der Freundschaft*, reacts sympathetically to the situation of the young Algerian men: '[S]chau dir die jungen Männer an, ihre Ohnmacht, ihre Verwahrlosung, ihre Wut! Von den Vätern abhängig, bis sie selbst Väter sind, nein, bis der Vater stirbt' (*GF*, p. 257). Here, once more, whole families are ruled by the dictatorship of an unsympathetic father.

In an article discussing the protests of the Arab Spring of 2011 in the *Frankfurter Allgemeine Zeitung*, Roes develops this portrayal of the Arab patriarchy and interprets the widespread protests as an 'Aufstand der Söhne im Medienzeitalter'. Roes narrates the story of one young Yemeni man as an example of conditions that are widely endured by youths in Yemen:

> Sary ist neunzehn. Er hätte gern studiert, musste aber im Geschäft des Vaters aushelfen. Er sympathisiert wie viele mit den Demonstranten in Sanaa. In Aden jedoch würde er es niemals wagen, auf die Straße zu gehen. Sein Vater würde ihn dafür wohl totprügeln.[28]

Further, Roes comments on the father: 'An manchen Tagen gibt er den fürsorglichen Familienvater, um dann plötzlich gewalttätig und brutal zu sein. Sary und seine Geschwister tyrannisiert er mit absurden Vorschriften und bestraft sie hart'. This picture of domestic violence is then generalized by the statement that 'Alle meine Freunde im Jemen können von väterlicher Gewalt erzählen'.

It may appear at times that the author reproduces negative stereotypes of Arab fatherhood – a stereotype of ethnicity, but also of gender and generation. It seems that all Algerian fathers are violent and abusive, and that all wives and children suffer behind closed doors and in silence. However, taking into consideration three of Roes's early works, the scope of his engagement with patriarchal oppression can be seen to extend much further. This broader context of father-son relationships aids in providing an understanding of how Roes approaches the examples presented in *Weg nach Timimoun*.

Roes's treatment of this theme can be traced back to the early volume *Jizchak: Versuch über das Sohnesopfer* (1992), which can be understood as the

28 Michael Roes, 'Die Söhne haben das Schweigegebot gebrochen', *Frankfurter Allgemeine Zeitung*, 8 February 2011, p. 30, http://de.qantara.de/wcsite.php?wc_c=15900 [accessed 8 August 2011].

first volume of a loose trilogy on the topic of the relationship between fathers and sons.[29] *Jizchak* is a travelogue in which a German traveller recounts a visit to Israel, an anthropological essay on the sacrifice of sons, and an art-historical study. Abraham's intended sacrifice of Isaac is the central topic of the book and Roes's text revolves around Caravaggio's artistic representation of the biblical scene. The Judeo-Christian vision of a father-son relationship is under the spotlight, a relationship that mirrors that between man and God. Indeed, the parallels are clear in the Christian tradition between the sacrifice of Jesus by His (heavenly) father in the New Testament and Abraham's willingness to sacrifice his son in the Old Testament. *Jizchak* shows that Roes, far from being fixated on negative portrayals of Arab fathers, exposes and critiques the son's fragile position in the face of oppressive fathers in all cultures. Like the Arab sons in his fictional work, the child in Judeo-Christian cultures is 'zu absolutem gehorsam verpflichtet' (*J*, p. 134). Abraham never doubts his 'right' to sacrifice Isaac: 'Das leben des sohnes unterliegt uneingeschränkt der verfügungsgewalt des vaters' (*J*, p. 170). Roes's narrator finds a similar situation existing in contemporary Israel, with young Israeli soldiers regarded as present-day Isaacs: 'bemitleidenswerte burschen, die für die erbarmungslose politik ihrer väter die köpfe hinzuhalten haben' (*J*, p. 34). The violence and oppression is a never-ending cycle with victimized sons becoming in turn the violating fathers. Indeed, Roes explains the bind in which men find themselves:

> Vaterschaft wird offenbar nicht nur als gewinn, sondern auch als zumutung, als herausforderung oder sogar als bedrohung empfunden. Die kindheitserfahrungen mit den eigenen eltern tauchen aus den tiefen des vergessens auf. Die erinnerung an demütigende und ohnmächtige empfindungen vor allem dem eigenen vater gegenüber müssen nun durch eine identifikation mit ihm ersetzt werden. Die strenge des vaters wird zum vorbild für die haltung zum eigenen sohn (*J*, p. 135).

Roes's engagement with this theme continues in his stage play *Cham: Ein Symposion* (1993), which takes as its basis the biblical passage in which Noah places a curse on his son Ham (or Cham). In Genesis 9:20–28, Noah, drunk after partaking of wine, is found naked in his tent by Ham. The son calls on his two brothers, who cover their father's nudity with a blanket. Ham's actions are interpreted by Noah as a transgression and the son and his line are cursed: 'Als der vater von der untat seines sohnes erfährt, verflucht er ihn: Von nun an seist du niedrigster der knechte deiner brüder. / Nichts verzeihen patriarchen weniger als blozsgestellt zu werden' (*C*, p. 79).

29 Cf. Martin Luedke, 'Stachel im Fleisch', *Die Zeit*, 19 May 1995, www.zeit.de/1995/21/Stachel_im_Fleisch [accessed 5 December 2011].

Lleu Llaw Gyffes (1994), Roes's first novel and the final volume of his trilogy on the topic, presents a counterfoil to the unsympathetic father. The novel draws inspiration from the medieval Welsh legends of *The Mabinogion*. The German director Ernst Töpfer has been filming a screen version of the myth of Math fab Mathonwy in Wales when his son Jonathan, who was playing the role of Lleu Llaw Gyffes, dies in an accident. The twelve chapters of the book represent twelve hours in an all-night vigil that the father holds for his son. Interspersed between these chapters are twelve scenes that comprise the film script, telling Lleu's story. According to the myth, Lleu is born to an uncaring mother, Arianrhod, and is brought up by a kindly father figure, his uncle Gwydion. Arianrhod puts her son under a series of spells, first preventing him from receiving a name, second from taking arms and armour, unless she is the one who provides them for him. Gwydion becomes a mentor to the young Lleu and helps him, through trickery and magic, to force Arianrhod to give him a name and to arm him with weapons. As a result she conjures a spell that will prevent him from ever taking a wife of human flesh. Gwydion therefore creates Blodeuwedd, a woman of flowers, and imbues her with life. Gwydion's care for Lleu, and Arianrhod's disregard and cruelty towards him, stand in stark contrast to the images of fatherhood that were engaged with in the volume on Abraham and Isaac. Roes has found in Welsh mythology the antithesis to the biblical story that serves as an archetype for father-son relationships. It is Gwydion, the father-figure, who provides the protection, nurturing and care, while the torment is inflicted upon the son by his cruel mother.

While fathers are largely demonized, mothers are characterized sympathetically in *Weg nach Timimoun*. While Aeschylus's Clytemnestra was a 'woman of monsterful will',[30] Zarouia is nothing of the sort. She kills Ibrahim and his new wife, Hafsa (who occupies Cassandra's role), in a scene marked by commotion and tumult, making motives ambiguous:

> Er schlägt der Mutter ins Gesicht, doch Zarouia läßt seine Hand mit der geladenen Waffe nicht los. [...] Ein Schuß fällt. Die fremde Frau schreit auf, die Kinder weinen. Erschrocken blickt Ibrahim auf den roten Fleck, der sich rasch auf Hafsas Kleid ausbreitet. Zarouia entwindet ihrem Mann die Pistole und richtet die Mündung auf ihn. [...] Er hebt die Hand, um sie ein weiteres Mal zu schlagen. Zarouia drückt ab. Diesmal trifft die Kugel Ibrahim in die Brust. Er blickt erstaunt, macht aber noch einen Schritt. Zarouia schießt ein drittes Mal (*WT*, pp. 92–93).

The text largely justifies the killing by the confusion that dominates the scene and Ibrahim's acts of domestic violence. Zarouia's actions are contextualized

30 Winnington-Ingram, *Studies in Aeschylus*, p. 96.

by Ibrahim's attempts to defy the first bullet – taking 'noch einen Schritt', presumably with the intention of hitting his wife again. Zarouia is also presented with an opportunity to explain matters from her perspective. These explanations are proffered in sections which represent a hypothetical future and are therefore to be regarded as fruits of Laid's imagination. Nevertheless they offer an interesting insight into Zarouia's situation. She reveals her weaknesses, admits to failures, and explains why she sent Laid away when he was still a youth, yet despite this claim to weakness she displays, like her Greek counterpart, a considerable degree of agency in taking a lover in defiance of social disapproval. However, her strength is rooted in weakness and her actions originate from a desire to conceal and control her deepest fears. Attempts to overcome her powerless situation as a woman in Algeria lead to trouble and conflict: 'Immer, wenn ich mich zwang, stark zu sein, ist es schlimmer gekommen, als wenn ich mich in die Rolle der duldsamen Frau gefügt hätte' (*WT*, p. 150).

These factors explain, up to a point, why Laid does not avenge his father's death by killing his mother. A further reason is the way in which gender roles are reversed in the novel: Laid is given feminine attributes and is characterized as a mother's boy, in contrast to the masculine attributes given to his sister Assia, who is very close to her father. Assia is her father's 'kleine Kriegerin' (*WT*, p. 65). He allows her to drive his car, a feat she accomplishes with 'Burschikosität' (*WT*, p. 65). Whereas Assia is described as strong and soldierly, Laid completely lacks such masculine characteristics. According to his own description of himself, Laid is:

> ein blasser, schmalbrüstiger Knabe, zu früh entwöhnt, um Jahre zurückgeblieben, bis in die Pubertät hinein Bettnässer, bis heute ein Gelegenheitsstotterer, ein Muttersöhnchen, das den Ball nicht fangen kann und ihn wie ein Mädchen wirft und statt mit dem Luftgewehr auf Hornvipern und Palmentauben mit seiner Leica Augenblicke schießt (*WT*, p. 15).

Father and son could not be more different. While Ibrahim is vain and fond of posing in front of the camera, Laid prefers the inconspicuousness of standing behind the lens. Laid's Leica is talked of in terms of a weapon, but for Ibrahim anything other than a real firearm is unworthy of a real man.

When Laid refuses to murder his mother, Assia questions his gender identity: 'Schon als Kind warst du eher das Mädchen als ich' (*WT*, p. 151). Assia's gender identity, in turn, is questioned when she insists on vengeance (*WT*, p. 124). Aggression and violence are firmly linked in the novel to men and masculinity. Even in Assia's case, when a woman displays a thirst for bloody vengeance, she is described in terms of her masculine traits and her femininity is negated. Her aggressive nature is revealed in Laid's memory of their cousin

Yasir's wedding. A twelve-year-old Laid stands watching the groom who is looking rather mournful considering that he is supposed to be celebrating his wedding. As they exchange glances that are laden with homoerotic desire, Assia surprises her brother with a beating. Firstly, she should not have been near the men's tent since the women are celebrating elsewhere according to custom. Her presence in the men's tent suggests an interest in men and masculinity, conveying a desire to be like a man. Moreover, in attempting to beat Laid's homosexuality out of him, she displays a hyper-masculine urge to maintain socially acceptable norms.

Laid's refusal to reclaim power on behalf of a patriarchal order may be understood as progress from the medieval values of Timimoun towards the Enlightenment values of modernity. Aeschylus's *Oresteia* shows how a self-perpetuating cycle of violence is brought to an end as a system of justice based on law and reason replaces the old order. The play represents a 'historical transition from vendetta justice to institutionalized trial by jury'.[31] In Aeschylus's play this violence ends after Orestes kills his mother in revenge for her murder of Agamemnon. After being pursued by the Furies, Orestes is tried in Athens, where he is acquitted by Athene and the curse on the House of Atreus is lifted. Laid in *Weg nach Timimoun* succeeds in ending the cycle of violence at an earlier stage, before killing his mother:

> Where will it end?
> where will it sink to sleep and rest,
> this murderous hate, this Fury?[32]

These last lines from *The Libation Bearers* communicate one of the main themes of Roes's novel. Laid's decision in turning his back on the patterns of violence that are portrayed as characteristic of traditional societies in Algeria is also symbolically advocating an end to the civil war that plays out in the background of the novel: violence against the mother is comparable to violence against the motherland. Laid's aspiration for peace echoes the hope voiced by the pacified Furies towards the end of *The Eumenides*:

> And the brutal strife,
> the civil war devouring men, I pray
> that it never rages through our city, no
> that the good Greek soil never drinks the blood of Greeks,
> shed in an orgy of reprisal life for life.[33]

31 Helene P. Foley, 'Introduction', in Aeschylus, *Oresteia*, trans. by Peter Meineck (Indianapolis: Hackett, 1998), pp. vi–xlvii (p. xvii).

32 Aeschylus, *Oresteia*, p. 226.

33 Aeschylus, *Oresteia*, p. 274.

Laid avoids the fate of his mythical counterpart. His story thematizes 'die Überwindung des mythischen Wiederholungsmusters'.[34] Even if at times he doubts his ability to act against societal expectations, Laid is ultimately in control of his own actions and fully determines his own fate. The intertextuality of the novel can therefore be described as 'demythologizing', with Roes using Aeschylus's play as a model from which he radically deviates, suggesting that the time has come to transcend the patterns of mythological archetypes.

The *Oresteia*'s tragic power is lost in Michael Roes's novel. This is inevitable considering Laid's decision not to kill his mother. The tragic model of the novel's hypotext is rejected in favour of a more tranquil ending. Other factors contribute to this diminished sense of tragedy. Ibrahim's decision to marry his daughter to a comrade smacks of pride and recklessness, but there is no intent to sacrifice, no causal link between his decision and Laila's death. Neither is there a sense that Ibrahim's house is cursed, as was the House of Atreus – the novel offers no equivalent to Thyestes' feast. No gods interfere in the action of the Algerian characters: their joys and their hardships are shown to result directly from their own decisions. The only force beyond their control lies in the power that is attributed to societal expectations. Roes's novel is not a blow-by-blow equivalent of the classical play but rather an adaptation that draws from a source but does not adhere religiously to it. As George Steiner has stated, tragedy is dead and 'the ancient is not a glove into which the modern can slip at will'.[35] Myths and archetypes may retain their power in our imaginations, but Roes is making the point that no honour is to be found in tragedy, in vengeance, or in violence. His novel is a critique of honour killings and the revenge culture in Algeria and elsewhere in the Arab world. The end of the novel shows that Laid has taken note of the art historian Lumière's baffling send-off early in the novel: 'Und vergeßt nicht, es gibt auch einen Heroismus der Zurückhaltung, ja der Untätigkeit. Adieu!' (*WT*, p. 52). Both the *Oresteia* and *Weg nach Timimoun* end 'with the discovery of the potential to avoid the unending violence of revenge and reversal'.[36] However, whereas in Aeschylus the solution is found in the establishment of law and order, in the novel Laid moves away from conflict altogether, negating the need for juristic intervention entirely.

34 Sibylle Cramer, 'Fieber, Ehre, Lust: Michael Roes' feine afrikanische Orestie "Weg nach Timimoun"', *Frankfurter Rundschau*, 8 November 2006, p. 16.

35 George Steiner, *The Death of Tragedy* (London: Faber & Faber, 1961), p. 329.

36 Goldhill, *Aeschylus*, p. 30.

Algerian Outsiders

The *Oresteia* serves as the main intertext in *Weg nach Timimoun*. There are, however, numerous other literary references in the novel, some unambiguous, others less so. For example, the scene in which Laid and Nadir safely negotiate a police roadblock by hiding under the skirts of two old Arab women who are travelling on the back of the same van (*WT*, p. 165–6) is surely a playful nod to the refuge found by Joseph Koljaiczek under Anna Bronski's wide skirts in the opening chapter of Günter Grass's *Die Blechtrommel* (1959).

Another intertextual reference can be detected as Laid describes Nadir's habit of letting him smoke the last drag of his cigarette butts. Laid does not otherwise smoke and 'bei niemandem sonst würde mir einfallen, seine speicheldurchtränkte Kippe zu Ende zu rauchen' (*WT*, pp. 9–10). He reasons that the ritual is a means of confirming their friendship: 'Es wird wohl dieselbe Bedeutung wie das Herumreichen der Friedenspfeife unter Indianern haben' (*WT*, p. 10). This is an allusion to Roes's earlier novel *Haut des Südens*, whose narrator reveres Herman Melville's *Moby Dick* for its portrayal of an intercultural friendship that was ahead of its time. The narrator quotes passages from Melville's novel, particularly from the scene in which Ishmael and Queequeg become acquainted: '"Und als unsere Pfeife ausgeraucht war, drückte er seine Stirn gegen meine, legte den Arm um mich und sagte, von nun an seien wir verheiratet, was in der Redeweise seiner Heimat wohl hieß, wir seien Blutsbrüder"' (*HS*, p. 87). The reference to smoking in *Weg nach Timimoun* is inevitably double-layered, pointing to Roes's previous novel as well as to the canonical text from which the motif of communal smoking is borrowed. Smoking together, be it a cigarette or a peace pipe, serves as a symbol of sealing or reaffirming a friendship. In *Weg nach Timimoun*, the reference to smoking serves to illustrate the nature of the friendship between Laid and Nadir and, as in *Moby Dick*, has distinctly homoerotic undertones. In Roes's novels friendships between men often defy the traditional distinction made between platonic friendship and homosexual relationships. While Laid is gay, Nadir is not, but the friendship is nevertheless a close one and remains so despite the strain imposed upon it by the long journey. The smoking motif recurs in *Geschichte der Freundschaft*, a novel in which Roes develops further his conception of friendship between men.

A final author whose work is directly quoted in *Weg nach Timimoun* is Albert Camus. In their shared hotel room in El Djelfa, Laid reads aloud from Nadir's copy of Camus' *L'étranger* (1942). That is not the only work by Camus evoked in Roes's novel. *Weg nach Timimoun* opens with the two main characters swimming in the agitated waves of the Mediterranean, just off the Cap Carbon near Bejaia. Despite the fact that Nadir proves himself to be the stronger swimmer, the scene conveys the bond that exists between the two as they plough through the waves in 'vollkommene Harmonie' (*WT*, p. 7). Indeed, the understanding that exists between the two is suggestive of a 'Zwillingspaar' (*WT*, p. 7). In Camus' novel *La Peste* (1947) the narrator, Dr Bernard Rieux, goes with his friend Tarrou for a midnight swim in the ocean. Their venturing out to sea at the dead of night is a rare respite from the gruelling work of diagnosing, treating and burying the victims of the plague that is scourging the city of Oran, also located on the Algerian coast. The swimming scene serves to establish the friendship, which is being officially sealed, as it were, on that very night. As Rieux tells Tarrou: 'J'ai de l'amitié pour vous. Mais jusqu'ici le temps nous a manqué' [Of course we're friends; only, so far we haven't had much time to show it].[37] Like Laid and Nadir, when they are in the water they intuitively share an understanding that allows them to maintain a harmonic rhythm, despite differing levels of ability:

> Rieux se retourna, se mit au niveau de son ami, et nagea dans le même rythme. Tarrou avançait avec plus de puissance que lui et il dut précipiter son allure. Pendant quelques minutes, ils avancèrent avec la même cadence et la même vigueur, solitaires, loin du monde, libérés enfin de la ville et de la peste.
>
> [Rieux turned and swam level with his friend, timing his stroke to his. But Tarrou was the stronger swimmer and Rieux had to put on speed to keep up with him. For some minutes they swam side by side, with the same zest, in the same rhythm, isolated from the world, at last free of the town and of the plague.][38]

The similarities between these two scenes and the two friendships are striking. They highlight Roes's interest in the theme of friendship between men and illustrate Camus' influence on the German writer.

It comes as no surprise that Roes refers to Camus in *Weg nach Timimoun*, since Camus was an Algerian *pied-noir* and *L'étranger* is set in and around Algiers. The reference to *L'étranger* is, however, more significant than simply a sharing of geographical location. In Camus' novel, Meursault receives news of his mother's death but responds with emotional detachment, even beginning a sexual relationship with Marie on the day following the death. He helps Raymond, an acquaintance of his, to gain revenge on his girlfriend, who had been unfaithful to him. While Raymond, Marie and Meursault spend a Sunday at a beach-house outside the city, the beaten girlfriend's brother injures Raymond with a knife. Shortly thereafter Meursault returns to the beach with

37 Albert Camus, *La Peste* (Paris: Gallimard, 1968), p. 196; English: Albert Camus, *The Plague*, trans. by Stuart Gilbert (Harmondsworth: Penguin, 1960), p. 235.

38 Camus, *La Peste*, p. 206; Camus, *The Plague*, p. 246.

Raymond's pistol and encounters the Arab again. Under the blinding light and oppressive heat of the afternoon sun, Meursault shoots the unnamed Arab five times and is later convicted of murder and sentenced to death. Meursault consistently emanates cool emotional detachment and it has been widely argued that he is found guilty not because he murdered the Arab but because he did not properly mourn the death of his mother.[39]

Meursault's conviction and sentencing, based on his unconventional response to his mother's death, is foreshadowed in the vigil scene at the residential home. On the night before the funeral Meursault is joined by ten of his mother's friends, the same number as there are jurors in court. Sitting there opposite this group Meursault states: 'J'ai eu un moment l'impression ridicule qu'ils étaient là pour me juger' [For a moment I had an absurd impression that they had come to sit in judgement on me].[40] In the actual trial for his shooting of the Algerian, the prosecutor emphasizes Meursault's moral vacuity, claiming that he is also:

> 'un homme qui tuait moralement sa mère [...] . J'en suis persuadé [...] vous ne trouverez pas ma pensée trop audacieuse, si je dis que l'homme qui est assis sur ce banc est coupable aussi du meurtre que cette cour devra juger demain [le meurtre d'un père].'
>
> [morally guilty of his mother's death [...] . I am convinced [...] that you will not find I am exaggerating the case against the prisoner when I say that he is also guilty of the murder to be tried tomorrow in this court [the murder of a father by his son].][41]

Gerry Brenner, in an original psychoanalytical reading of Camus' text, develops this interconnection between the murder of the Arab and the death of Meursault's mother. Meursault's misogyny is clear from the way he treats his lover, as well as the way in which he so readily and coldly assists Raymond in avenging his own mistress's alleged infidelity. Further, Brenner argues that Meursault places the blame for his father's absence squarely on his mother's shoulders. His attack on the Arab can therefore be understood as displaced violence:

> [I]nasmuch as [Meursault] blames his shooting of the Arab on the dazzling spears of sunlight glinting off the Arab's knife blade and stabbing at his 'stinging

39 Cf. Gisela Dischner, 'Albert Camus: Der Fremde im Büro', *Die Stimme des Fremden* (Hofheim: Wolke, 1992), pp. 101–12 (p. 110); John Robert Maze, *Albert Camus: Plague and Terror, Priest and Atheist* (Bern: Lang, 2010), p. 35.

40 Albert Camus, *L'étranger* (Paris: Gallimard, 1942), p. 19; English: Albert Camus, *The Outsider* trans. by Stuart Gilbert (Harmondsworth: Penguin, 1961), p. 20.

41 Camus, *L'étranger*, p. 154; Camus, *The Outsider*, p. 102.

> eyes'; and inasmuch as a man's eyes are a classic displacement of his testicles (vide Oedipus's self-mutilation); and inasmuch as the Arab is a condensation for Mr Meursault of women turned aggressive, then it would seem fair to conclude, in classical fashion, that Mr Meursault's shooting of the Arab is a retaliatory act against his mother's castration of his father and, thus, her threat to himself as well.[42]

Camus, like Aeschylus, is interested in parricide. Meursault did not kill his mother in a literal sense but he is convicted of murder and punished by society, as represented by a court of law. In *Weg nach Timimoun* Laid, in contrast, is urged by a traditional code of honour to avenge the death of his father by killing his mother. What the two protagonists have in common is that they are able to maintain a certain level of freedom from prevailing societal expectations. Meursault, despite incarceration and impending execution, remains free mentally and maintains a detached, objective attitude. Laid also maintains a certain level of independence of thought, even after travelling from his adopted seaside home in Bejaia back to the landscape of his childhood where familial, social and religious expectations still retain a powerful hold. The close of the novel confirms that Laid resists this pressure and chooses a different path, a path that confirms his place as an outsider himself.

Laid is an outsider well before he chooses not to adhere to the traditional code of blood-vengeance. Already during his teenage years he feels set apart, not least due to the fact that he is gay. His mother's decision to send him away after his father's death reinforces the image which he has of himself: 'Für ihn war es wie eine Verbannung' (*WT*, p. 149). In Bejaia, his new home, he is different from the local population, never fitting in with what is typically expected. He is a 'Zugereiste[r]', a 'Zugewanderte[r]', and is therefore set apart from the members of the 'alteingesessene[n] Familien' (*WT*, p. 10). He joins a boxing club but never feels comfortable with the 'übertriebene[n], demonstrative[n] Brüderlichkeit' (*WT*, p. 16) of his fellow fighters. In Nadir he finds a rare friend with whom he shares an interest in books. This too sets them apart:

> Hätten wir das vor den Augen der anderen gemacht, den Austausch von Büchern, dann hätten wir wieder das übliche Gespött gehört: Nun schaut euch diese Leseschwuchteln an! Lesen scheint noch unanständiger zu sein als nicht mit ihnen um die Wette zu saufen (*WT*, p. 17).

Laid's interest in photography also sets him apart. Photography functions in the novel as a recurring symbol of Laid's status as an outsider. He has latent

42 Gerry Brenner, *Performative Criticism: Experiments in Reader Response* (New York: State University of New York Press, 2004), p. 219.

ambitions as an artist and is scornful of his customers' demand for artificially blithe family photographs: 'Sie wollen keine Kunst von mir, sondern genau diese farbenfrohe grellgeschminkte Lüge, wie sie bereits die Eltern von ihrem glücklichsten Tag schießen ließen und goldgerahmt auf den Fernseher platzierten' (*WT*, p. 13). He is the prototypical artist-as-outsider, observing the masses from the outside, pained by the hypocrisy that he perceives. This compels him to keep his distance from that which he observes through the lens of his camera, perpetuating his status as outsider. His occupation as a photographer is an expression of his desire to remain distanced and passive, it is an 'Akt der Nichteinmischung' (*WT*, p. 161). There are echoes here of Susan Sontag's view of photography as 'essentially an act of non-intervention'.[43] Laid's admission that 'ein professioneller Fotograf, der vor die Wahl gestellt ist, eine Aufnahme zu machen oder sich einzumischen, selbstverständlich die Aufnahme vorzieht' (*WT*, p. 161) is either a direct reference to, or at the very least an unconscious confirmation of, Sontag's assertion that 'it has become [plausible], in situations where the photographer has the choice between a photograph and a life, to choose the photograph. The person who intervenes cannot record; the person who is recording cannot intervene'.[44] Laid's chosen profession therefore reflects his personality as a natural observer, always watching but not comfortable when forced to become actively involved. The call to avenge his father comes, therefore, as all too great a demand. To intervene and to become involved in such a drastic and violent manner is well outside his natural domain. When the moment comes to intervene in the politics of his family home it is understandable that he chooses to remain distant, favouring the emptiness of the desert landscape over the complex politics of the family home.

Laid's enthusiasm for photography develops as a substitute for going hunting with guns – an endeavour he seems to be constitutionally unsuited to. After the first unsuccessful hunt with his father he is given the Leica camera, which is presented as an alternative to a real weapon. Ibrahim, his father, says:

> Auch damit kann man auf die Jagd gehen. Doch frage Ali, den Drogisten, wie man das Ding handhabt. Er hat es mir verkauft und mir versprochen, auch noch die nötige Munition, das heißt die Filme dafür zu besorgen. Er wird dir zeigen, wie man sie einlegt und damit schießt. Und das ganz ohne Explosionen (*WT*, p. 61).

Laid's status as an outsider is emphasized in that a man who is unable or unwilling to handle weapons is not quite complete, at least not in the eyes

43 Susan Sontag, *On Photography* (London: Penguin, 1979), p. 11.
44 Sontag, *On Photography*, p. 12.

of his father, or of Algerian society. It is of great significance, in terms of the novel's intertextual status, that Roes chooses to illustrate his metaphor of the camera as weapon by using the hunt. Susan Sontag also uses and explores the use of the metaphor of the camera as a weapon or as weapon-ersatz and she, too, illustrates her point using the scenario of a hunt:

> One situation where people are switching from bullets to film is the photographic safari that is replacing the gun safari in East Africa. The hunters have Hasselblads instead of Winchesters, instead of looking through a telescopic sight to aim a rifle, they look through a viewfinder to frame a picture.[45]

The parallels between Roes and Sontag are clear: both recount how hunters now hunt with film where once they used bullets, but whereas Sontag reasons that this change is due to the endangered status of the animals, in Roes's novel, it is simply due to Laid's inability to use a weapon. By resorting to the camera as a more peaceful alternative to the gun, he foreshadows his later refusal to turn to violence when he returns to Timimoun.

Although Ibrahim looks upon the camera as a poor substitute for a real gun, Laid regains a certain sense of power through his photography. It is a solution to perceived weakness without having to resort to physical violence. He takes pictures of family members in compromising situations, gaining power through observing voyeuristically (*WT*, p. 36). He also comes to the rescue of an assault victim by scaring away the attacker with the flash of his camera (*WT*, p. 34). The power that the camera bestows upon the photographer does not even necessitate him becoming involved. Photography is 'a defense against anxiety, and a tool of power'[46] even as non-intervention is maintained. Milan Kundera, in his novel *The Unbearable Lightness of Being* (1984), makes comparable use of the metaphor. The motif appears in the novel twice in two contexts in close succession. It is used, first, when Tereza and Sabina, Tomas's wife and his lover, are taking nude photos of each other: 'Tereza took off her clothes. There she stood before Sabina naked and disarmed. Literally *disarmed*: deprived of the apparatus she had been using to cover her face and aim at Sabina like a weapon.'[47] The motif reappears in the context of Tereza's work photographing the Russian soldiers during the Prague Spring of 1968. The soldiers 'had been carefully briefed about how to behave if someone fired at them or threw stones, but they had received no directives about what to do when someone aimed a lens.'[48] This second example is of particular relevance

45 Sontag, *On Photography*, p. 15.

46 Sontag, *On Photography*, p. 8.

47 Milan Kundera, *The Unbearable Lightness of Being*, trans. by Michael Henry Heim (London: Faber & Faber, 1999), pp. 64–65.

48 Kundera, *The Unbearable Lightness of Being*, p. 65.

here. The motif is ideally suited to represent resistance by a weak or oppressed individual or group (Laid, the Czechs) – be that weakness physical or political. Using the camera is a form of defence against a stronger foe when drawing real weapons is impossible or not desired. The moral high ground is retained and the subversive nature of the resistance baffles the oppressor and leaves him vulnerable on an intellectual or ethical level.

Of the four novels focused upon in this study, *Weg nach Timimoun* is unique for a number of reasons. It features a non-German narrator, whose voice is supplemented by a third-person perspective. The novel is also different in that it features no marked quotations. The relation between the novel and its intertexts is rather a hypertextual one, based largely on thematic concerns. This chapter has revealed how the main themes of *Weg nach Timimoun* – familial obligation, revenge, gender roles – are all illuminated by the novel's intertexts. The *Oresteia* functions as the most important of these but it is clear that Roes deviates from this model in fundamental ways. In *Haut des Südens* and *Geschichte der Freundschaft* (as the following chapter will show), some of the intertexts (Melville, Foucault) represent a way of life towards which to aspire. In contrast, the main intertext of *Weg nach Timimoun* represents calamitous patterns of violence and vengeance. The main literary model, although still relevant and applicable to the contemporary situation, is deviated from and revealed to be an unhelpful pattern for a peaceful and intelligent existence.

CHAPTER 4

International Borders and Interpersonal Bonds in *Geschichte der Freundschaft*

In *Geschichte der Freundschaft* (2010) Michael Roes examines once more the theme of intercultural encounters in a novel that tells the story of a friendship between Matthias Kahn, a German pathologist, and Yanis Choukri, a student from the predominantly Berber-speaking mountainous Kabylia region of Algeria. The novel also recounts the cultural history of male-male friendship by referring to literary, philosophical and historical works in chapters that are separate from the main narrative. The interplay between these two strands reinforces the contrast between the difficulties in the relationship between the novel's two main characters and a utopian ideal of friendship as described in works such as Michel de Montaigne's essay 'De l'Amitié' ['On Friendship'] (1580), Jacques Derrida's *Politiques de l'amitié* [*Politics of Friendship*],[1] and in interviews by Michel Foucault.[2] Roes is, on the one hand, telling the *story* of a friendship, the 'Geschichte *einer* Freundschaft'. On the other hand, by including sections that reflect on specific representations of friendship in culture, Roes widens the scope of his novel, and in so doing presents a 'Geschichte *der* Freundschaft', a *history* of male-male friendship in a much broader sense.

Matthias Kahn is travelling in Algeria in the summer of 1998, a time of political unrest not only due to the sporadic atrocities of the continuing Algerian Civil War (1991–2002), but also because of the demonstrations by the Kabyle people who are calling on Algeria's government to recognize Tamazight, a Berber language, as an official language. Matthias settles in Tichy for the summer, a small seaside town in the province of Bejaia, 250 kilometres east of Algiers. He is there with his sketchbook to seek artistic inspiration. Far

1 Jacques Derrida, *Politiques de l'amitié* (Paris: Galilée, 1994); English version: *The Politics of Friendship*, trans. by George Collins (London: Verso, 1997).

2 Cf. Michel Foucault, 'Sexual Choice, Sexual Act: Foucault and Homosexuality', from an interview conducted and translated by James O'Higgins, in *Michel Foucault: Politics, Philosophy, Culture: Interviews and Other Writings 1977–1984*, ed. by Lawrence D. Kritzman (New York; London: Routledge, 1988), pp. 286–303; Michel Foucault, 'Sex, Power, and the Politics of Identity', in *Ethics: Subjectivity and Truth*, ed. by Paul Rabinow (New York: New Press, 1998), pp. 163–73.

from treading in the footsteps of other Western artists who have ventured to the Maghreb[3] before him (Eugène Delacroix's Orientalist paintings come to mind),[4] Matthias's subject matter is more mundane: he paints animal corpses (*GF*, p. 8), fishermen's nets (*GF*, p. 17) and 'abstraktes Zeug' (*GF*, p. 310). During his 'kurze[n] Sommer in Tichy' (*GF*, p. 9) the German holidaymaker is drawn towards Yanis, a student of English at Bejaia University. After an intense but vacillating friendship that lasts the whole summer, Matthias is on his way home to Germany when he learns that Yanis is in trouble after an Algerian policeman is seriously wounded during a violent demonstration. Matthias decides to look for Yanis, who is now a fugitive, and eventually finds him severely injured and in a weakened state, in hiding under the guardianship of a Touareg desert tribe.

Matthias pays for the pair to be smuggled across the border into Mali, a five-day journey across the Sahara desert, before they go onward to Germany, where they enter into a civil partnership and live together. Matthias and Yanis's arrival in Berlin is not the end of their troubles. It soon becomes apparent that the trauma Yanis experienced in Algeria, and the cultural differences of the West, hinder his attempts to settle down to a life in the German capital. He had envisioned the city as a 'Stadt des Glücks' (*GF*, p. 147), where he could enjoy freedom and luxury unheard of in Algeria,[5] but in reality he is a misfit and an outsider, he gets lost repeatedly and never adapts to the pace of city life. Differing cultural concepts lead to severe difficulties in the relationship, with Yanis portrayed as being blind to European cultural norms. This is surprising since Yanis had been described by Matthias as a particularly able interpreter and mediator between cultures when they were in Algeria. However, the maturity that Matthias had previously identified in Yanis has faded, leaving a stubborn, recalcitrant, helpless man paralysed by life in the West. As the age difference between the two men becomes more apparent, the relationship evolves to resemble that of a father and son. However, whereas in Algerian society the father is respected to the point of fear, in Berlin Yanis's

3 The Maghreb comprises five countries on the Mediterranean coast of Africa which have been Arabized since the middle of the sixth century: Morocco, Algeria, Tunisia, Libya and Mauritania. It also includes Western Sahara, which remains disputed territory. The Arabic word *maghreb* means 'the land where the sun sets', referring to the area's westerly position from the perspective of the rest of the Arab countries.

4 Cf. Roger Benjamin, ed., *Orientalism: Delacroix to Klee* (Sydney: Art Gallery of New South Wales, 2001), pp. 6–11.

5 There exist parallels between Roes's novel and some recent works by migrant Francophone authors in that they challenge 'both stereotypes of immigrants and stereotypes of France [or Germany in Roes's case], more specifically myths of Paris [or Berlin], as paradise' (*New Approaches to Twentieth-Century Travel Literature in French*, ed. by Forsdick, Basu and Shilton), p. 112.

attitude towards Matthias oscillates between contempt and indifference. Yanis's immaturity is further emphasized when Natascha, a Ukrainian woman with whom he has an affair, also likens him to a child (*GF*, p. 184). Matthias and Natascha come together without Yanis's knowledge to form a surrogate parental unit that functions to make decisions on behalf of the young Algerian, and to discuss important issues affecting the peculiar love triangle. Later in the novel, faced with Yanis's physical deterioration, Matthias describes himself as his partner's nurse: 'Liege ich neben ihm im Bett, dann wie neben einem alten, schwerkranken Mann, mehr Nachtschwester als Liebhaber' (*GF*, p. 224). The two characters' roles have been reversed with regard to seniority: Yanis is now debilitated, helpless and reliant on Matthias's care. He is at the same time a little child unable to fend for himself, and an old man made immobile by the ailments of advancing age.

In comparison with the problems posed by migration and by cultural differences, Yanis's ambiguous sexuality poses far fewer problems in the relationship than might have been expected. Matthias accepts this ambiguity, noting: '[Du v]ersteckst deine Liebe zu Frauen, maskierst deine Heterosexualität, als sei sie ein verbotenes Begehren' (*GF*, p. 167). While Matthias identifies himself as gay and expresses his love for Yanis (*GF*, p. 296), Yanis seems to identify himself largely as heterosexual but open to sexual relations with men. As was indicated in the discussion of the relationship between Daniel and the narrator of *Haut des Südens*, it is of particular significance that the friend is of a different cultural background, since this cultural 'gap' affords a space in which new modes of relating can be negotiated. In addition, the distinction that is perceived in the West between 'heterosexuals' and 'homosexuals' is not made as readily in the Arab world. This is an important distinction in Roes's concept of male-male friendships, which includes physical intimacy as well as emotional affinity. Brian Whitaker writes that:

> Arabs who engage in same-sex activities do not necessarily regard themselves as gay, lesbian, bisexual etc. Some do, but many (probably the vast majority) do not. This is partly because the boundaries of sexuality are less clearly defined than in the West but also because Arab society is more concerned with sexual acts than sexual orientations or identities.[6]

Joseph A. Massad also suggests that those in the Arab world who identify themselves as 'gay' in the (imported) Western sense are a small minority, usually belonging to the richer classes. Their self-identification is 'part of the package of the adoption of everything Western by the classes to which

6 Whitaker, *Unspeakable Love*, p. 10.

they belong'.[7] In contrast, the majority of men 'who engage in same-sex relations [...] do not identify as "gay" nor express a need for gay politics'.[8] Yanis's sexual identity appears to accord to this more flexible view: 'Mit einem Jungen zusammenzusein ist ja nichts Schlechtes. Doch mit einem Mädchen zusammenzusein bedeutet mir mehr' (*GF*, p. 43). In Berlin, however, he becomes disillusioned with his experiment in homosexuality, confiding in his diary: '*Mit einem Mann zusammenzuleben ist kein Weg. Es ist vielleicht ein Zwischenhalt, aber selbst darüber kann ich mit niemandem reden*' (*GF*, p. 262).

Yanis's relationship with Natascha leads to a pregnancy, but the baby is raised, according to the mother's wishes, by the two men, who together with the baby thus form yet another family unit. On hearing news that the Algerian government has declared an amnesty for all political fugitives Yanis travels there together with his young son, thus taking him away from both his biological mother and his second father. A 'broad amnesty for past abuses that covered members of state security forces and armed groups'[9] was declared by Abdelaziz Bouteflika, the Algerian president, on 1 November 2005, and it is this news that prompts Yanis's return to his homeland. In Algeria, Yanis mysteriously dies during an evening swim in the sea with Slimane, his older brother. The reader is led to suspect that Slimane has drowned his brother according to their father's commands in what would have constituted an honour killing, in order to put an end to the perceived shame brought upon the family by Yanis's lifestyle in Berlin. Milan, the boy, is held by Yanis's family and is denied contact with Matthias, even when the latter travels to Algeria once more. With the aid of Zubaida, a strong, emancipated young woman whom Matthias befriends during a bus journey, and Nadira, Yanis's sister, Matthias successfully implements a daring rescue mission to wrench Milan away from Yanis's family and take him back to Berlin. The close of the novel shows Matthias and Milan at the airport in Algiers anxiously awaiting their return flight to Germany, a repetition of the novel's opening passage. The narration of the plot is therefore a flashback from the present tense parenthesis of the airport scene,[10] with the reader left unsure at the end whether Matthias and Milan return to Germany safely.

7 Joseph A. Massad, *Desiring Arabs* (Chicago: University of Chicago Press, 2007), p. 173.

8 Massad, *Desiring Arabs*, p. 173.

9 Martin Evans and John Phillips, *Algeria: Anger of the Dispossessed* (New Haven and London: Yale University Press, 2007), p. 290.

10 Here Roes, a film-maker as well as an author, borrows a well-established film technique for use in his novel. Volker Schlöndorff uses a similar framing technique in *The Voyager* (1991), a film adaptation of Max Frisch's *Homo Faber* (1957). The film begins and ends in Athens Airport, with the story told in one long flashback. Although Frisch's novel opens in an airport (La Guardia, New York) and features numerous movements backwards and forwards in time, it does not employ such a framing technique.

Life in Kabylia

Recent Algerian and Kabyle political history function as important background elements to Roes's novel. The Bejaia district of Algeria which Matthias Kahn visits is part of the Kabylia region. Algeria's Kabyle population totals 8.7 million, around two million of whom live in Algiers. A further two million live in France. The Kabyles are Berbers, the indigenous people of North Africa, and are 'the most sizeable, politically best organized and most sophisticated of the various Berber groups'.[11] Although they played an active and important part in the War of Independence against the French (1954–62), their language and culture were denied official recognition in the new independent Algerian state as part of the policy of creating a unified Algerian identity. In 1980 tensions between the Kabyles and the Algerian government escalated, leading to the unrest of the 'Tizi Ouzou Spring', named after the main city in the region, or the 'Berber Spring', the 'first serious outbreak of Berberist frustration in independent Algeria'.[12] The violence erupted when the Kabyle activist and intellectual Mouloud Mammeri was banned from delivering a lecture at the university in Tizi Ouzou. Thirty people were killed and a further two hundred were injured in the resulting violence. Although the uprising resulted in little change in terms of official government policy, it was 'an important landmark in the development of the Berberist movement in Algeria [...] [and] prepared the ground for the outbreak of anti-government sentiment' in later riots.[13]

Towards the beginning of *Geschichte der Freundschaft* reference is made to one of the later riots. Although not explicitly stated, the novel's opening is set in the summer of 1998, a date that can be identified from an outburst by Yanis's father: 'Hast du gehört? Sie haben unseren Sänger ermordet!' (*GF*, p. 18). The reference is to the murder of the popular Kabyle singer and prominent campaigner for the Berberist cause, Lounès Matoub, on 25 June 1998. Matoub's music was 'militant and uncompromising' in 'championing the linguistic and cultural rights of the Kabyles';[14] and his death has variously been attributed to Algerian authorities and to Islamic extremists without ever being satisfactorily explained. The murder triggered weeks of rioting and it is one of these demonstrations that Yanis is urged by his father to join. Yanis gladly obeys his father's instruction and joins his comrades on the streets, 'um dort zu demonstrieren und mich mit den Polizisten zu prügeln' (*GF*, p. 18). He is eager to portray the protests as 'ein lustiges Räuber-und-Gendarm-Spiel' (*GF*, p. 18) and does not dwell on the number of dead and injured. It is an incident

11 Stone, *The Agony of Algeria*, p. 198.

12 Stone, *The Agony of Algeria*, p. 205.

13 Stone, *The Agony of Algeria*, pp. 207–08.

14 Evans and Phillips, *Algeria*, p. 248.

during a violent demonstration later that summer that leads to his fugitive escape from Algeria to Berlin.

Violence erupted in Kabylia once more in the spring of 2001,[15] after the eighteen-year-old Massinissa Guermah died in police custody. Whereas the police had had orders not to shoot during the demonstrations following Matoub's death, during the 'Black Spring' of 2001 they made frequent use of their weapons, even shooting one fleeing protester in the back. The protesters responded with 'reckless indifference to the shoot-to-kill policy, shouting, "You cannot kill us, we are already dead"'.[16] In *Geschichte der Freundschaft*, soon after Matthias's arrival in Kabylia in 1998, the demonstrators are said to shout 'Schießt doch! Wir sind längst tot!' (*GF*, p. 11), clearly foreshadowing the cries of the real demonstrators in 2001. The novel's use of the slogan as a poignant and symbolic expression of frustration and resentment illustrates how Roes's fiction is embedded in recent Algerian history. Its use conveys the 'absence of hope'[17] which was at the root of the violence in 1998 and 2001, and the state of helplessness which continues to afflict many young Arab and Kabyle Algerians today.

Roes shows unemployment, dissatisfaction and boredom to be a part of quotidian reality for many Algerian youths. It is suggested in the novel that one of the root causes of this hopeless situation is the unquestionable power of patriarchal structures in Algerian society, with young men living in their fathers' shadow, and young women constantly supervised and controlled. Yanis explains: 'Der Respekt vor dem Vater ist ein so wesentlicher Teil unserer Tradition, dass du ihm nicht entkommen kannst' (*GF*, p. 44). Achmed Choukri abuses his position of power as the head of the family; domestic violence is a spectre that haunts the household (*GF*, p. 273), preventing close bonds from being formed between the generations. For Yanis this leads to a greater recognition of the value of friendships. He explains: '[D]ie einzige Zuneigung, die uns zum Überleben bleibt, ist die Zuneigung unserer Freunde' (*GF*, p. 45). The Café de la Jeunesse and the drinks booth on the beach serve as a 'vorübergehendes Exil für die der Aufsicht und den Verpflichtungen des Elternhauses Entkommenen' (*GF*, p. 43), places where affection and friendship can be experienced and enjoyed. This is an escape that is, however, denied to their female counterparts.

Matthias sympathizes with the young Algerians, exclaiming during his second visit to Algeria:

15 Roes's first journey to Algeria was during the summer of 2001, when he spent two months in Tichy.

16 Evans and Phillips, *Algeria*, p. 277.

17 Evans and Phillips, *Algeria*, p. 277.

> [S]chau dir die jungen Männer an, ihre Ohnmacht, ihre Verwahrlosung, ihre Wut! Von den Vätern abhängig, bis sie selbst Väter sind, nein, bis der Vater stirbt, ohne Arbeit, ohne Frauen, ohne Einkommen, nur Gott am Anfang jeden Satzes und einen Joint am Ende jedes leeren Tages, als ob sie allein ihr Dasein noch erträglich machen könnten (*GF*, p. 257).

Matthias's passion and anger regarding the situation of Algeria's youth, fuelled by grief over Yanis's suspected murder, is expressed through the use of classic rhetorical devices such as three-part lists, used twice in the short quotation above. Listing three nouns, each preceded by the same possessive pronoun 'ihr', naturally intensifies the sentence, creating a sense of crescendo. The technique is swiftly repeated with another three nouns, now preceded by the preposition 'ohne', emphasizing the powerlessness and impotence of the young Algerians. Another rhetorical device is used here, that of contrasting opposites. Young Algerian men are said to invoke God's name at the beginning of each sentence, and to smoke a joint at the end of each day. Not only do the ideas 'Anfang' and 'Ende' contrast, giving the sentence a satisfying antithesis, but the two methods used by Algerian youths to make their existence bearable, 'Gott' and 'Joint', are placed in an ironic juxtaposition that suggests that neither will ultimately provide a solution to their predicament. The repetition of various forms of the word 'Vater' underlines the status accorded to the patriarchal head of the family and Matthias's mid-sentence correction ('nein, bis der Vater stirbt') is an anticlimactic slump, a linguistic reflection of the young men's stagnating lives. Despite the use of such rhetorical devices, not dissimilar to those used widely by political speech-writers to persuade and elicit support, Zubaida is not influenced by Matthias's eloquent tirade. She counters with a rhetorically less sophisticated but nevertheless convincing reply that gives the feminist side of the story: 'Ich glaube nicht, dass ich sie [die jungen Männer] bedauere, antwortet Zubaida. Jahrhunderte lang hatten sie die Macht. Und du siehst ja selbst, was sie damit angestellt haben' (*GF*, p. 257).

Zubaida's succinct response foregrounds gender themes and raises the matter of the repression of women. The novel highlights the complex issues surrounding the position of women in Algerian society, with differences in attitudes between generations becoming apparent. Yanis's mother suffers at the hand of her husband, in some instances physically. A woman's place, traditionally, is in the home or the courtyard: 'Kabylenfrauen gehen selten und so gut wie nie allein aus dem Haus' (*GF*, p. 268). The dictates of honour preclude Yanis's mother from bathing in the sea, leaving her to gaze 'Richtung Meer, von dem sie nur einen schmalen Spalt zwischen den eng aneinandergebauten Häusern auf der gegenüberliegenden Seite der ungepflasterten Straße sehen kann' (*GF*, pp. 268–69). She has reluctantly accepted her position and does not even dare to challenge her husband after being 'krankenhausreif geprügelt'

(*GF*, p. 65). The novel does not, however, make generalizations about Algerian or Kabyle women and some of the women of the younger generation are marked as headstrong and bold. Yanis's sister, Nadira, lives, like her mother, under the restrictions of the Choukri household, 'eine Sklavin im eigenen Elternhaus' (*GF*, p. 259). Her confinement is the result of disobedience. After defying her family's wish that she marry her cousin she was forced to abandon her degree in Philosophy and now lives at home under close scrutiny. However, her rebellious spirit is not quashed and she plays a central part in Matthias's plan to take Milan away from his Kabyle grandparents, despite the possible consequences she might face.

Zubaida is the most obvious example of an independent, determined woman. The 'junge, kettenrauchende Frau' (*GF*, p. 262) studies languages and speaks German fluently. She has an open and friendly nature, and an intuitive and intelligent understanding of other people (*GF*, p. 256). She makes Matthias's acquaintance after he returns to Algeria after Yanis's death, and she soon becomes involved with his problem, agreeing to help find Milan. When visiting Matthias in his hotel room she is not concerned with appearances, despite the fact that the 'merkwürdiges Verhältnis' (*GF*, p. 264) could be misinterpreted as prostitution. She is portrayed as a modern woman, open to cosmopolitan influences. Zubaida is, in some ways, reminiscent of the female Deputy Minister in the Yemeni government, Raufa Rachman asch-Schu'aib, whom the narrator of *Leeres Viertel* meets in Sana'a. Zubaida speaks 'akzentfreie[s] Deutsch' (*GF*, p. 255), while the Deputy Minister speaks 'perfekte[s] Oxford-englisch' (*LV*, p. 453). The Deputy Minister 'braucht keinen männlichen beschützer. Sie strahlt [...] souveränität aus' (*LV*, p. 453); and the anthropologist remarks: 'Hier sehe ich zum ersten mal eine sich unterordnende, ergebene haltung von männern – einer frau gegenüber' (*LV*, p. 453). Zubaida is younger and does not enjoy a similar position of authority, but she has a comparable audacity and confidence, suggesting that Roes is keen to counter stereotypical images of oppressed, veiled Arab/Berber women with a differentiated representation that reflects the heterogeneity of the lives of women in the Middle East.

As if to emphasize the point that women do not need men's protection there is a passage in *Geschichte der Freundschaft* in which Matthias observes a student demonstration outside his hotel. The women of the group 'bilden ein weibliches Schild zwischen den behelmten Männern mit den Hartgummiknüppeln und ihren unrasierten Kommilitonen' (*GF*, p. 265). They take up this position presumably in the belief that the police will exercise more restraint against them than they would against the men. By exploiting their femininity they are able to protect their male colleagues and serve as mediators between the two male factions. The masculinity of both the police

('Hartgummiknüppeln') and the male students ('unrasiert') is emphasized. The police helmets and batons are contrasted in particular with the softness of the women's 'knöchellangen Kleidern und Kopftüchern' (*GF*, p. 265). The strength of the women lies, however, precisely in that softness, which distinguishes them from their masculine opposition. The 'weibliches Schild' formed by holding hands possesses a moral authority and intelligence that the masculine forces, characterized by sheer power, do not have. However, while Roes reverses the stereotypical picture of Arab women by attributing to them an element of agency and emancipation, he also resorts to using imagery that reinforces the traditional binaries: men are hard, women are soft. The deconstruction of the cliché thus remains only partially successful. On the whole, however, Roes avoids facile stereotypes of '"Oriental woman"'[18] by portraying a spectrum of female characters in both *Leeres Viertel* and *Geschichte der Freundschaft*.

Migrant Characters in German Literature

The transposition of the cross-cultural encounter between a white European and an Algerian to within Germany's national borders is a recent development in Roes's *oeuvre*. His earlier novels were set largely outside Germany. It is also unusual for a German-born author to write about the life of immigrants in Germany, a task that has largely been left to writers with a non-German background.[19] As Monika Albrecht notes, it was the novelist and veteran 68er Peter Schneider who was the first to describe this division of roles with outspoken criticism. In an article published in *Die Zeit* in 2006, he writes: 'Die Migranten-Schriftsteller sind für das Ausländerthema zuständig – so wie früher die DDR-Autoren für die deutsche Teilung zuständig waren. Die Schriftsteller deutscher Herkunft schreiben über ein Deutschland, in dem Nichtdeutsche so gut wie gar nicht vorkommen'.[20] Paul Michael Lützeler, in a review of Barbara Frischmuth's novel *Die Schrift des Freundes* (1998), also comments on this situation, describing how those well-travelled German writers, '[die] mit postkolonialem Blick die spannungsreiche Beziehung zwischen unterschiedlichen Zivilisationen geschildert [haben]', have largely failed to bring 'die kulturelle und politische Gemengelage zur Sprache, die sich

18 Negar Mottahedeh, 'Images of Women: Middle East', in *Routledge International Encyclopedia of Women: Global Women's Issues and Knowledge*, III, *Identity Politics – Publishing*, ed. by Cheris Kramarae and Dale Spender (London: Routledge, 2001), pp. 1118–20 (p. 1119).

19 Monika Albrecht, 'Selim's Sisters: Muslim Women in Novels by Uwe Timm and Hermann Schulz', *German Life and Letters*, 63 (2010), 20–36 (pp. 20–22).

20 Peter Schneider, 'Selim blieb ein Einzelkind', *Die Zeit*, 19 (2006), www.zeit.de/2006/19/Selim_blieb_ein_Einzelkind [accessed 29 November 2010].

aus der Präsenz türkischer Minderheiten in deutschen Großstädten ergeben hat'.[21] Schneider cites only two exceptions in his article: Sten Nadolny's *Selim oder die Gabe der Rede* (1990) and the Frischmuth novel mentioned above, two works which feature migrant protagonists. Schneider's article refers to works in which immigrants play a central role. The list can, of course, be extended considerably when literary works featuring migrant workers only as peripheral characters are taken into account. Heinrich Böll's novel *Gruppenbild mit Dame* (1971) was the first work of German literature to feature a Turkish guest worker – Mehmet, Leni Pfeiffer's lover.[22] Siegfried Lenz's short story 'Wie bei Gogol' concerns a traffic accident in which a Turkish *Gastarbeiter*, Herr Üzkök, is hit by the first-person narrator's car.[23] Botho Strauß's play *Groß und Klein* (1978), which features a character known simply as Der Türke, was the first German-language play to require the services of a Turkish-born actor. There have also been a number of works of reportage in which German writers attempt to understand and represent the experience of so-called guest workers and their families.[24] Günter Wallraff's *Ganz unten* (1985) is the most famous work in this category, although Wallraff's project, in which he disguised himself as a Turk and entered the world of the guest-worker, has been criticized for not 'really [being] about Turks at all, but rather about creating a vehicle in which Wallraff may present his own views of the Federal Republic'.[25] Two other works of reportage from this period are Max von der Grün's *Leben im gelobten Land: Ausländer in Deutschland* (1975) and Paul Geiersbach's *Bruder, muss zusammen Zwiebel und Wasser essen!* (1982). While Teraoka criticizes the former for perpetuating stereotypes about immigrant workers, she praises the latter for allowing 'the Other's own voice [to speak] to us directly in its own idiom [...] . They speak, we learn to listen'.[26] In post-Reunification literature, one can point to Günter Grass's *Unkenrufe* (1992), in which Grass 'lets the German language be hybridized while showing how it sounds when spoken by emigrants and immigrants'.[27] Hermann Schulz's

21 Paul Michael Lützeler, 'Ein Derwisch verschwindet', *Die Zeit*, 36 (1998), www.zeit.de/1998/36/Ein_Derwisch_verschwindet [accessed 29 November 2010].

22 Cf. Rita Chin, *The Guest Worker Question in Postwar Germany* (Cambridge: Cambridge University Press, 2007), p. 62.

23 This was written in 1973 and published in *Einstein überquert die Elbe bei Hamburg* (Hamburg: Hoffmann & Campe, 1975).

24 Cf. Arlene Akiko Teraoka, 'Talking "Turk": On Narrative Strategies and Cultural Stereotypes', *New German Critique*, 46 (1989), 104–28 (Special Issue on Minorities in German Literature).

25 Teraoka, 'Talking "Turk"', p. 117.

26 Teraoka, 'Talking "Turk"', p. 127.

27 Marja-Leena Hakkarainen, 'German Home and Hybridity: Reclaiming New Cultural Identities in Selected German Migrant Narratives from the 1990s', in *Cultural Identity in Transition: Contemporary Conditions, Practices and Politics of a Global Phenomenon*, ed. by

Iskender (1999) is also important as one of the few novels that feature central characters of non-German ethnicity. Uwe Timm's *Rot* (2001) is also significant in that it features the character Nilgün, a 'well-integrated social climber, one of those of the second generation of former Turkish-German guest-workers who have successfully made their way into German society'.[28]

Despite the fact that this list of works by German and Austrian writers featuring migrant characters can be extended far beyond that compiled by Schneider, its brevity is still striking. What is more significant is the fact that in many of these works migrant characters are marginal figures, giving the impression that German authors have a conception of the immigrant as an ambiguous, imperceptible figure on the periphery of society. As B. Venkat Mani notes:

> While the guest worker as a literary character claims centrality in a body of literature that came to be known as *Gastarbeiterliteratur*, marginality through sporadic visibility and limited mobilizing power over the narrative mark his presence in works by authors of German ethnic heritage.[29]

Schneider provides a plausible reason as to why this is so when he suggests that writers are often reluctant to write about issues of which they have no direct experience. More interesting is his idea that '[z]wischen der physischen Ankunft und der formalen Einbürgerung einer Migrantengruppe und ihrer Einbürgerung in die Wahrnehmung und Fantasie der Einheimischen [...] eine unvorstellbar lange Zeit vergehen [kann]'.[30] The presence of migrants from the Mediterranean countries has, of course, long been an issue of debate in the German media, and there are numerous popular TV dramas and films that have featured immigrants. Schneider cites Rainer Werner Fassbinder's *Angst essen Seele auf* (1974) as a pioneering work in this respect, although it has been claimed elsewhere that the film, along with Günter Wallraff's *Ganz unten*, helped establish the stereotypical 'Ali' figure in the German mindset: 'the naïve migrant worker on the fringes of German society with limited powers of communication and few opportunities to control his own fate: an object of others' gazes, discourses and action'.[31] Schneider argues that the development of a character in a novel demands 'mehr Vertrautheit und psychische Arbeit als

Jari Kupiainen, Erkki Sevänen and John A. Stotesbury (New Delhi: Atlantic, 2004), pp. 191–204 (p. 194).

28 Albrecht, 'Selim's Sisters', p. 24.

29 B. Venkat Mani, *Cosmopolitical Claims: Turkish-German Literatures from Nadolny to Pamuk* (Iowa City: University of Iowa Press, 2007), pp. 50–51.

30 Schneider, 'Selim blieb ein Einzelkind'.

31 Tom Cheesman, *Novels of Turkish German Settlement: Cosmopolite Fictions* (Rochester: Camden House, 2007), p. 146.

die eines Serienhelden oder einer Solidaritätserklärung' and that this explains why German-born authors have largely been reluctant to include immigrants as central characters in their works.

In contrast, there are a growing number of fictional works by German writers of non-German origins that offer a varied representation of minorities. Writers such as Sherko Fatah, Emine Sevgi Özdamar, Rafik Schami and Zafer Şenocak (examples from whose work are discussed below) have found a place for themselves in contemporary German literature. Their representations of life in Germany for minority groups engage with themes such as 'migration, integration, multiculturalism, and racism'.[32] The great challenge that remains for minority writers is the problem of compartmentalization: 'even as [the industry] celebrates transformations and progress within German culture, those transformations are accomplished by reasserting notions of absolute difference and locking writers into the role of cultural representatives of ethnic and national minority communities'.[33]

Roes has long been writing with a 'postkoloniale[n] Blick'[34] regarding German characters venturing abroad and interacting with people of other cultures. However, he has recently addressed the void in contemporary post-colonial German literature that Schneider and Lützeler identify by engaging with the issue of how foreign immigrants live their lives in Germany, and how German characters interact with foreign people in their own backyard. Roes's novel *Ich weiß nicht mehr die Nacht* (2008) is a retelling of the Phaedra myth set in modern Germany, the protagonists being a Greek immigrant family living in a small town in the Lower Rhine region. The first section of his next novel, *Die Fünf Farben Schwarz* (2009), features a young Chinese man who had come to Germany to study; and his novel *Die Laute* (2012) features a Yemeni man who migrates to Poland. The fact that Roes has included immigrant characters in four recent novels is an indication that he is attempting to break the silence that has, according to one critic, 'become the very element of communication'[35] between Germans and ethnic minorities living in Germany.

'Die Immigration macht krank': Yanis in Berlin

Yanis leaves Algeria as a fugitive and his status as he arrives in Berlin is ambiguous. Although his departure from Algeria was due to fear of criminal prosecution and political persecution he does not hold the status of an asylum

32 Cheesman, *Novels of Turkish German Settlement*, p. 56.

33 Cheesman, *Novels of Turkish German Settlement*, p. 35.

34 Lützeler, *Postmoderne und postkoloniale deutschsprachige Literatur*, p. 102.

35 Azade Seyhan, 'Introduction', *New German Critique*, 46 (1989), 3–9 (p. 3).

seeker in Germany. Neither is he an economic migrant in the traditional sense. His history and ambitions are very different from those of the foreign guest-workers who arrived in West Germany from the 1950s onwards. A cynical view of Yanis's relationship with Matthias could interpret it as an alternative kind of economic migration – trading on the back of the relationship for a German visa. In reality Yanis's reasons for emigration range from the political to the legal, from economic to personal. Yanis, like all immigrants, is also simultaneously an emigrant and the challenge facing him is twofold. He must attempt to overcome the pain of leaving home while dealing with the difficulties of settling abroad. The Berlin section of *Geschichte der Freundschaft* focuses on Yanis's attempt to settle in Germany and his efforts to overcome feelings of alienation in the face of his new environment. It becomes clear that much of Yanis's psychic energy is directed towards home. He is preoccupied with the trauma he experienced there and is struggling to process feelings of yearning, homesickness and loss. His focus is divided between the processes of immigration and emigration: he suffers what Abdelmalek Sayad calls a 'double absence', in which he 'remains psychically both in the former home and the new, host country, or in both the past and the present'.[36]

Zafer Şenocak, whose volume of essays *Zungenentfernung* (2001) will be discussed later, states in one of his essays that it is impossible to leave a city in which one has lived for a considerable length of time: 'Orte, die man vergessen will, werden zu Alpträumen. Orte, die man unfreiwillig verlassen hat, zu magnetischen Anziehungspunkten'.[37] In Yanis's case Tichy simultaneously represents both a nightmarish past from which he is glad to have escaped and a home to which he longs to return. In contrast to this negative interpretation of migration as a 'double absence', Emine Sevgi Özdamar sees considerable creative potential in such a situation. She argues that:

> In order to be creative [...] you needed to leave your native country, indeed to betray it, and then you could be in two places simultaneously. That's how it really is, in my experience, when you're living in a foreign country. Whether you want to or not, you find yourself in two places at once. [...] the whole thing runs like a simultaneous film in which images and yearnings merge without any gaps. When the two come together in this way, it makes for a beautiful encounter.[38]

36 Madelaine Hron, *Translating Pain: Immigrant Suffering in Literature and Culture* (Toronto: University of Toronto Press, 2009), p. 26.

37 Zafer Şenocak, *Zungenentfernung: Bericht aus der Quarantänestation* (Munich: Babel, 2001), p. 23.

38 David Horrocks and Eva Kolinsky, 'Living and Writing in Germany: Emine Sevgi Özdamar in Conversation with David Horrocks and Eva Kolinsky', in *Turkish Culture in German Society Today*, ed. by David Horrocks and Eva Kolinsky (Oxford: Berghahn, 1996), pp. 45–54

Özdamar's real-life experience is a world away from that of the suffering immigrant in Roes's novel. For her the new perspective gained through the experience of immigration outweighs the loss and she utilizes this as an impetus for her creative literary work.

Matthias is aware of the difficulties that Yanis faces in this liminal space between his homeland and the new, alienating culture. Observing the breakdown in Yanis's behaviour and wellbeing, Matthias identifies displacement and homesickness as the causes and comments: '[D]ie Immigration macht krank. [...] Migration macht nicht nur krank. Migration ist die Krankheit' (*GF*, pp. 177–78). Yanis atrophies and seems powerless to reverse the decline. His affliction manifests itself as both a depression and a physical disease as his mind and body seem incapable of withstanding the loss of his home culture and the adaptation to a Western lifestyle. He often complains of vague illnesses; and a fungal infection appears in the corners of his mouth and in his armpits, signifying stagnation, laziness and an inability to change. The fungus 'dringt tief in die unteren Hautschichten, breitet sich rasch aus' (*GF*, p. 155), suggesting that it becomes a part of him, growing deeper, spreading wider, indicating his failure to settle down to life in Germany and foreshadowing his death in Algeria. Yanis also neglects issues of hygiene, eats sloppily, and leaves a trail of blood, skin and hair when he shaves. The only matter in which he continues to take pride is his hair, which he continues to style as he always did.

According to psychologists working with immigrants, the difficulties associated with adapting to a foreign country are intensified 'je unfreiwilliger die Migration stattfindet und damit ohne Vorbereitungen erfolgt'.[39] Yanis's sudden, forced departure from Algeria clearly exacerbates the difficulties he has in adapting to life in the West. His experience of travel is far removed from that Matthias enjoys. For Yanis, forced migration leads to a sense of rootlessness and displacement. He is not afforded time to grieve for the loss of his native culture, and as a result he reacts negatively towards the German way of life as represented more often than not by Matthias. Yanis obstinately rejects Matthias's advice and help, and contradicts him in infuriating ways: 'Reflexartig behauptet er das Gegenteil von dem, was ich gerade gesagt habe, auch wenn er damit seiner eigenen früheren Aussage widerspricht. [...] ein Widersprechen ohne nachzudenken' (*GF*, p. 155). At times he regrets his

(pp. 53–54). The interview was conducted (in English) when Emine Sevgi Özdamar was the guest of the German Section of the Modern Languages Department of Keele University in October 1994.

39 Meryam Schouler-Ocak, 'Sind Migrantinnen und Migranten anders depresiv?', in *Migration und psychische Gesundheit: Belastungen und Potentiale*, ed. by Theda Borde and Matthias David (Frankfurt am Main: Mabuse, 2007), pp. 83–94 (p. 83).

decision to leave Algeria (*GF*, p. 249), insisting that Matthias was wrong to have brought him to Germany.

Yanis's story of suffering is typical in the history of immigration. The Swiss physician Johannes Hofer published a thesis on the 'Heimweh-Krankheit' in 1688, in which he conceives of homesickness as an illness that makes the patient compulsively dream of his homeland 'in übermäßig schönen Bildern [...], welchen die Heimat selbst gar nicht entspricht'.[40] The illness was said to be located in the imaginary powers, with the connection between mind and body causing physical symptoms. Young Swiss men were considered to be especially susceptible and the only cure was a swift return home. Although Hofer's medical theory has by now been consigned to the history books, Osman Gürlük, a Turkish immigrant who is profiled in Max von der Grün's *Leben im gelobten Land: Ausländer in Deutschland* (1975), agrees with Hofer on this point: 'Heimweh ist eine Krankheit, und diese Krankheit ist nur in der Türkei zu heilen'.[41] In Tahar Ben Jelloun's novel *Partir* (2006), which will be examined later in more detail, the Spanish character Miguel 'prit brusquement conscience de l'urgence qu'il y avait à renvoyer Azel et Kenza au Maroc. Leur retour était certainement la seule chose qui leur permettrait de retrouver leur repères et de guérir' [understood how urgent it was to send Kenza and Azel home to Morocco, since their return was certainly the only thing that would help them find their footing again and begin to heal].[42]

Almost three hundred years after Hofer, in 1952, Frantz Fanon, the influential psychiatrist and revolutionary, described the symptoms of North African immigrants in France, noting that 'they insistently complain of indefinable, yet ubiquitous, body pain, that they often dramatize performatively'.[43] More recently the 'study of "immigrant psychology" is an emerging field of research',[44] with the specific difficulties and problems faced by migrants being increasingly recognized by the medical profession. Maghrebi immigrants in France have been said to be particularly susceptible to a *mal partout* (pain everywhere) that is not dissimilar to that expressed by Yanis: 'Vague, poorly expressed, and lacking in imagery, this pain appears as "inclassable"'.[45] Contemporary research has shown that depressive conditions among immigrants are caused largely

40 Simon Bunke, *Heimweh: Studien zur Kultur- und Literaturgeschichte einer tödlichen Krankheit* (Freiburg im Breisgau: Rombach, 2009), p. 29.

41 Max von der Grün, *Leben im gelobten Land: Ausländer in Deutschland* (Munich: DTV, 1994), p. 11.

42 Tahar Ben Jelloun, *Partir* (Paris: Gallimard, 2006), p. 243; English: *Leaving Tangier*, trans. by Linda Coverdale (Mount Pleasant: Arcadia, 2009), p. 199.

43 Hron, *Translating Pain*, p. 65.

44 Hron, *Translating Pain*, p. xi.

45 Hron, *Translating Pain*, p. 66.

by the stress perceived in unfamiliar surroundings, but are not an inherent or unavoidable aspect of life for adoptive citizens. Ilhan Kizilhan, a clinical psychologist, gives a useful summary of the situation:

> Der Prozess der Migration beinhaltet nicht nur die Verarbeitung vieler neuer Erfahrungen und Umstände, sondern auch den Umgang mit Verlusten und zieht normalerweise langwierige Adaptionsprozesse nach sich. Dieser Akkulturationsvorgang kann sehr stressbelastet sein und sowohl zu körperlicher als auch psychischer Anspannung führen. Der individuelle Verarbeitungsprozess wird in erheblichem Ausmaß mitbestimmt durch den psychosozialen Kontext und das soziale Klima, in dem die Migranten leben. Migrations- und Akkulturationsprozesse sind jedoch nicht per se Ursache für psychische Erkrankungen, beeinflussen aber die gesundheitlichen Belastungen, da sie besondere Stressoren darstellen.[46]

Yanis's impromptu egress from Algeria constitutes an abrupt separation from his home culture, his family, and all the familiarities of daily life and he lacks a vital element of migrant life, the cultivation of a feeling of continuity between life in the country of origin and life in the adopted country. There are also emotional issues relating to his family, to his father in particular, that are unresolved as he leaves Tichy, issues which continue to occupy his mind in Berlin.

In addition to these 'problems of emigration', there are those 'problems of immigration', those issues associated with integrating into his new German surroundings. Isolation, alienation, and prejudice are often a part of the immigrant experience; and as an Arab migrant in a Western setting he faces discrimination that a white migrant would not have to tolerate. Yanis is ignored and overlooked; and if he is seen at all, it is as the Other. Yanis expresses the frustration he feels in the face of this xenophobia, as well as the pain of homesickness, in a notebook that Matthias finds only after learning of Yanis's death. These passages are included in Matthias's narrative in italicized sections and will be discussed later in this chapter. Quite apart from the feelings of worthlessness and depression that he records in those notes, the young Algerian also expresses his pain directly through his body: his psychological pain is somatized and manifests itself in headaches, vague pains and a fungal infection. In her study of immigrant suffering and its representation in literary works, Madelaine Hron states that 'immigrants are always confronted with the problem of conveying their pain in language – be it the language of words, the language of the body, or the language of psychological signs and symptoms'.[47]

46 Ilhan Kizilhan, 'Potentiale und Belastungen psychosozialer Netzwerke in der Migration', in *Migration und psychische Gesundheit*, ed. by Borde and David, pp. 53–67 (pp. 54–55).

47 Hron, *Translating Pain*, p. 32.

Although Yanis appears uncommunicative and is reluctant to discuss his problems with Matthias, subconsciously and involuntarily he communicates all his anguish and utilizes all three channels mentioned by Hron with which to do so. His frustration and despair are expressed through depression, physical discomfort and through the written word.

The 'migration as illness' trope used in the depiction of Yanis's experience of life in Berlin can be clearly distinguished from the more troubling 'immigrant as disease-carrier' trope. Historically, illness was associated with immigrants. They were feared as the carriers of disease, with 'specific immigrant groups [...] associated with particular diseases: Asians with bubonic plague, Italians with polio, and Jewish immigrants with tuberculosis'.[48] Yanis's illness is clearly not intended in this tradition. Rather than bringing the disease with him, Yanis is 'infected' by the disease after arrival in Berlin. By stating that 'Migration ist die Krankheit' (*GF*, p. 178), Roes highlights the difficulties immigrants face in a foreign environment and he does this by using the language of the body. Hron notes the prevalence of physical imagery in works by migrant Maghrebian writers in French, stating that they:

> draw on the universal signifier of the body to convey their emotional distress and social alienation as clearly, critically, and efficiently as possible. Physical bodily pain renders the sufferings of immigration concrete and tangible, graphically explicit, and even viscerally understandable for the reader.[49]

This is reminiscent of Roes's statement regarding the 'elementare körperliche Erfahrungen' (*KT*, p. 127) that humanity has in common, elements that can be exploited to enhance understanding between people of different backgrounds. The universal element of the body functions as a bridge between the reader – who may well have little or no knowledge of the migrant experience – and the immigrant population. By drawing on physical sensations of pain and illness, Roes makes the immigrant's experience, which may otherwise remain abstract, more palpable for his readership.

To thematize illness in relation to immigration is not without risks. Although Roes's treatment of disease is far removed from overtly racist discourses that have deployed the 'immigrant as disease-carrier' trope, the thematization of the immigrant's diseased mind and body could nevertheless result in subtle associations being made in the reader's mind between immigrants and ill-health. There is a danger that depictions of migrant characters as sick, lazy and unable to adapt to Western society could become representative of immigrants in general. If immigrants are described exclusively in terms of their suffering

48 Hron, *Translating Pain*, p. 120.
49 Hron, *Translating Pain*, p. 81.

then the question might be raised as to whether migration is advantageous to the migrant at all; and it is not such a leap to the more contentious issue of whether migration is advantageous to the host country – an issue that is often raised by right-wing, anti-immigration political parties. To counter such an interpretation, Roes expands the picture by including all travel as problematic: 'Nicht erst die Migration ist eine Krankheit, sondern schon das Reisen, jedes Reisen' (*GF*, p. 297). It is not only economic migrants and asylum seekers that are at risk from the disease of immigration, the Western traveller is equally challenged. Illness is presented as part of the process of adapting to a foreign climate and culture, but 'die Krise des Reisens ist zugleich eine Kritik des Reisens, mein Körper ist ein Eindringling, ein Krankheitsherd im Organismus der Fremde' (*GF*, p. 297). Travel is portrayed as unnatural, an activity that induces crises and illnesses. Roes's use of medical imagery of infections and foreign organisms operates on traditional binary opposites, a 'precarious metaphor' since it seems to advocate 'differences between the self and the other, the nation body and the alien invader, the citizen and the immigrant'.[50] For Roes the critical situation, the crisis or illness, is an opportunity to be relished, not to be shied away from. The language suggests that an evolutionary process is underway: 'Überlebt der Körper die Infektion, geht er gestärkt aus der Krise hervor. Die Kontaminierung mit Fremdem führt zu einer gesteigerten Immunabwehr, aber auch zu Hybridbildungen, Bastardisierungen, Fehllesungen. Sie machen Entwicklung erst möglich' (*GF*, p. 298). Even traditionally controversial terms such as 'Kontaminierungen' and 'Bastardisierungen' express for Roes the potential that lies in an encounter with foreign climates and cultures. Being 'contaminated' by the foreign may be an experience fraught with dangers and difficulties but it is nevertheless an experience that he seeks since the crisis that is triggered as a result of such a contamination leads to increased strength and regeneration. It is an evolutionary experience.

Roes's metaphor of illness has a parallel in a similar metaphor employed by the Turkish-German writer Zafer Şenocak, who discusses a question he is often asked concerning origins. Rather than regarding the question as a 'lästige Gängelung', Şenocak recommends responding to it in a creative manner. He regards stating one's place of birth as one's origin to be an unsatisfactory and often misleading answer. He would rather replace such definitive and unambiguous statements of identity with a 'persönliche Geographie, in der Grenzen anders verlaufen als auf der Landkarte'.[51] As the title of his essay – 'Die Heimat trägt der Mensch in sich' – suggests, Şenocak emphasizes

50 Hron, *Translating Pain*, p. 12.

51 Şenocak, *Zungenentfernung*, p. 23.

the importance of bringing along one's personal history when moving to a new location, saying that he would not have stayed in Berlin 'wäre es mir nicht möglich gewesen, diese Stadt für meine Erinnerungen bewohnbar zu machen'.[52] Speaking of such relocations, he states that 'Jeder Umzug in eine andere Stadt ist eine Art Transplantation. Es kann vorkommen, daß der Körper die neue Umgebung abstößt wie ein fremdes Organ'.[53] Şenocak is not speaking exclusively of immigration here; he is also referring to resettlements within one country. He was born in Ankara but the family soon moved to Istanbul. Later, when Şenocak was eight years old, they emigrated to Germany and settled in Munich. Since 1990 Şenocak has been living in Berlin, which he regards as 'die einzige Metropole Deutschlands'.[54]

Like Roes, Şenocak uses medical terminology to express the idea of migration. In the above quotation organ transplantation, a drastic and invasive medical procedure, is used as a metaphor to convey the process of settling in a foreign city. The metaphor implies change and a degree of hybridity since the body, after undergoing the procedure, is a composite of organs from different bodies. Despite their similarities, Roes and Şenocak's metaphors operate in opposite ways. In Roes's novel the traveller or immigrant is the 'Eindringling', who is a 'Krankheitsherd' in the organism of the foreign culture. As such, not only is he suffering the 'crisis' of travel, he is also at risk of being eliminated in the foreign organism's attempts to deal with this infection. The traveller is vulnerable and fragile and the onus is on him to adapt and become stronger, to evolve so as to overcome this crisis. In contrast, Şenocak's essay portrays the position of the traveller as being far more stable. When moving from one location to another the migrant may reject his new surroundings as an unsuitable geography for his personal history. Here it is the new 'Umgebung' that is at risk of rejection, in which case the migrant will simply move onwards to a more suitable place. For Şenocak the process of migration was not easy. Much of his poetry, essays and fiction deals with the challenge the migrant faces in creating a new identity for himself. It appears, however, that Şenocak attributes to the migrant a greater degree of agency than Roes does in *Geschichte der Freundschaft*. Yanis fails miserably to create an identity for himself as an Algerian in Berlin, but this failure is represented in the novel as Yanis being rejected as an outsider by his new surroundings. It is never suggested that Berlin has proved, as Şenocak might put it, an unsuitable home for Yanis's memories.

Despite the intensity of Yanis's suffering, his is, in many ways, a privileged position compared to that of many migrants living in Germany. He is in

52 Şenocak, *Zungenentfernung*, p. 23.
53 Şenocak, *Zungenentfernung*, p. 23.
54 Şenocak, *Zungenentfernung*, p. 23.

an ideal situation to take advantage of the 'neue[n] interkulturelle[n] Potential[s]' that Kizilhan speaks of, and he certainly does not fit into the category of the exploited immigrant worker as portrayed in works such as Rafik Schami's *Die Sehnsucht fährt schwarz* (1996). Schami's work has been described as 'Widerstandsliteratur', a call on migrants to refuse to accept 'die bestehenden Zwänge und Ausgrenzungsversuche'[55] that face the immigrant in Germany daily. Through his relationship with Matthias, Yanis is largely able to avoid such exploitation. In fact he is often seen exploiting Matthias's generosity and love, living a life of leisure, avoiding housework and paid employment as much as possible. He is welcomed, albeit cautiously, by Matthias's family, and makes astounding progress in his learning of the German language. However, although Yanis does not face overt racist abuse in Germany, he does face subtle, invisible barriers to integration. When Yanis enters a restaurant to seek employment (*GF*, p. 284) he describes the strange look in the owner's eyes, a look that fills him with defeatism and disillusionment, a look not unlike those that Mesut, in Sten Nadolny's novel *Selim oder die Gabe der Rede*, describes: 'jene Beleidigungen etwa, die man nur an den Gesichtern erkannte, nicht an den schnell gesprochenen Worten. Dann mußte man so tun, als hätte man nichts bemerkt, um sein bißchen Würde zu wahren'.[56]

Nadolny depicts a German society in which the immigrant is overlooked. The Turkish guest-workers face an 'alles durchdringende Gleichgültigkeit, Desinteresse und Kommunikationsunwilligkeit'.[57] They also experience instances of more overt racism, something to which Yanis in *Geschichte der Freundschaft* is not exposed. Indeed Alexander, Selim's German friend, identifies four possible reactions to the question of the foreigner in Germany: 'die "Haßtirade" (selten), den "Antrag auf Nichtbefassung" (vorherrschend, in der Regel mit heuchlerischen Bemengungen), die sachliche Rede (selten) und die "erzählerische Partizipation" (so gut wie unbekannt)'.[58] Mahmut Karakus, writing about *Selim*, discusses this distinction between the less common openly xenophobic abuse ('selten') and the more widespread apathy ('vorherrschend') facing foreigners in Germany. Karakus points out, however, that 'diese Nichtbefassung, das Ignorieren, eigentlich alles andere als harmlos

55 Moustafa Al-Slaiman, 'Autor/innen aus dem arabischen Kulturraum', in *Interkulturelle Literatur in Deutschland. Ein Handbuch*, ed. by Carmine Chiellino (Stuttgart: Metzler, 2007), pp. 235–47 (p. 241).

56 Sten Nadolny, *Selim oder Die Gabe der Rede* (Munich: Piper, 1992), p. 71.

57 Anke Bosse,'Ost und West im Fadenkreuz des Erzählens: Selim oder die Gabe der Rede', in *Sten Nadolny*, ed. by Wolfgang Bunzel (Eggingen: Isele, 1996), pp. 192–225 (p. 200).

58 Nadolny, *Selim*, p. 350.

ist',[59] since this 'Nichtbefassung' implies rejection and has a negative impact on the Turks' sense of identity. Ayse, a young Turkish woman, voices exactly this thought:

> Daß die Deutschen die Türken hassen, kann man eigentlich nicht sagen. Es ist schlimmer: sie wollen mit uns nichts zu tun haben. Das heißt, ihnen ist egal, was mit uns passiert – Hauptsache, sie haben keine allzu deutliche Schuld daran – die scheuen sie. [...] Haß kann man abbauen, sogar ins Gegenteil verwandeln durch Wärme und Humor. Aber Gleichgültigkeit, egal, ob die nette oder feindselige, ist wie eine Glasscheibe, alles tropft ab. Dahinter verändert sich nichts.[60]

The invisible barrier facing Yanis in Roes's novel can likewise be read as a critique of German society and its alleged indifference towards ethnic communities living in its midst.

Certain elements of the description of Yanis's life in Berlin may strike the reader as perpetuating and reinforcing negative stereotypes concerning foreigners and immigrants. In Yanis's case these include laziness with regard to paid employment, untidiness around the home, and a clumsy and almost disastrous attempt to navigate the streets of Berlin. A more positive stereotype is also alluded to, that of the 'Oriental storyteller' who can entrance an audience with his narrating skills.[61] Yanis's portrayal also transcends common stereotypes of the foreigner. In Yanis, Roes has created a character that partially conforms to unsavoury images of the undesirable immigrant, while also displaying attributes that set him apart. By endowing Yanis with an individual character and identity, Roes challenges stereotypes of the foreigner or immigrant. Yanis's ambiguous sexuality, his excellent knowledge of English and swift acquisition of German, and his position outside the ghetto of migrant life in Berlin make him an interesting and multifaceted character. In addition, Germany's so-called *Ausländerproblem* is often discussed in terms of a *Türkenproblem*,[62] ignoring the fact that Germany's foreign population originates from a variety of countries across Europe, the Mediterranean, and

59 Mahmut Karakus, *Interkulturelle Konstellationen: Deutsch-türkische Begegnungen in deutschsprachigen Romanen der Gegenwart* (Würzburg: Königshausen & Neumann, 2006), p. 103.

60 Nadolny, *Selim*, p. 380.

61 Yanis's storytelling abilities do not match those of the title character in Sten Nadolny's *Selim oder die Gabe der Rede*. In that novel the trope of the story-telling Oriental – 'so waren ja die Orientalen' (Nadolny, *Selim*, p. 48) – is invoked but the novel as a whole makes 'careful use of [both German and Turkish] stereotypes [...] [to] enable alternative reading strategies for majority representations of minorities' (Mani, *Cosmopolitical Claims*, p. 66).

62 Cf. Chin, *The Guest Worker Question*, p. 149; Sabine von Dirke, 'Multikulti: The German Debate on Multiculturalism', *German Studies Review*, 17 (1994), 513–36 (p. 523).

even further afield. Were he a real person, Yanis would belong to a relatively small group of Algerians resident in Germany: only 16,798 in 2000, a figure that had decreased to 13,948 by 2005.[63] The depiction of Yanis's origins in an Algerian seaside village and the description of life for young men in the Maghreb provide a back story that the German public rarely hears (or listens to). This story draws the reader in and makes it possible to sympathize more readily with Yanis's plight in Berlin. Yanis becomes an individual figure with whom the reader begins to feel affinity, even if the Algerian's experience is too far removed for it to be truly understood.

The fact that Matthias's narration begins in Algeria also affords the reader an insight into Yanis's cultural background and gives an impression of the influences that formed the young Algerian. Some of his perceived failures in Berlin are related to the differences between the lifestyles of Algeria and Germany. The depiction of Yanis's life in Algeria before he meets Matthias illuminates our understanding of his reaction to life in Berlin. His refusal to help Matthias with housework ('Das ist Frauenarbeit!' (*GF*, p. 158)) appears arrogant and bigoted. Regarded in the context of his home culture, where housework is solely the responsibility of the women, his reaction can be understood (if not commended) as culturally conditioned. Similarly his inability to hold down a job in Berlin can be understood in the light of the pervasive unemployment among youths in Algeria. Having little experience of the demands of paid work, especially of the working culture in Germany, Yanis's shortcomings can be better comprehended.

Matthias admits to his own personal failings, which can also be linked to differences in cultural background. In the final passage of the novel, Matthias ruefully concludes that his friendship with Yanis failed to flourish as it might have partly due to their failure to acknowledge their respective rhythms: 'Viel zu spät erst habe ich verstanden, was ich von dir, Yanis, hätte lernen können: Verlangsamung' (*GF*, p. 315). Perhaps there is an admission here that he had had unrealistic expectations with regard to Yanis settling down swiftly and without problems in Berlin. Read in this light, Yanis's recalcitrance might be reinterpreted as a reaction to a perception that Matthias failed to understand his problems. Although Matthias regards himself as relatively enlightened in matters of interculturality, in this case he appears to have met his limits.

These limits to Matthias's intercultural competence are also hinted at in this statement of his: 'Mein Leben lang habe ich versucht, das Andere, Fremde interessant zu finden, ohne es überwinden oder mir vertraut machen zu müssen' (*GF*, p. 201). Matthias claims that he does not feel the need to overcome

63 Cf. Statistisches Bundesamt, *Population and Employment: Foreign Population. Results of the Central Alien Register* (Wiesbaden: Statistisches Bundesamt, 2007).

Otherness or difference in his engagements with the Other. However, his position also betrays an aspect to which he appears to be oblivious. His claim that he has always *tried* to find the Other interesting has undertones of guilt or obligation. Furthermore, in his efforts to be interested it seems that he rather reinforces the division between Self and Other. In his acknowledgement that he has something to learn from Yanis, there is not only a sign of respect to his friend and his cultural heritage, but also an element of Othering that sets the two apart.

This section concludes with a brief examination of Milan, the child born as a result of Yanis's affair with Natascha. Not only does he play an important role in the development of the plot, he is also a highly symbolic figure. His unplanned birth arguably keeps the two men together, and the child's presence as a go-between in their apartment helps to illustrate and define the difficulties in the relationship between the two adults. With Yanis's death, Milan, together with a few diary notes, is the only token of remembrance that Matthias retains of his deceased friend. During their time together in Berlin, Matthias says of his friendship with Yanis that it is like a 'zwiespältige[s] Feuer, diese verkohlten Zweige, unter denen immer wieder neues Grün sprießt' (*GF*, p. 232). The friendship has a fiery, destructive force but, as in nature, destruction leads to renewal. The 'Findling Milan' (*GF*, p. 232) is an example of this regeneration, and is born from the ashes of the two men's relationship, but he also symbolizes possibilities for the future of German society. Milan is the biological progeny of Algerian and Ukrainian migrants but due, on the one hand, to Natascha's wishes and, on the other, to the fatal circumstances that befall Yanis, he will be raised by Matthias alone. In a nation that has traditionally 'define[d] "Germanness" according to descent',[64] Milan will be a part of a growing minority of ethnic non-Germans who are culturally German and who hold German nationality. He becomes, as such, a model of hybridity that stands as a symbol for the potential of transcending divisive social demarcations.

Tahar Ben Jelloun's *Partir* and Michael Roes's *Geschichte der Freundschaft*

Although there is no evidence to suggest that Roes uses Tahar Ben Jelloun's *Partir* (2006)[65] as an intertext, the numerous similarities between that novel and *Geschichte der Freundschaft* merit some examination. The two novels share common themes and a similar plot but vastly different protagonists.

64 Arlene Akiko Teraoka, 'Detecting Ethnicity: Jakob Arjouni and the Case of the Missing Detective Novel', *The German Quarterly*, 72 (1999), 265–89 (p. 273).

65 Jelloun, *Partir* (Paris: Gallimard, 2006); English: *Leaving Tangier*, trans. by Linda Coverdale (Mount Pleasant: Arcadia, 2009).

As a result, a comparison of the two Western travellers will illuminate our understanding of Roes's conception of intercultural encounters with men from the Maghreb.

Ben Jelloun was born in Morocco but emigrated to France in 1971. His novel *Partir* deals with the experience of young Moroccan men who, like Yanis and his friends in Algeria, have 'un avenir bouché, pourri, rien à l'horizon' [blocked, rotten futures, nothing on the horizon].[66] Azel, the protagonist, is obsessed with leaving Morocco for Spain. It becomes 'une sorte de folie qui le travaillait jour et nuit' [a kind of madness that ate at him day and night].[67] He has his chance when he becomes involved with a wealthy Spanish art dealer, Miguel, who invites him to live with him in Barcelona. Azel becomes a 'domestique le jour' [servant by day] and an 'amant la nuit' [lover by night],[68] a situation that quickly destroys any sense of well-being or self-esteem he may have had before leaving Tangier. Like Yanis, Azel experiences immigration as illness and suffers considerable physical and emotional deterioration. His relationship with Miguel comes to an acrimonious end and, facing deportation, Azel negotiates his freedom by informing on Islamist groups for the Spanish police. It is a move that seals his fate. By the end of the novel he is dead, lying with his throat cut in a pool of blood.[69] Immigration, illness, ambiguous sexuality and wounded masculinity are all themes that surface in both novels. I wish now, however, to focus on the foreign traveller in both works – Miguel in *Partir* and Matthias in *Geschichte der Freundschaft*. Doing so will reveal two very different positions chosen by gay Western travellers in the Maghreb.

Miguel is not a philanthropic traveller who helps Azel out of the kindness of his heart. One passage in particular reveals Miguel's attitude to the Moroccan men with whom he becomes involved:

> Chaque fois que Miguel forçait un homme à entamer avec lui une histoire, il le regrettait, mais cela ne lui déplaisait pas de souffrir et de se plaindre dans sa solitude. Il aimait la peau mate des Marocains, leur maladresse, mot qu'il utilisait pour parler de leur ambiguïté sexuelle. Il aimait leur disponibilité, qui marquait l'inégalité dans laquelle les liens se tissaient. Ainsi, tantôt domestique le jour, tantôt amant la nuit.
>
> [Whenever Miguel forced a man to become involved with him, he regretted it, but he found a kind of perverse pleasure in feeling lonely and sorry for himself. He loved the 'awkwardness' of Moroccan men, by which he meant

66 Jelloun, *Partir*, p. 152; *Leaving Tangier*, p. 120.

67 Jelloun, *Partir*, p. 23; *Leaving Tangier*, p. 10.

68 Jelloun, *Partir*, p. 47; *Leaving Tangier*, p. 32.

69 Cf. Sherko Fatah's *Das dunkle Schiff* (2008), which features a Kurdish immigrant in Berlin who meets a similar end at the hands of Islamic extremists.

> their sexual ambiguity. He loved the olive sheen of their skin. And he loved their availability, which marked the inequality in which the relationship was formed, for the lover by night was thus the servant by day.][70]

Miguel's attitude here is clearly revealed by the narrator to be manipulative and neo-colonial. There is a very clear dynamic of power in which the Westerner holds all the cards. As Sophie Smith states:

> Here, sex is not an act to be shared by mutually respecting, loving or desiring partners, but a form of currency, a service to be carried out for the colonial master. Miguel does not challenge this exploiter/exploited power dynamics, hinting at his manipulative intentions and once more consigning Azel to a position of inferiority and submission.[71]

Azel's submission is at its most obvious in a scene in which he is forced by Miguel to dress as a female Oriental dancer to perform for a party of gay European men. Miguel introduces Azel as follows:

> Mes amis, je suis heureux de vous présenter ma dernière conquête : un corps d'athlète sculpté dans le bronze, avec en supplément un chouia de féminité. C'est un étalon rare ; [...] Azel [...] est simplement un très bel objet, un objet de toutes les tentations.
>
> [My friends, I'm delighted to present my latest conquest to you: the body of an athlete sculpted in bronze, with a piquant soupçon of femininity. Quite a stud! [...] Azel [...] is simply a most beautiful object, an object to tempt every eye.][72]

Not only is Azel totally emasculated, his 'animalisation is a neo-colonial objectification of the Moroccan male as born to be exploited, and in this context sexually so'.[73]

Matthias positions himself as a very different traveller to Miguel and regards his interaction with the Maghreb and its people in a different way. He is an insecure traveller, constantly observing his surroundings and questioning his motives for being there. He is considerate of the culture that he is visiting and although aware of the probable limitations he faces in terms of understanding the local culture and fitting in, he makes an effort to be accepted. He attempts to live a lifestyle that resembles that of the locals and rents an apartment rather than staying in a hotel – the latter described by Hans Magnus Enzensberger

70 Jelloun, *Partir*, pp. 46–47; *Leaving Tangier*, p. 32.

71 Sophie Catherine Smith, 'Negotiations of Masculinity in Francophone Men's Writing' (unpublished doctoral thesis, University of Swansea, 2009), p. 152.

72 Jelloun, *Partir*, p. 112; *Leaving Tangier*, p. 87.

73 Smith, 'Negotiations of Masculinity', p. 154.

as the 'Schloß des Großbürgertums' and 'Kathedrale des Tourismus'.[74] Indeed, there is general suspicion of hotels and what they stand for among travel writers in the post-colonial era. As Lützeler notes, hotels are often regarded as neo-colonialist palaces, 'Villa der westlichen *middle-class* [...] [wo] Einheimische [...] vor allem als Dienstpersonal vor[kommen]'.[75]

One feature of writing by travellers with a colonialist mindset is the prevalence of the 'Monarch-of-all-I-survey' trope,[76] or of the 'commanding view'.[77] Whereas the nineteenth-century African explorer would stand on a hilltop surveying his newly conquered territory, the modern-day tourist often stands on a hotel balcony and enjoys a clear view over the city visited. This all-seeing figure claims to understand the issues and problems of the (often Third World) country and offers possible solutions. Descriptions of landscapes and cityscapes are thus often indications of an attempt to establish a position of authority and a gaze of mastery. David Spurr states that:

> the writer who engages this view relies for authority on the analytic arrangement of space from a position of visual advantage. [...] the organization and classification of things takes place according to the writer's own system of value. Interpretation of the scene reflects the circumspective force of the gaze, while suppressing the answering gaze of the other. In this disproportionate economy of sight the writer preserves, on a material and human level, the relations of power inherent in the larger system of order.[78]

Matthias, however, admits that he cannot see clearly, he cannot really grasp the scene. His 'Blick aufs Meer' is 'verstellt' (*GF*, p. 11). He asks questions far more often than he offers answers, and he does not claim to understand what happens before him. His gaze is not a controlling one and he presents himself as a traveller who engages with the foreign country on equal terms. He arrives in Algeria already equipped with a theory of travel that explains this stance: 'Genau so sollte das ideale Reisen sein: den Gesten des Anderen angepasst, ja unterworfen, seine rasierklingenscharfen Zärtlichkeiten erleidend. Das sich selbst behauptende, erobernde Reisen ist das koloniale Reisen, das die Begegnung mit dem Anderen immer nur als Machtkampf begreift' (*GF*, p. 258). Matthias makes a distinction between a post-colonial approach (which he clearly aims to embody) and a neo-colonial approach (which Miguel takes to

74 Enzensberger, 'Eine Theorie des Tourismus', pp. 201–02.

75 Lützeler, *Postmoderne und postkoloniale deutschsprachige Literatur*, p. 121. For a more light-hearted attitude to hotels and their significance see Urs Widmer's short essay 'In Hotels' in the volume *Vor uns die Sintflut* (Zurich: Diogenes, 1998) pp. 132–38.

76 Cf. Pratt, *Imperial Eyes*, pp. 197–223.

77 Cf. David Spurr, *The Rhetoric of Empire: Colonial Discourse in Journalism, Travel Writing and Imperial Administration* (Durham, NC: Duke University Press, 1993), pp. 13–27.

78 Spurr, *The Rhetoric of Empire*, pp. 16–17.

the extreme in Ben Jalloun's novel). The post-colonial traveller is humble and vulnerable – attributes that make room for the acquisition of new knowledge and understanding of the host culture. As if to demonstrate this vulnerability and openness Matthias goes to visit a local barber in the first few days of any journey:

> Voller Hingabe und Vertrauen in seine Kunst sitze ich auf dem sich schuppenden Kunstledersessel, jede Bewegung meines Kopfes ahne ich voraus, ehe der sanfte Druck seiner Hände ihn zwingt, voller erregend ängstlicher Phantasien, wozu die scharfe Klinge, sein und mein alltägliches Handwerkzeug, fähig ist, die Empfindsamkeit der Kehle, der Wange, des Augapfels. Kein Blick, kein Wort, keine Bewegung zu viel (*GF*, pp. 257–58).

Matthias relinquishes his position as Western subject, in so far as that is possible, to assume a position that resembles that of the locals. By placing himself in the skilful hands of the Algerian barber he not only adopts the style of the local Berber men, he also signals his vulnerability and trust. There is an unmistakeable element of sexual tension entwined in Matthias's experience of vulnerability, with fear and arousal merging and compounding as he sits awaiting the feel of the razor on his throat. Whereas Miguel's liaison with Azel is distinguished by displays of power, the sexual aspect of Matthias's interaction with Yanis and the Maghreb more generally is characterized by submission and vulnerability. Matthias's relationship with Yanis is characterized by affinity and attraction, despite the frequent problems they experience. While Matthias strives never to exploit his position as a Western traveller, Miguel is the epitome of the enduring colonialist mindset, 'conquering' Moroccan men and entwining them in games of power and domination.

The Body

In *Geschichte der Freundschaft*, as in *Leeres Viertel*, Roes posits that the body is the essential element in any intercultural encounter. The first chapter of this book argues that the final scene of *Leeres Viertel* shows the narrator going beyond attempting to understand the Yemeni tribesmen through intellectual processes, for example in his anthropological research, and transcending cultural barriers by interacting with the people and their culture in a physical way, via the medium of traditional Yemeni dance. The importance of physical contact is demonstrated early in Matthias's friendship with Yanis when they pay a visit to the *hammam*, the public baths, together. During the visit they wash each other thoroughly, a 'selbstverständliche[r] Freundesdienst' (*GF*, p. 26) in most Arab countries. In contrast to much of the rest of the Arab world, however, close physical contact between men is unusual in Kabylia. Yanis is enthusiastic about this new experience and scrubs Matthias so thoroughly 'dass ich noch Tage später an Hals und Brust die Schürfwunden von seiner Schmirgel- und Hobelarbeit, vom salzigen Meerwasser zusätzlich aufgeraut, zur Schau trage' (*GF*, p. 26). Yanis exclaims afterwards: 'Nie habe ich so intensiv meinen eigenen Körper gespürt [...] . Ich habe keine Angst vor diesen Berührungen, fährt er fort. Sie verletzen uns nicht. Im Gegenteil!' (*GF*, p. 26). The friendship between the two men is intensified as a result of this physical interaction. Soon afterwards the two spend an afternoon together on the beach, with the image of their bodies 'Haut an Haut mit ihm im weißen feinkörnigen Sand' (*GF*, p. 35) reminding the reader of the 'Schürfwunden' that may well have remained on Matthias's skin. Non-linguistic means of communication are repeatedly claimed to be superior to speech and to intellectual attempts at cross-cultural understanding: 'Nicht das Gespräch steht im Mittelpunkt des Zusammenseins, sondern der Körper' (*GF*, p. 99). Through the common experience of physical sensations two people can come to understand each other in a way that is impossible through language, which is often a source of confusion: 'Vor allem in den Worten liegen die Missverständnisse, und im gnadenlosen Funktionieren unserer Sozialmaschinerie' (*GF*, p. 172). Matthias regards even the simple act of lending Yanis his clothes as exemplifying this physical closeness: 'Dass du auch meine Kleidung trägst, schafft eine direkte körperliche Nähe und Vertrautheit, die Worte nicht herstellen könnten' (*GF*, p. 165).

The image of the Tower of Babel is repeatedly invoked as a symbol of the complexity of communication in a world where languages, cultures and beliefs interact in multifarious convolutions. On the one hand it is clear that intercultural communication has become a more intricate endeavour since God decided to 'confound their language, that they may not understand one another's speech' (Genesis 11:7). Roes makes the point, however, that a common language is not sufficient to guarantee successful communication between two people. One indispensable prerequisite for communication, according to Roes, is empathy, defined as: 'im Anderen ein mir, meinem Körper und seinem Empfinden ähnliches Wesen zu entdecken' (*GF*, p. 99). Here again the emphasis is on the body and the emotions, rather than on language and the intellect. The concept of empathy that Roes advances in *Geschichte der Freundschaft* is comparable to the 'gemeinsame[n] oder vergleichbare[n] erfahrung' (*LV*, p. 745) that the narrator of *Leeres Viertel* considers essential to any productive communication. Where this common experience or empathetic attitude is found, communication is possible even when language barriers pose considerable difficulties. Despite this faith in the body as a means of overcoming linguistic barriers Roes and his narrators are simultaneously aware of the limitations of any communication. In *Leeres Viertel* the narrator expresses his inability to convey deeper truths, asking: 'wie verständigen wir uns über das unzeigbare, das verborgene in uns, das uns selber fremde. Wir wissen darum, doch fehlen uns nicht selten selbst die worte' (*LV*, p. 746). These incommunicable feelings and ideas are also detectable in *Geschichte der Freundschaft*, for example in Yanis's emotional turmoil after his arrival in Berlin, which is discussed privately in his notebook and expressed psychosomatically through his body but never comprehensively communicated.

It is significant that the examples of close physical contact between the two men cited above take place in Algeria. They are passages full of vitality, warmth and excitement, passages that exude an undeniable eroticism. Matthias is entranced by the sight of Yanis's body (*GF*, p. 13, pp. 34–35) and enjoys a heightened awareness of his own (as in the *hammam* scene discussed above). This new experience of the body is not exclusively positive. Matthias has physical symptoms that he relates to his fear of the violence that still plagues Algeria: 'Bei jeder Berührung zuckt der Körper in paranoider Furcht vor einem neuen Gewaltakt zurück' (*GF*, p. 37). Similarly, when he is alone in Algiers after Yanis has returned to his hometown, Matthias's body feels heavy and lifeless, his veins filled with 'flüssigem Blei' (*GF*, p. 67); and on the bed where Yanis had previously slept lies Matthias's battered rucksack like a 'lebloser Körper' (*GF*, p. 67), a meagre replacement for Yanis's 'durchtrainierten Körper' (*GF*, p.13). When Yanis returns to Algeria from Germany, Matthias again experiences physical symptoms due to the separation, this time 'Nervenschmerzen in der linken Gesichtshälfte' (*GF*, p. 239). The body clearly functions, for both Yanis and Matthias, as an instrument that communicates emotions that would otherwise be unexpressed.

During his first visit to Algeria one important change that can be observed in Matthias is his reduced faith in intellectual attempts to understand the foreign: 'Der Körper ist plötzlich wichtig geworden. Die körperliche Schönheit ist es, die mich verführt, und der gelingt, was ein Monopol des Intellekts schien: zum Begreifen herauszufordern und sich berühren zu lassen' (*GF*, p. 138). When one compares descriptions of physical appearances and bodily functions in Algeria and in Germany one can distinguish a tangible difference. After their arrival in Berlin both communication and physical proximity between the two men are limited. Matthias still examines and describes Yanis's body with admiration (*GF*, p. 152) but the dynamics of the relationship are vastly different to what they had been in Algeria: '[E]s [ist] hier anders. Ein Fremder liegt neben mir im selben Zimmer' (*GF*, p. 153). As the novel progresses and Yanis's health declines, descriptions of him portray his body in a negative light. His heavy body, the viral fungus and rotting teeth all contrast with the beautiful young man previously depicted. He is like Frankenstein's monster, 'zusammengestückelt aus den als unheilbar amputierten Abfällen der Chirurgie' (*GF*, p. 177). Matthias comments: '[H]ier in Deutschland bewegt Yanis sich, als sei er nicht nur in ein fremdes Land, sondern in einen ihm fremden Körper hineingeraten' (*GF*, p. 230). As his physical condition declines, so too does the quality of communication between the two. After Yanis's incarceration for petty theft he finds it impossible to communicate his feelings and there is often 'Streit in der Luft' (*GF*, p. 222) of their apartment. Yanis retreats into his own world, staying in the flat as much as possible, finding solace in a world of coffee, cigarettes and internet pornography. It could thus be suggested that while Matthias, during his travels, exploits the potential of the body to maximize success in his encounter with Algerian culture, Yanis fails even to recognize this potential. As Yanis comes face to face with a foreign culture his body contracts in fear and remains paralysed. However, to claim that Yanis neglects the body in the process of communication would be misleading. Although he does this subconsciously, he uses his body to communicate the pain of immigration, expressing feelings that can be only inadequately expressed in words.

The Voice: Narrative Characteristics

Geschichte der Freundschaft is mainly narrated in the first person, from Matthias's perspective. He sometimes slips into the second person and addresses Yanis directly in passages that convey the narrator's devotion to the young Algerian. This mode of address is intensely personal and gives the impression that the world at large is shut out from the narrator's consciousness. His focus is solely on his friend to the exclusion of all else. The reader of the novel, however, is not shut out from their world and is afforded the privilege of accessing the personal sphere and emotional lives of these two men. Yanis's own voice is at times heard in the text, in sections that appear only towards the end of the novel. These are notes that Yanis has been writing since his arrival in Berlin, but which Matthias does not find until after Yanis's death. In addition to these two voices, numerous quotations from philosophical and literary works on the topic of male-male friendship are interwoven into the novel. Roes has, in previous novels, used a multitude of narrative voices, with particular success in *Der Coup der Berdache* (1999), a novel told by three narrators, each of whom has a second, alternative identity. Multivocal narrative is a particular trait of postmodern fiction and Roes uses it as a technique for giving voice to the marginalized, be they the third-gender characters of *Der Coup der Berdache*, or the alienated immigrant in *Geschichte der Freundschaft*.

That Yanis's voice is only heard posthumously says much about the position of the migrant in contemporary Germany. Yanis is excluded, alienated and powerless. In life he had, metaphorically speaking, no voice – an unfamiliar situation for one who belongs to Algeria's '*Mundkultur*' (*GF*, p. 246). The diary notes can also be read as symptomatic of the failure in Matthias and Yanis's relationship. According to Nietzsche's writing on friendship, he who lives with 'unzureichender Gesellschaft, wird gewöhnlich ein guter Briefschreiber sein'.[79] Yanis has no one to whom he can write letters, leaving him the only recourse of writing without a readership. It is only after Yanis's death, when it is too late, that Matthias and the reader hear that voice which he has been struggling to express.

In his diary notes, which are all italicized in the novel, Yanis expresses feelings of unworthiness, inferiority and fear, comparing himself at one point to a dirty fly: '*Jedes Mal, wenn ich etwas sagen will, Matthias, fühle ich mich so stumm und hässlich wie diese haarige Mülleimerfliege*' (*GF*, pp. 246–47). He also uses other animal imagery, describing himself as '*ein Wildtier*' (*GF*, p. 245) and '*ein Parasit*' (*GF*, p. 262). There are examples in history of animal and insect imagery being used to ostracize a minority. The National Socialists, drawing on associations made since the Middle Ages, infamously dehumanized the Jews by portraying them as vermin and parasites, thereby justifying their extermination.[80] There is no evidence in *Geschichte der Freundschaft* that Yanis suffers such explicitly xenophobic abuse in Berlin, so it seems unlikely that Yanis's application of this imagery is an indication that he has internalized such conceptions. A much more convincing explanation for Yanis's use of animal metaphors can be found by looking to his formative years in Algeria. According to Yanis, his father and older brother '*tun so, als ob sie Löwen seien*' (*GF*, p. 312). Yanis thinks of them rather as '*Hyänen*' (*GF*, p. 312), cowards that attack the weak and vulnerable. Yanis, in contrast, was a beautiful child who looked like a '*Prinzessin*' (*GF*, p. 313) and who learned to hate his own beauty, feeling a constant sense of fear '*wie ein Hund*' (*GF*, p. 313). It becomes clear here that Yanis's internalization of animal hierarchy has its roots not in racist ideology but in the patriarchal regime of fear with which he grew up, showing that the traumas of childhood still affect him long after he has left his home town behind.

Yanis applies this animal imagery to his new situation in Berlin and reveals an inferiority complex that relates to his home culture. He associates

79 Friedrich Nietzsche, *Sämtliche Werke*, ed. by Giorgio Colli and Mazzino Montinari, 15 vols, II, *Menschliches Allzumenschliches* (Munich: DTV, 1999), p. 244.

80 Philippe Burrin, 'Nazi Antisemitism: Animalization and Demonization', in *Demonizing the Other: Antisemitism, Racism and Xenophobia*, ed. by Robert S. Wistrich (Amsterdam: Harwood, 1999), pp. 223–35 (p. 226).

Algeria with the animal kingdom, saying that '[*man*] [*i*]*n meiner Heimat* [...] *kein Mensch sein* [*kann*]' (*GF*, p. 245). Germany is, on the other hand, inhabited by humans. To adapt to life there he has to sell his '*Tierseele* [...] , *um ein Mensch zu werden*' (*GF*, p. 245). Before he met Matthias, Yanis claims, he was already '*sprachlos, augenlos, ein Zombie, den man nur in mondloser Nacht für einen Menschen halten konnte*' (*GF*, p. 293). To describe Algeria as a '*Vorhölle mit Untoten*' (*GF*, p. 293) is to evoke images of strife and civil war, and to recall the hopelessness felt by many young Algerians. Yanis is ashamed of the primitiveness of his culture when compared to the perceived sophistication of Western attitudes, practices and technology; and bashfully admits that his Berber language – '*dieses Kindergebrabbel*' (*GF*, p. 272) – has no word for 'Werbung', 'Neurose' or 'Bundestagabgeordneter'. Coming to Germany has meant losing his past, which now seems meaningless '*als sei es nur ein zerlesener Comic*' (*GF*, p. 292). Having failed to create a new identity for himself in Berlin he is left feeling like a '*Fälschung, eine Kopie irgendeines Phantoms*' (*GF*, p. 292). In the attempt to become assimilated into German life Yanis has lost his cultural identity, as characterized by the 'Tierseele', and is now left without reference points by which he can orient himself. The migrant thus perceives himself as inferior to the Germans but cannot maintain the animal metaphor since he has sold that animal soul and lost that part of his heritage.

While the animal metaphor is used to portray Yanis's life in Algeria, in Berlin the metaphor employed is that of the blind man. It is revealing that Yanis does not use animal metaphors to describe his position in Germany. To have done so would, perhaps, have drawn too direct a parallel between himself and the victims demonized in National Socialist propaganda. The metaphor of the blind man nevertheless encapsulates the anonymous, neglected position of a migrant in Germany at the beginning of the twenty-first century. Yanis first claims that a 'Blinder ist *noch* ein Mensch' (*GF*, p. 248, my italics), referring to the position of immigrants as second-class citizens in Germany. They may not be as highly regarded as the Germans but they still qualify as human. However, he goes on to say that if all others ignore the blind man's presence, if they turn a blind eye towards him, so to speak, 'dann ist er weniger als ein Tier, dann ist er nichts!' (*GF*, p. 248). The immigrant's existence is entirely dependent upon the Germans' acceptance or rejection of him. The immigrants' status as 'Blinde', their disadvantaged situation, is a condition pressed upon them. Ironically, the Germans are also portrayed as blind, in their case, blind to the presence of the millions of foreign residents who live among them, but this blindness is, in contrast to the metaphorical blindness of the disadvantaged migrant, a chosen position that reflects ignorance of, if not arrogance or racism towards, the foreign population.

A History of Friendship: Nietzsche, Foucault and Co.

Jacques Derrida, in his study *Politiques de l'amitié*, remarks that 'les grandes méditations canoniques sur l'amitié [...] appartiennent à l'expérience du deuil, au moment de la perte – celle de l'ami ou de l'amitié' [the great canonical meditations on friendship [...] belong to the experience of mourning, to the moment of loss – that of the friend or of friendship].[81] Not only are some of these canonical works quoted in *Geschichte der Freundschaft*, the novel can also be read as being part of the same tradition. Matthias writes his first-person narrative from a position similar to that of Montaigne writing after Etienne de la Boëtie's death, or of Nietzsche, who wrote many of his aphorisms on friendship in the period around 1878 to1879, after the 'break with his old friend Carl von Gersdorff and the death of Albert Brenner' and following the collapse of his friendship with Wagner.[82] Matthias is narrating a story of loss, grief and tragedy. The novel's plot is a flashback from the present tense of the airport scene in Algiers, giving the novel a sense of retrospection. Matthias's narrative, however, is clearly not to be read as an uncritical eulogy to a friend and a friendship now lost. His style is largely unsentimental and honest regarding the failings of the relationship, and critical of his own and his deceased friend's many weaknesses. Matthias works by day as a pathologist, examining corpses and identifying causes of death and disease. In *Geschichte der Freundschaft* he probes the dead friendship, analysing mistakes, limitations and failures of communication. It is an analysis executed with admirable candour and precision; and he takes responsibility for his 'analytische Blamagen' (*GF*, p. 190) and the failure of both parties to recognize 'des jeweils eigenen Rhythmus' (*GF*, p. 315), which he believes led to the failure of the friendship. He also admits that the friendship was more than likely doomed from the start: 'Die Untersuchungen zu den Schwierigkeiten multikultureller Beziehungen sind doch Legion, ihr vorprogrammiertes Scheitern eine Binsenweisheit' (*GF*, p. 178).

Matthias and Yanis's difficulties are contrasted in the novel to the broader picture of the history of friendship in cultural and philosophical works. For example, Roes has taken the title of his novel from a quotation by the French philosopher and historian of ideas, Michel Foucault. In an interview two years before his death, Foucault argued that the tradition of close friendships between men had been on the decline since the sixteenth century; and that since the

81 Jacques Derrida, *Politiques de l'amitié* (Paris: Galilée, 1994), p. 322; English: *The Politics of Friendship*, p. 290.

82 Ruth Abbey, 'Circles, Ladders and Stars: Nietzsche on Friendship', in *The Challenge to Friendship in Modernity*, ed. by Preston T. King and Heather Devere (Ilford: Frank Cass, 2000), pp. 50–73 (p. 51).

eighteenth century one had seen how 'homosexuality became a problem'.[83] Foucault suggests that it would be productive, after examining the history of sexuality (published in his three-volume *Histoire de la sexualité* (1976–84), known in German as *Sexualität und Wahrheit*), to 'try to understand the history of friendship, or friendships'.[84] The excerpt from this interview given by Foucault is only one of the many asides in *Geschichte der Freundschaft* that refer to a selection of cultural or intellectual works that engage with the theme of friendships between men – ranging from the Hollywood film *Brokeback Mountain* (2005) to the story of David and Jonathan in the Bible, from Neal Stephenson's science-fiction novel *Snow Crash* (1992) to Batman and Robin's crime-busting partnership. Through these cultural references a programme or template for successful or ideal friendship is explored, thereby extending the novel's scope to reach far beyond the example of Matthias and Yanis.

These sections, although set apart from the novel's main plot and introduced by Roman numerals, can be attributed to Matthias, the first-person narrator. Although they are mostly direct quotations or anonymous musings on cultural issues, Matthias's voice can be identified clearly behind at least one of these sections. When quoting from *Menschliches Allzumenschliches* (1878–80), Matthias modifies Nietzsche's original words and makes them applicable to his own friendship with Yanis. Nietzsche, in the passage 'Von den Freunden', alludes to an apocryphal statement attributed to Aristotle: 'Freunde, es giebt keine Freunde!'.[85] Nietzsche's response is to counter this statement, claiming: 'ja es giebt Freunde, aber der Irrthum, die Täuschung über dich führte sie dir zu; und Schweigen müssen sie gelernt haben, um dir Freund zu bleiben'.[86] When Matthias quotes from the passage, he says: 'Ja, es gibt Freunde, aber der Irrtum, die Täuschung über dich führt *dich mir* zu; und Schweigen müssen *wir* gelernt haben, um *Freunde* zu bleiben' (*GF*, p. 267, my italics). Matthias has changed key personal pronouns in Nietzsche's text in order to

83 The interview was conducted in Toronto (in English) in June 1982 by B. Gallagher and A. Wilson: cf. Michel Foucault, 'Sex, Power, and the Politics of Identity', in Paul Rabinow (ed.), *Ethics: Subjectivity and Truth* (New York: New Press, 1998), pp. 163–73 (here p. 171). Quoted by Roes in German, *GF*, p. 7. The German translation of the interview from which Roes quotes can be found in full in Michel Foucault, 'Sex, Macht und die Politik der Identität', in *Kritik des Regierens: Schriften zur Politik* (Berlin: Suhrkamp, 2010), pp. 386–400.

84 Michel Foucault, 'Sex, Power, and the Politics of Identity', p. 171. Quoted by Roes in German, *GF*, p. 6.

85 It would appear that this is a corruption (introduced in Diogenes Laertius's work *Lives and Opinions of Eminent Philosophers* (third century)) of Aristotle's statement in his *Nicomachean Ethics* that 'those who have many friends and who greet everyone with familiarity (*oikeiôs*) seem to be friends to no-one' (Bruce Rosenstock, 'Derrida *Polutropos*: Philosophy as *Nostros*', in *Derrida and Antiquity*, ed. by Miriam Leonard (Oxford: Oxford University Press, 2010), pp. 235–66 (p. 256)).

86 Nietzsche, *Menschliches Allzumenschliches*, p. 263.

make explicit the relevance of the passage to his own relationship with Yanis. It becomes clear that this passage is not part of a series of quotations compiled by a neutral, non-participating anthologizer, but is assembled and arranged by Matthias and presented alongside the narration of his story.

Two sections in Matthias's narrative support the argument that his voice is to be heard behind both strands of the novel. In one section Matthias refers to Nietzsche's *Menschliches Allzumenschliches* in a context separate from the quotation discussed above. Referring to the stresses and strains that Yanis's chronic state of ill-health inflicts on their relationship, Matthias is tempted to read aloud to him the section 'Nicht zu lange krank zu sein' from Nietzsche's work, in which the philosopher comments with irony on the danger of prolonged illness: 'bald werden die Zuschauer durch die übliche Verpflichtung, Mitleiden zu bezeigen, ungeduldig' (*GF*, p. 190). An over-long period of illness leads observers (or friends) to conclude that the illness is deserved and that they consequently need not sympathize. Shortly before this Matthias writes a short passage that sounds comparable to some of the novel's clearly labelled theoretical or cultural-historical sections. He speculates that everyone needs friends, only that 'der eine [...] einen Freund [braucht], der ein Spiegelbild seines eigenen Ichs sein soll, der andere einen Lehrmeister oder ein Vorbild, ein dritter einen Unterstützer und Förderer' (*GF*, p. 176). He then proceeds to offer examples of anthropological studies that demonstrate exotic or unusual practices or belief as regards friendship. This leads him to ask the question that is at the heart of the novel's engagement with the theme of friendship between men: 'Wovon sprechen wir, wenn wir über die Freundschaft reden?' (*GF*, p. 176). As a result the distinction between the two separate narrative strands is rendered less defined than it first appears as Matthias is revealed to be the author of both.

To return briefly to the first Nietzsche quotation, it is striking that the passage chosen by Matthias is remarkably pessimistic regarding the nature of friendship: it is based as a matter of necessity on a limited understanding and knowledge of the friend. That Matthias adapts the personal pronouns to reflect his and Yanis's friendship demonstrates the resonance within him of the pessimism of the passage. In a line from the same passage not quoted in the novel, Nietzsche exclaims: 'Nach alledem wirst du dir sagen: wie unsicher ist der Boden, auf dem alle unsere Bündnisse und Freundschaften ruhen, wie nahe sind kalte Regengüsse oder böse Wetter, wie vereinsamt ist jeder Mensch!'.[87] Friendship is presented by Nietzsche as fragile, unstable and based on incomplete communication. Every human being ultimately stands alone. However, far from being a purely pessimistic testimony, Nietzsche's aphorisms

87 Nietzsche, *Menschliches Allzumenschliches*, p. 263.

can also be read as affirmations of the value of friendship, for 'what begins as an apparent attack on the illusions of solidarity becomes an injunction to celebrate the reality of human relationships rather than lament their imperfections'.[88] For Matthias this means interpreting his 'analytische Blamagen' (*GF*, p. 190) that lead to the difficulties within the friendship with Yanis as the exact proof, the 'Zeugnis meiner Freundschaft zu ihm' (*GF*, p. 267).

This 'middle period' when he wrote *Menschliches Allzumenschliches* was one in which Nietzsche 'was setting greater than usual store by friendships'.[89] However, although he acknowledges in that volume that 'not only can friendship foster self-overcoming, but that the talent for friendship is one of the marks of a higher human being',[90] it becomes increasingly clear in his later works that he prescribes solitude and autonomy for the higher human being. The only type of human contact that will benefit the *Übermensch* is 'adversarial engagement'.[91] The idea of the friend as foe is alluded to in some quotations in Roes's novel (none of which are from Nietzsche) but they seem difficult to apply to Matthias's story. Neither he nor Yanis is portrayed as a higher human being and their relationship, although fraught with difficulty, is hardly an adversarial contest designed to foster personal growth. Matthias's selection of quotations from *Menschliches Allzumenschliches*, as a work that exemplifies Nietzsche's attitudes towards human friendships in his middle period, is therefore suitable as the quotations demonstrate the fragility and imperfection of any friendship, while also pointing towards the value and merit of human relations.

It is worth pausing at this stage to consider the nature of Yanis and Matthias's friendship. Is the novel's title misleading in calling the story one of friendship? Would it not be more precise to call it a story of love between men?[92] Matthias

88 Abbey, 'Circles, Ladders and Stars', p. 55.

89 Duncan Large, 'Proust on Nietzsche: The Question of Friendship', *The Modern Language Review*, 88 (1993), 612–24 (p. 621).

90 Abbey, 'Circles, Ladders and Stars', p. 51. In 'Von den Freunden', for example, Nietzsche reveals that friendships offer a chance for self-recognition, self-improvement and the abandonment of illusions: 'Es ist wahr, wir haben gute Gründe, jeden unserer Bekannten, und seien es die grössten, gering zu achten; aber eben so gute, diese Empfindungen gegen uns selber zu kehren. – Und so wollen wir es mit einander aushalten, da wir es ja mit uns aushalten' (Nietzsche, *Menschliches Allzumenschliches*, p. 263).

91 Abbey, 'Circles, Ladders and Stars', p. 66.

92 The passage on the website gaybooks.de regarding *Geschichte der Freundschaft* is very revealing. It pokes fun at the 'inhaltlich korrekten, aber "total weichspülenden" Verlagstext' by supplementing it with an additional, more explicit commentary. For example: 'Inmitten politischer Unruhen lernt Matthias, ein deutscher Urlauber, in Algerien den jungen Kabilen Yanis kennen (*er verliebt sich in ihn*). Im Laufe seines Aufenthalts freunden sie sich an (*sie haben Sex miteinander*), bis Yanis kurz vor Matthias' Abreise bei einer politischen Demonstration verschwindet', www.gay-and-lesbianbooks.de/Roes-Michael/61-Neue-Romane/1258823808-Geschichte-der-Freundschaft.html?keyword=roes [accessed 22 March 2011].

applies numerous labels to the relationship over the course of the novel but most often describes it as a 'Freundschaft' (*GF*, p. 141, p. 157, p. 171, p. 188, p. 190, p. 198). This label is used, however, in the broadest possible sense and its meaning shifts according to use. To quote one of the above uses of the word 'Freundschaft' in full is to reveal this ambiguity: 'Nicht an erkaltender Liebe, sondern an dieser Überforderung wird unsere Freundschaft scheitern' (*GF*, p. 198). It is clear that love plays a part in the friendship, despite the assertion made in the theoretical parts of the novel that friendship is superior to love (*GF*, pp. 234–35). In another passage Matthias insists: 'Nun, Gott sei Dank sind wir kein Paar. Wir sind weit davon entfernt. [...] ich bin mit dir zusammen, aber du nicht mit mir' (*GF*, pp. 166–67). In yet another, however, he contradicts himself, telling the gay couple he meets in an Algerian café: 'Ich bin sein Freund gewesen. Wir haben zusammen in Berlin gelebt' (*GF*, p. 285). Moreover, he describes himself and Yanis at one point as being 'wie jedes gewöhnliche Ehepaar' (*GF*, p. 222), remaining together only because of their child. Their relationship is clearly one in which they struggle to find a clear identity, it is 'eine "unmögliche" Freundschaft' (*GF*, p. 141) in which they must attempt to resist and overcome social norms and create or invent new ways of being. The representation of the friendship thus thematizes and engages with the challenge that Foucault is issued by his interviewer, that of exploring 'anew the possibilities of friendship [...] . Isn't the real task to set up new social relations, new value structures, new family structures, and so on?'.[93] In another interview Foucault explains that one task facing gay men is to:

> develop relationships that are intense and satisfying even though they do not at all conform to the ideas of relationship held by others [...] [to] learn to express their feelings for one another in more various ways and develop new life-styles not resembling those that have been institutionalized.[94]

Matthias's ambiguous or ever-changing labelling of the relationship is an effect that results from attempting to formulate and bring into existence new ways of being and relating. On the whole Matthias appears to advocate a return to classical antiquity, when 'die Freundschaft, *philia*, noch nicht von der Liebe geschieden [war]' (*GF*, p. 20). The etymological roots of the word *friend* are examined and found to contain 'alle wesentlichen Attribute einer Freundschaft [...] : De[n] freie[n] Zusammenschluss von Gleichen, die Liebes-, Schutz-, und Bestandsgemeinschaft' (*GF*, p. 20).

93 Foucault, 'Sex, Power, and the Politics of Identity', p. 171.

94 'Sexual Choice, Sexual Act: Foucault and Homosexuality' from an interview conducted and translated by James O'Higgins, quoted in Lawrence D. Kritzman, ed., *Michel Foucault: Politics, Philosophy, Culture: Interviews and Other Writings 1977–1984* (New York; London: Routledge, 1988), pp. 286–303 (p. 301).

Matthias speculates that love and war share a semantic field – 'erobern, rauben, gefangennehmen, treffen, verwunden, fallen' (*GF*, p. 234) – and proceeds to outline the superiority of friendship over love relationships. Although both spring from a desire for intimacy, they are directed towards opposite aims: 'In der Freundschaft vereine ich mich mit einem mir Gleichen, in der Liebe suche ich die Vereinigung mit einem mir Wesensfremden' (*GF*, p. 235). Matthias seems here to have identified what he believes to have been the central problem of his relationship with Yanis: the lover will always be the Other, a 'ständige Quelle der Scham, denn er lässt mich verwundbar, ja lächerlich erscheinen' (*GF*, p. 235), whereas the friend is not 'der Andere, der Fremde, [...] er ist die selbstverständliche zweite Hälfte meines Selbst' (*GF*, p. 173). Love relationships are presented as being inherently unequal and self-destructive, while friendships are characterized by egalitarianism and homology. Although not mentioned or quoted in this context in the novel, Nietzsche too was convinced of the superiority of male-male friendships over love relationships. In *Die fröhliche Wissenschaft* (1882–7) Nietzsche equates love with egoism and greed, while friendship is 'eine Art Fortsetzung der Liebe, bei der jenes habsüchtige Verlangen zweier Personen nacheinander einer neuen Begierde und Habsucht, einem gemeinsamen höheren Durste, nach einem über ihnen stehenden Ideale, gewichen ist'.[95] Michel de Montaigne, three centuries earlier, had also regarded male-male friendships as superior to love relationships, which he described as 'volage, ondoyant et divers' [fickle, fluctuating and variable]. Friendships, in contrast, are like 'une chaleur generale et universelle, temperée au demeurant et égale, une chaleur constante et rassize, toute douceur et pollissure, qui n'a rien d'aspre et de poignant' [general universal warmth, temperate moreover and smooth, a warmth which is constant and at rest, all gentleness and evenness, having nothing sharp nor keen].[96] Marriage is a 'marché qui n'a que l'entrée libre, [...] là où en l'amitié, il n'y a affaire ny commerce que d'elle mesme' [bargain where only the entrance is free, [...] whereas in friendship there is no traffic or commerce but with itself].[97] Although there is no suggestion that Yanis has read either Montaigne or Nietzsche, he appears to subscribe to this view, blaming Matthias's love for him for their troubles: 'Aber es ist wohl die Liebe schuld. Sie ist es, die seiner Väterlichkeit [towards Milan] die Milde und Gelassenheit gibt. Und sie ist es, die unserer Freundschaft im Weg steht' (*GF*, p. 296–7).

95 Friedrich Nietzsche, *Die fröhliche Wissenschaft* (Stuttgart: Kröner, 1986), p. 47.

96 Michel de Montaigne, 'De l'Amitié', in *Les Essais* (Paris: Gallimard, 2007), pp. 189–201 (p. 192); *On Friendship*, trans. by M. A. Screech (London: Penguin, 2004), p. 5.

97 Montaigne, 'De l'Amitié', p. 193; *On Friendship*, p. 6.

The story of Matthias and Yanis is one in which the attempt to establish a new kind of friendship fails. Juxtaposed with the quotations from and references to the theoretical and cultural-historical sources, however, it points towards the possibility of finding new ways of relating, new types of relationships. Matthias and Yanis encounter countless difficulties due to inadequate communication, cultural differences and Matthias's possessive love. By means of the secondary strand other approaches and examples are presented, examples that serve to prompt a reconsideration of how friendships between men can function. Matthias comes to regard the abandonment of claims to possession and total equality of the partners as essential in any relationship. The narrator of *Leeres Viertel* also considers the idea of equality between partners within relationships of central importance. He described heterosexuality as 'ein verhältnis zwischen ungleichen, zwischen stärkeren und schwächeren, tätigen und duldenden, also ein gewaltverhältnis, "homosexualität" hingegen eine beziehung zwischen gleichen, die ihre rollen in jeder begegnung neu definieren müssen und können' (*LV*, p. 302). Manfred Koch, writing for the *Neue Zürcher Zeitung* in what was the only review of *Geschichte der Freundschaft* to appear in a major German-language daily newspaper, focuses on this idea in his appraisal and summarizes this point:

> Mit Foucault (den er zu Beginn ausführlich zitiert) versteht Roes unter Freundschaft eine ideale Beziehungsform, in der alle Beteiligten zugleich geborgen und frei, einander leidenschaftlich zugetan und doch souverän zusammenleben können. Auch für ihn ist Freundschaft als "Gemeinschaft von Gleichen" der Gegenbegriff zu "Liebe", die in der westlichen Kultur seit dem 18. Jahrhundert vor allem als Sexual- und damit Machtverhältnis definiert wird.[98]

This utopian ideal is not realized in the novel. Indeed, it is not clear whether the author believes that this ideal form for friendship exists or can be created. *Geschichte der Freundschaft* portrays one attempt at such a relationship and frames that effort in the context of over two thousand years of philosophical discussion on the topic. By employing such a broad temporal perspective Roes indicates that the 'ideale Beziehungsform' may well change gradually over time. While each generation is advised to look back to find inspiration and guidance, it must ultimately find or create its own answers.

98 Manfred Koch, 'Der kurze Sommer des Liebesglücks: Michael Roes' philosophisch-ethnologischer Roman über Männerfreundschaft', *Neue Zürcher Zeitung*, 12 October 2010, p. 17.

Conclusion

To avoid a dilution of focus, this book has had to limit its scope to certain aspects of these four novels. As a result, a number of potential research questions remain and a number of avenues for further research are open. The interpretation presented in this study has been generally approving of Roes's work, reading the novels as depictions of post-colonial intercultural engagement. The novels may, however, invite a number of other possible interpretations, some of which are far more hostile to Roes's literary approach. One issue that must be left somewhat unresolved at the conclusion of this book concerns Roes's choice of intertexts. I have noted how the majority of the intertexts belong to the Western/Northern cultural sphere, with only a scattering of references to non-Western texts. It could be argued here that Roes, while producing a discourse of his own regarding the Middle East, is ignoring that region's own discourse about itself. Western travel writing is much more visible in Roes's depiction of the Arab world than the Arabs' representations of themselves. The danger here is that such a choice of reading appears unwittingly to advocate the superiority of Western over Eastern literature, reinforcing the Western Orientalist discourse that speaks on behalf of the East.

Related to this issue is the possibility that traces of a colonialist attitude are detectable in what is otherwise a post-colonial approach. Future research could focus on more critical readings that explore whether the author, although clearly well-intentioned and widely read in the theory of post-colonialism, is at times blind to aspects of his own intercultural engagement. One character who embodies this ambiguity is the art historian Gérard Lumière in *Weg nach Timimoun*. He could be read as the archetypal colonialist, albeit a benevolent one who regards himself as bringing the Enlightenment (as his name suggests) to Algeria. The novel gives voice to Laid's anxieties but the young Algerian is never in a position to provide solutions. The key to solving Laid's problems is provided by the Frenchman Lumière. The advice he imparts (*WT*, p. 52) reflects the novel's broader message that there is an alternative to Algeria's tradition of violence and revenge. Lumière's position reflects in many ways Roes's own as the Western author of a novel that advocates reason against tradition. It appears that Roes intends Lumière as an ironic comment on the presumption he and other Westerners display in dispensing advice to developing countries. If that is the case, this clever sleight-of-hand displays an admirable level of self-awareness but fails to mitigate the arrogance of presuming to offer answers to the problems of other countries and cultures. That an author who aims to embody post-colonial approaches to travel and intercultural engagement is at times liable to reproduce colonialist discourse demonstrates how deeply rooted such power dynamics are embedded in the Western psyche.

Potentially fruitful avenues of research may also be pursued in readings of Roes informed by the field of White Studies, which problematizes the position of white subjects. Such an approach draws attention to the fact that 'white people have had so very much more control over the definition of themselves and indeed of others than have those others'.[1] This is related to the point made above regarding the lack of non-Western intertexts and the resulting dynamics of power. As Michel Foucault argues, 'power is everywhere',[2] not least in the acts of reading, writing and representation. This is a fundamental problem in the genre of Western travel writing in particular, whose narratives are usually centred on the white, well-educated and therefore powerful, travelling subject. Future research that analyses Roes's replication or contestation of the dynamics of whiteness would be valuable. This could be explored in conjunction with the issue of homosexuality and colonialism. Some critics have asked whether 'homosexual cross-racial love always contest[s] colonial relations and ideology'.[3] Further exploration of Roes's work with regard to this question is sure to reveal more about the connection between sexuality, power and (post-) colonial intercultural engagement and it is to be hoped that further studies of his complex work will be carried out to augment our understanding of these important questions regarding identity and the contemporary, globalized world.

***

This study has limited its focus to four of Roes's novels, each of which shares a highly intertextual approach to writing about the intercultural experience. Taking the four novels as a collective, it becomes clear that some of the intertexts are intercultural in their own right (Carsten Niebuhr's *Reisebeschreibungen*, Herman Melville's *Moby Dick*), while others are not (Aeschylus's *Oresteia*, Nietzsche's aphorisms on friendship). In most cases, however, Roes's use

1 Richard Dyer, *White* (London: Routledge, 1997), p. xiii.

2 Michel Foucault, *The Will to Knowledge. The History of Sexuality*, 3 vols, I, trans. by Robert Hurley (London: Penguin, 1998), p. 93.

3 Katrin Sieg, *Ethnic Drag: Performing Race, Nation, Sexuality in West Germany* (Ann Arbor: University of Michigan Press, 2002), p. 188.

of texts from the latter category is geared towards a commentary on travel, intercultural relations and cultural exchange. The variety of intertexts used contributes to the richness and complexity of the novels and attests to Roes's boldness as an intertextualist. Furthermore, the processes used by the author to embed these older literary works into the new ones are diverse and highly inventive. As I have shown in the four chapters, even though he constantly reverts to using second-hand material as a source for his literary production, the means by which he recycles that material testifies to his originality and resourcefulness.

The instances of intercultural encounter depicted by Roes in his fictional work range from successful transcultural bridge-building to tragic situations caused by catastrophic failures of communication. Between these two poles, Roes shows most encounters to be characterized by partially successful attempts at expression, understanding and exchange. The subtlety of Roes's depiction of intercultural meetings is due at least in part to the fact that much of his fiction originates from his own life experience. In *Leeres Viertel*, the narrator spends a considerable amount of time and effort learning the language and studying the customs of his hosts. He opens himself to the Yemeni culture in a manner most Westerners could not endure. Anthropological information is not the only output of this work: he also attains broader insights into the nature of the differences between one culture and another, and how these can be partially overcome. He repeatedly encounters problems, stumbles over cultural differences and faces the overwhelming alienation that is an inevitable part of anthropological research. When facing the incomprehensibility of the foreign, the traveller comes to realize how enslaved he is to his own culture. As Schnittke remarks in *Leeres Viertel*:

> Nun bin ich so lange und so weit forth von der Heimath gereist, doch bin ich ihr nicht wirklich entronnen. Vielmehr scheint es, als hätte ich mich in dem gleichen Maasse der Entfernung dem Tieferen, dem Eigentlichen des Heimath Genannten angenähert (*LV*, p. 101).

In this light, the reader understands Roes's practice of intertextuality as a link to his home culture. Some examples can be found of references to non-Western literature (Mohamed Choukri, Ibn Battuta, Hafis, *The Epic of Gilgamesh*), but the engagement with Western writers and thinkers is deeper and wider-ranging. As a traveller and representative of German and Western culture, Roes continues to draw from his own culture as he enters into intercultural situations. It is, perhaps, not so surprising that he refers mainly to Western literature since he would naturally be more intimately familiar with it. Roes's library of mainly Western texts is his window onto the world. The intertextuality of his travel fiction reveals that to encounter other cultures one needs a culture of one's own. In this case it means using the cultural tradition from which one comes as a tool with which one may begin to approach, dissect and understand what is foreign.

The relevance of this research to the broader field of German Studies lies in the significance and nonconformity of Roes's *oeuvre*. Although not the recipient of wide public recognition, his work is important because of the innovative way his narratives incorporate complex positions with regard to some of the major intellectual debates of contemporary society. Throughout his writing career, Roes has been preoccupied with some of the same questions that fascinate society and dominate in the media: questions regarding identity, (homo-)sexuality, race and racism, gender, and relations between the West and Islam. However, Roes's work offers an alternative perspective on these contemporary debates about identity. By interweaving paradigm-changing theories into his novels he impels his readers to rethink and revise perceptions of the world, both with regard to their home culture and to societies further afield.

As the chapter on *Leeres Viertel* has shown, the novel uses intertexts to exhibit its place within the Western tradition of exploration, anthropology and travel writing. It appears that it is no longer possible to experience the world unmediated through texts. Everything has been said and written, each blade of grass has been seen and described already. Despite this, and despite the extensive reliance on historical travelogues in *Leeres Viertel*, the novel simultaneously emphasizes the importance of face-to-face contact with real people, the representatives of other cultures. Roes's novel reminds its readers that literary and intellectual engagement with the Other is no substitute for personal experience. His emphasis on the body as a medium for intercultural encounters makes this clear: 'Doch können wir uns verständigen. Denn gemeinsam haben wir unseren körper. Nicht kulturen begegnen einander, sondern gesichter, gerüche, stimmen' (*LV*, p. 800).

The central question of this study regarding the connection between intertextuality and interculturality remains an unsolved problem. Roes apparently believes that it is possible to take a dual approach that combines a reliance on intertextuality with a claim to truth and authenticity deriving from real-life experience. These two approaches to travel – the intertextual and the corporeal – appear to be in direct conflict, but Roes views them as complementary ways of drawing near to, and learning about, foreign countries. Such a position is contrary to the logical argument that the greater the reliance on intertexts, the further away one moves from the real world. Intertextuality is an infinite network of texts that is, ultimately, closed off from the real world. Within this network there is no need for real experience because that void is filled by the presence of texts. However, while Roes appears to enjoy exploiting the potential of intertextual 'play', he simultaneously seems reluctant to abandon all claims of real-world authenticity. He presents his anthropological insights, confident that they have an inherent truth-value deriving from what Rabinow calls the 'experiential "I was there" element'.[4] This tension between textual knowledge and personal experience cuts to the very heart of the field of intertextuality and will continue to occupy the attention of scholars drawn to study Roes's travel literature in future.

Since the end of the Cold War the West has tended to look towards the Middle East for its enemies and counterfoils. This urge to detect the presence of an enemy, no matter how ill-defined, assists in the creation of a strong identity for the Self. It is an ironic coincidence that *Leeres Viertel* was published in the same year as Samuel P. Huntington's *The Clash of Civilizations*; and the two volumes can be regarded as embodying opposite sides of the debate on international relations.[5] While Huntington regards clashes between cultures as inevitable, Roes works on establishing a communicative process between East and West that would make conflict less likely. Since the 9/11 terrorist attacks, the debate surrounding Islam's relationship with the West has intensified. Roes's response has been to continue publishing works that depict human, and often mundane, aspects of life in the Arab world that the Western media fail to show. His fiction contributes to public debate by increasing differentiation in the representation of life in the Middle East, providing an element of proportionality to Western perception of Muslim countries.

Haut des Südens is the only one of the four novels in which Roes draws on intertexts 'native' to the country visited. Since Roes is German, the focus on American writers in *Haut des Südens* is already intercultural. The novel's intertextuality is largely metatextual and assumes the form of literary criticism. The narrator's interest in the racial dynamics of the American South is largely directed towards literary works that feature 'inter-racial' friendships. This focus is mirrored in the novel by the German narrator's friendship with the Nigerian Daniel, which takes on 'hypertextual' (Genette) contours when their friendship becomes a pastiche of Queequeg's and Ishmael's in *Moby Dick*. This novel takes an important position on the question of race. The political debate in the West surrounding the issue centres on ending discrimination and promoting equality for black/Arab/Asian populations. While *Haut des Südens* unquestionably contains a strong anti-racist message, Roes approaches race from a different angle. While careful not to negate the weightiness of the

4 Rabinow, 'Representations are Social Facts', p. 244.

5 In much the same way, *Geschichte der Freundschaft* can be regarded as a counterpoint to Thilo Sarrazin's *Deutschland schafft sich ab*, which also appeared in the same year. Fictional representations of the lives of migrants in Germany can provide balanced depictions that eschew the extremes of argument employed by books such as Sarrazin's bestseller.

issue, he subverts the notion of race and reveals its hollow essence as a cultural construct. The misery imposed on blacks in the American South is shown to be predicated upon an artificial racial hierarchy implemented as a tool of control and exploitation. While well-meaning contemporary debates surrounding race focus on improving relations between 'races', Roes draws attention to the fact that race itself is a dubious concept with no biological basis.

The intercultural encounter staged in *Weg nach Timimoun* is of a very different nature because it is the only novel to feature a non-German narrator. As a result, the novel presents not so much an intercultural encounter as an encounter within one culture, albeit from the perspective of an outsider. However, the literary work originates from Roes's interest in Algerian culture and builds upon years of intercultural work. The novel's unusual blending of third and first person narration is a reflection of the author's position outside this culture and his narrator's perception of himself as a man who exists on the margins of his own culture. The novel's main intertext is also different from the previous two novels in that its main theme is revenge and familial obligations rather than interculturality. Through the relocation of the action of the *Oresteia* to contemporary Algeria, Roes is commenting on the transcultural role literature can assume, and on the applicability of Greek myth to non-Western societies in the present day. However, as the chapter on *Weg nach Timimoun* has shown, the narrator advocates a rejection of tragedy and revenge, suggesting that, in this regard, the time has come to turn away from the destructive elements of myth as they manifest themselves in the modern world. Roes responds to this collision between tradition and modernity with an attempt to negotiate the border between a permissive cultural relativism that turns a blind eye to objectionable cultural norms on the one hand, and an offensive interference in the internal affairs of foreign countries on the other. The fascination of the West with a culture in which the values of honour and vengeance dominate is understandable. However, Roes avoids exoticization and sensationalism in his involvement with this debate and engages his readers with a novel that encourages a reconsideration of how the West responds to cultural difference.

Again in *Geschichte der Freundschaft*, the collection of intertexts is not primarily centred on the theme of interculturality, but in this case on the theme of male-male friendships. These intertexts illuminate the novel's main narrative, the development of a friendship between the German narrator and an Algerian student. It is argued in all four chapters that Roes's conception of sensual friendships between men is particularly suited to intercultural situations because the liminal space between cultures offers a freedom that invites a more creative approach to relationship-building. The novel's narrative, and its collection of quotations, illuminate each other in a manner which could be termed 'contrapuntal'. While the intertexts on the topic of friendship have a universal applicability and shed light on the reader's understanding of interpersonal relations, the manner in which Roes applies them is specific to an intercultural and all-male situation. Whereas Matthias fails to establish new ways of overcoming the intercultural divide and establishing a lasting bond with his partner, the accompanying theories and quotations suggest that the search for viable alternatives can continue.

The novel demonstrates again that Roes offers new perspectives from which current debates can be understood. Although Roes presumably supports the campaign for gay equality he has not entered recent public debate in support of gay marriage.[6] Instead, Roes transcends the contemporary political debate by offering an alternative view of male-male 'friendship' that leaves the distinction between homo- and heterosexuality nebulous. At a time when the debate surrounding gay marriage is intensifying in Germany and elsewhere, Roes is already advancing a position that goes beyond the conventional binary understanding of sexuality. Ironically, however, while Roes's deliberately enigmatic concept of male-male relationships seems to be progressive in the context of the current media discourse, his intertexts reveal that his model of sexuality is not as modern as it may appear. As I show in the chapter on *Geschichte der Freundschaft*, Roes's vision is actually inspired by pre-modern conceptions of sexuality which were more concerned with specific sexual activities than with an all-encompassing sexual identity. His conception of male sexuality presents a challenge both to the conservative faction opposed to same-sex marriage and to the liberal campaign promoting gay rights.

This book argues that while the intertexuality of Roes's fiction is at times superficially postmodern, he actually resists the postmodernist tendency to abandon political values and aesthetic judgement. I have shown how each of the four novels engages with important contemporary debates concerning identity, politics and interculturality, demonstrating that the author is unafraid of taking a strong stance on ethical issues. In each case the intertextual processes underpinning the novel are a vital element in the way these political points are communicated. Roes engages with his intertexts and draws from them alternative approaches to understanding and explaining the world. In the process, he formulates radical concepts of identity that provide an important contrast to mainstream concepts that dominate popular discourse.

6 This hesitancy could well be attributed to a perception that, as Ole von Beust, the gay former CDU mayor of Hamburg recently asserted, 'Schwulenehe ist etwas sehr Konservatives'. See Ole von Beust (with Mira von Gajevic), 'Interview mit Ole von Beust: "Schwulenehe ist etwas sehr konservatives"', *Berliner Zeitung*, 29 March 2013, www.berliner-zeitung.de/politik/interview-mit-ole-von-beust--schwulenehe-ist-etwas-sehr-konservatives-,10808018,22241288.html [accessed 15 April 2013].

Bibliography

Primary Sources

Roes

Roes, Michael, *Jizchak: Versuch über das Sohnesopfer* (Berlin: Gatza, 1992)
— *Cham: Ein Symposion* (Berlin: Gatza, 1993)
— *Lleu Llaw Gyffes* (Berlin: Gatza, 1994)
— *Leeres Viertel. Rub' al-Khali: Invention über das Spiel* (Frankfurt am Main: btb, [1996]1998)
— *Durus Arabij / Arabische Lektionen* (Frankfurt am Main: Eichborn, 1997)
— *Der Narr des Königs: Madschnun al-Malik. Ein Schelmenstück* (Frankfurt am Main: Gatza bei Eichborn, 1997)
— *Der Coup der Berdache* (Berlin: Berlin Verlag, 1999)
— *Haut des Südens: Eine Mississippi-Reise* (Berlin: Berliner Taschenbuch Verlag, [2000] 2002)
— *David Kanchelli* (Berlin: Berlin Verlag, 2001)
— *Nah Inverness* (Berlin: Parthas, 2004)
— *Kain: Elegie* (Berlin: Parthas, 2004)
— *Weg nach Timimoun* (Berlin: Matthes & Seitz, 2006)
— *Krieg und Tanz* (Berlin: Matthes & Seitz, 2007)
— *Perversion und Glück* (Berlin: Matthes & Seitz, 2007)
— *Ich weiß nicht mehr die Nacht* (Berlin: Matthes & Seitz, 2008)
— *Die Fünf Farben Schwarz* (Berlin: Matthes & Seitz, 2009)
— *Geschichte der Freundschaft* (Berlin: Matthes & Seitz, 2010)
— *Engel und Avatare* [with Hinderk Emrich] (Berlin: Matthes & Seitz, 2011)
— *Die Laute* (Berlin: Matthes & Seitz, 2012)
— *Die Legende von der Weißen Schlange* (Berlin: Matthes & Seitz, 2014)

Other Authors

Aeschylus, *The Oresteia*, trans. by Robert Fagles (London: Penguin, 1979)
Camus, Albert, *Carnets: mai 1935 – février 1942* (Paris: Gallimard, 1962)
— *La Peste* (Paris: Gallimard, 1968)
— *The Plague*, trans. by Stuart Gilbert (Harmondsworth: Penguin, 1960)
— *L'étranger* (Paris: Gallimard, 1942)
— *The Outsider*, trans. by Stuart Gilbert (Harmondsworth: Penguin, 1961)
Canetti, Elias, *Die Stimmen von Marrakesch: Aufzeichnungen nach einer Reise* (Frankfurt am Main: Fischer, 1980)
Davidson, Robyn, ed., *The Picador Book of Journeys* (London: Picador, 2001)
Derrida, Jacques, *Politiques de l'amitié* (Paris: Galilée, 1994)
— *The Politics of Friendship*, trans. by George Collins (London: Verso, 1997)
Fatah, Sherko, *Das dunkle Schiff* (Salzburg: Jung und Jung, 2008)
Faulkner, William, *Intruder in the Dust* (London: Vintage, 1996)
— *Light in August* (London: Vintage, 2005)
Fichte, Hubert, *Der Platz der Gehenkten* (Frankfurt am Main: Fischer, 1989)
— *Alte Welt* (Frankfurt am Main: Fischer, 1992)
Gernhardt, Robert, *Die Madagaskar-Reise: Ein Bericht* (Frankfurt am Main: Zweitausendeins, 1980)
Goethe, Johann Wolfgang von, *West-östlicher Divan* (Frankfurt am Main: Insel, 1974)
— *Italienische Reise* (Frankfurt am Main: Fischer, 2009)
Grass, Günter, *Die Blechtrommel* (Munich: DTV, 1993)
Jelloun, Tahar Ben, *Partir* (Paris: Gallimard, 2006)
— *Leaving Tangier*, trans. by Linda Coverdale (London: Arcadia, 2009)
Koeppen, Wolfgang, *Amerikafahrt* (Fischer: Frankfurt am Main, 1962)
Kundera, Milan, *The Unbearable Lightness of Being*, trans. by Michael Henry Heim (London: Faber & Faber, 1999)
Melville, Herman, *Typee & Billy Budd* (London: Dent, 1958)
— *Moby Dick* (London: Penguin, 1994)
Montaigne, Michel de, 'De l'Amitié', in *Les Essais* (Paris: Gallimard, 2007), pp. 189–201
— *On Friendship*, trans. by M. A. Screech (London: Penguin, 2004)
Nadolny, Sten, *Selim oder Die Gabe der Rede* (Munich: Piper, 1992)
Niebuhr, Carsten, *Reisebeschreibung nach Arabien und andern umliegenden Ländern* (Zurich: Manesse, 1997)
Nietzsche, Friedrich, *Sämtliche Werke*, ed. by Giorgio Colli and Mazzino Montinari, 15 vols, ii, *Menschliches Allzumenschliches* (Munich: DTV, 1999)

Orwell, George, *The Collected Essays, Journalism and Letters of George Orwell*, i, *An Age Like This 1920–1940*, ed. by Sonia Orwell and Ian Angus (London: Secker & Warburg, 1968)

Philby, John, *The Empty Quarter* (London: Century, 1986)

Raban, Jonathan, *Old Glory: An American Voyage* (New York: Simon & Schuster, 1981)

Schami, Rafik, *Die Sehnsucht fährt schwarz* (Munich: DTV, 1988)

Schirmer, Bernd, *Die Hand der Fatima auf meiner Schulter: Algerische Reisebilder* (Leipzig: Mitteldeutscher Verlag, 1984)

Schrott, Raoul, *Finis Terrae* (Munich: DTV, 1997)

Seetzen, Ulrich Jasper, *Reisen durch Syrien, Palästina, Phönicien, die Transjordan-Länder, Arabia Petraea und Unter-Aegypten* (Berlin: Reimer, 1854)

Şenocak, Zafer, *Zungenentfernung: Bericht aus der Quarantänestation* (Munich: Babel, 2001)

Sterne, Laurence, *A Sentimental Journey* (Oxford: Oxford University Press, 1984)

Timm, Uwe, *Morenga* (Munich: DTV, 2000)

Twain, Mark, *Life on the Mississippi* (London: Penguin, 1984)

— *The Adventures of Huckleberry Finn* (London: Penguin, 1994)

Wittgenstein, Ludwig, *Philosophische Untersuchungen / Philosophical Investigations* [Bilingual edition. English trans. by G. E. M. Anscombe, P. M. S. Hacker and Joachim Schulte] (Chichester: Wiley-Blackwell, 2009)

Secondary Literature

Abbey, Ruth, 'Circles, Ladders and Stars: Nietzsche on Friendship', in *The Challenge to Friendship in Modernity*, ed. by Preston T. King and Heather Devere (Ilford: Frank Cass, 2000), pp. 50–73

Abbott, H. Porter, *The Cambridge Introduction to Narrative* (Cambridge: Cambridge University Press, 2008)

Achebe, Chinua, *Hopes and Impediments: Selected Essays* (New York: Doubleday, 1989)

Adams, David, and Galin Tihanov, eds., *Enlightenment Cosmopolitanism* (London: MHRA and Maney, 2011)

Adams, Percy G., *Travelers and Travel Liars, 1660–1800* (New York: Dover, 1980)

— *Travel Literature and the Evolution of the Novel* (Lexington: University Press of Kentucky, 1983)

Adelson, Leslie A., 'Migrant's Literature or German Literature? TORKAN's *Tufan: Brief an einen islamischen Bruder*', *The German Quarterly*, 63 (1990), 382–89

Adra, Najwa, 'Dance and Glance: Visualizing Tribal Identity in Highland Yemen', *Visual Anthropology*, 11 (1998), 55–102, www.najwaadra.net/danceglance.pdf [accessed 3 January 2011]

Albrecht, Monika, 'Selim's Sisters: Muslim Women in Novels by Uwe Timm and Hermann Schulz', *German Life and Letters*, 63 (2010), 20–36

Allen, Graham, *Intertextuality*, 2nd edn (London: Routledge, 2011)

Al-Slaiman, Moustafa, 'Autor/innen aus dem arabischen Kulturraum', in *Interkulturelle Literatur in Deutschland. Ein Handbuch*, ed. by Carmine Chiellino (Stuttgart: Metzler, 2007), pp. 235–47

Anz, Thomas, 'Das Spiel ist aus? Zur Konjunktur und Verabschiedung des "postmodernen" Spielbegriffs', in *Postmoderne Literatur in deutscher Sprache: Eine Ästhetik des Widerstands?*, ed. by Henk Harbers (Amsterdam: Rodopi, 2000), pp. 15–34

Apel, Friedmar, 'Sein Algerien', *Frankfurter Allgemeine Zeitung*, 3 July 2006, p. 38

Ashcroft, Bill, Gareth Griffiths, and Helen Tiffin, *Post-Colonial Studies: The Key Concepts*, 2nd edn (London: Routledge, 2007)

Augé, Marc, *Non-places: Introduction to an Anthropology of Supermodernity*, trans. by John Howe (London: Verso, 1995)

Bakhtin, Mikhail M., 'Epic and Novel: Toward a Methodology for the Study of the Novel', in Bakhtin, Mikhail M., *The Dialogic Imagination*, trans. by Caryl Emerson and Michael Holquist (Austin: University of Texas Press, 1981), pp. 3–40

Barthes, Roland, 'The Death of the Author', in Barthes, Roland, *Image – Music – Text*, trans. by Stephen Heath (London: Fontana, 1977)

Baumbach, Kora, 'Verdrängte Kolonialgeschichte: Zu Uwe Timms Roman *Morenga*', *Monatshefte*, 97 (2005), 213–31

Bay, Hansjörg, 'Going Native?: Mimikry und Maskerade in kolonialen Entdeckungsreisen der Gegenwartsliteratur (Stangl; Trojanow)', in *Ins Fremde Schreiben: Gegenwartsliteratur auf den Spuren historischer und fantastischer Entdeckungsreisen*, ed. by Christof Hamann and Alexander Honold (Göttingen: Wallstein, 2009), pp. 117–42

Becker-Cantarino, Barbara, 'Introduction: German Literature in the Era of Enlightenment and Sensibility', in *German Literature of the Eighteenth Century: The Enlightenment and Sensibility*, ed. by Barbara Becker-Cantarino (Rochester: Camden House, 2005), pp. 1–32

Benjamin, Roger, ed., *Orientalism: Delacroix to Klee* (Sydney: Art Gallery of New South Wales, 2001)

Benjamin, Walter, 'Der Erzähler', in Benjamin, Walter, *Gesammelte Schriften*, ed. by Rolf Tiedemann and Hermann Schweppenhäuser, 12 vols, ii, 2, pp. 438–65

Bennett, Andrew, and Nicholas Royle, *An Introduction to Literature, Criticism and Theory*, 4th edn (Harlow: Pearson, 2009)

Benthien, Claudia, *Haut: Literaturgeschichte - Körperbilder - Grenzdiskurse* (Reinbeck bei Hamburg: Rowohlt, 1999)

Berman, Nina, *German Literature on the Middle East: Discourses and Practices, 1000–1989* (Ann Arbor: University of Michigan Press, 2011)

Beust, Ole von (with Mira von Gajevic), 'Interview mit Ole von Beust: "Schwulenehe ist etwas sehr konservatives"', *Berliner Zeitung*, 29 March 2013, www.berliner-zeitung.de/politik/interview-mit-ole-von-beust--schwulenehe-ist-etwas-sehr-konservatives-,10808018,22241288.html [accessed 15 April 2013]

Biernat, Ulla, *"Ich bin nicht der erste Fremde hier": Zur deutschsprachigen Reiseliteratur nach 1945* (Würzburg: Königshausen & Neumann, 2004)

Blanton, Casey, *Travel Writing: the Self and the World* (New York: Routledge, 2002)

Borm, Jan, 'Defining Travel: On the Travel Book, Travel Writing and Terminology', in *Perspectives on Travel Writing*, ed. by Glenn Hooper and Tim Youngs (Aldershot: Ashgate, 2004), pp. 13–26

Bosse, Anke, 'Ost und West im Fadenkreuz des Erzählens: Selim oder die Gabe der Rede', in *Sten Nadolny*, ed. by Wolfgang Bunzel (Eggingen: Isele, 1996), pp. 192–225

Bourquin, Christophe, *Schreiben über Reisen: zur ars itineraria von Urs Widmer im Kontext der europäischen Reiseliteratur* (Würzburg: Königshausen & Neumann, 2006)

Boyle, Nicholas, *Goethe: The Poet and the Age*, 2 vols, i, *The Poetry of Desire* (Oxford: Oxford University Press, 1991)

Braun, Michael, 'Michael Roes: Leeres Viertel. Rub' al-Khali', *Die Woche*, 4 October 1996, p. 9

Brenner, Gerry, *Performative Criticism: Experiments in Reader Response* (New York: State University of New York Press, 2004)

Brenner, Peter J., 'Die Erfahrung der Fremde: Zur Entwicklung einer Wahrnehmungsform in der Geschichte des Reiseberichts', in *Der Reisebericht: Die Entwicklung einer Gattung in der deutschen Literatur*, ed. by Peter J. Brenner (Frankfurt am Main: Suhrkamp, 1989), pp. 14–49

Bunke, Simon, *Heimweh: Studien zur Kultur- und Literaturgeschichte einer tödlichen Krankheit* (Freiburg im Breisgau: Rombach, 2009)

Burrin, Philippe, 'Nazi Antisemitism: Animalization and Demonization', in *Demonizing the Other: Antisemitism, Racism and Xenophobia*, ed. by Robert S. Wistrich (Amsterdam: Harwood, 1999), pp. 223–35

Caillois, Roger, *Man, Play and Games*, trans. by Meyer Barash (Urbana and Chicago: University of Illinois Press, 2001)

Caselli, Daniela, *Beckett's Dantes: Intertextuality in the Fiction and Criticism* (Manchester: Manchester University Press, 2005)

Certeau, Michel de, *The Practice of Everyday Life*, trans. by Steven Randall (Berkeley: University of California Press, 1984)

Chandler, Daniel, *Semiotics: The Basics*, 2nd edn (Abingdon: Routledge, 2007)

Chase, Richard, 'Melville and *Moby Dick*', in *Melville: A Collection of Critical Essays*, ed. by Richard Chase (Englewood Cliffs: Prentice-Hall, 1962), pp. 49–61

Cheesman, Tom, *Novels of Turkish German Settlement: Cosmopolite Fictions* (Rochester: Camden House, 2007)

Chin, Rita, *The Guest Worker Question in Postwar Germany* (Cambridge: Cambridge University Press, 2007)

Clifford, James, 'On Ethnographic Authority', *Representations*, 2 (1983), 118–46

— 'Introduction', in *Writing Culture: The Poetics and Politics of Ethnography*, ed. by James Clifford and George E. Marcus (Berkeley: University of California Press, 1986), pp. 1–26

Cramer, Sybille, 'Jede Wirklichkeit hat ihre eigene Sprache', *Neue Zürcher Zeitung*, 7 November 1996, p. 33

— 'Fieber, Ehre, Lust: Michael Roes' feine afrikanische Orestie "Weg nach Timimoun"', *Frankfurter Rundschau*, 8 November 2006, p. 16

Crotty, Kevin M., *Law's Interior: Legal and Literary Constructions of the Self* (Ithaca: Cornell University Press, 2000)

Dallmayr, Fred, *Beyond Orientalism: Essays on Cross-cultural Encounter* (Albany: State University of New York Press, 1996)

Davis, Mary Kemp, 'The Veil Rent in Twain: Degradation and Revelation in *Adventures of Huckleberry Finn*', in *Satire or Evasion?: Black Perspectives on* Huckleberry Finn, ed. by James S. Leonard, Thomas A. Tenney and Thadious M. Davis (Durham, NC: Duke University Press, 1992), pp. 77–90

Desmond, Jane C., ed., *Meaning in Motion: New Cultural Studies of Dance* (Durham, NC: Duke University Press, 2003)

Dietsche, Petra, 'Einleitung', in *Das Erstaunen über das Fremde* (Frankfurt am Main: Peter Lang, 1984), pp. 5–11

Dillmann, Martin, *Poetologien der Kontingenz: Zufälligkeit und Möglichkeit im Diskursgefüge der Moderne* (Cologne: Böhlau, 2011)

Dirke, Sabine von, 'West meets East: Narrative Construction of the Foreigner and Postmodern Orientalism in Sten Nadolny's *Selim oder die Gabe der Rede*', *The Germanic Review*, 69 (1994), 61–69

— 'Multikulti: The German Debate on Multiculturalism', *German Studies Review*, 17 (1994), 513–36

Dischner, Gisela, 'Albert Camus: Der Fremde im Büro', in *Die Stimme des Fremden* (Hofheim: Wolke, 1992), pp. 101–12

Drabble, Margaret, 'Of Beasts and Men: Orwell on Beastliness', in *On* Nineteen Eighty Four: *Orwell and our Future*, ed. by Abbott Gleason, Jack Goldsmith and Martha C. Nussbaum (Princeton: Princeton University Press, 2005), pp. 38–48

Dunker, Axel, '"Als wisse ich endlich Alles oder doch wenigstens mehr vom Oriente als die Orientalen selbst": Zu Michael Roes' *Rub al-Khali. Leeres Viertel. Invention über das Spiel*', in *Ins Fremde Schreiben: Gegenwartsliteratur auf den Spuren historischer und fantastischer Entdeckungsreisen*, ed. by Christof Hamann and Alexander Honold (Göttingen: Wallstein, 2009), pp. 203–25

Durzak, Manfred, 'Zitat und Montage im deutschen Roman der Gegenwart', in *Die deutsche Literatur der Gegenwart: Aspekte und Tendenzen*, ed. by Manfred Durzak (Stuttgart: Reclam, 1971), pp. 211–29

Dyer, Richard, *White* (London: Routledge, 1997)

Eder, Walter, 'Zu Hause in der Fremde?: Der Verlust der Raumerfahrung als Verlust des Erfahrungsraums beim Reisen', in *Das Fremde: Erfahrungsmöglichkeiten zwischen Faszination und Bedrohung*, ed. by Ortfried Schäffter (Opladen: Westdeutscher Verlag, 1991), pp. 158–72

Eichler, Klaus-Dieter, ed., *Philosophie der Freundschaft* (Leipzig: Reclam, 1999)

Enzensberger, Hans Magnus, 'Eine Theorie des Tourismus', in *Einzelheiten 1: Bewußtseins-Industrie* (Frankfurt am Main: Suhrkamp, 1962), pp. 179–205

Evanoff, Richard J., 'Universalist, relativist, and constructivist approaches to intercultural ethics', *International Journal of Intercultural Relations*, 28 (2004), 439–58

Evans, Martin, and John Phillips, *Algeria: Anger of the Dispossessed* (New Haven and London: Yale University Press, 2007)

Federman, Raymond, 'Imagination as Plagiarism [an unfinished paper…]', *New Literary History*, 7 (1976), 563–78

— 'What are Experimental Novels and Why Are There So Many Left Unread?', in *Critifiction* (Albany: State University of New York Press, 1993), pp. 65–75

Fendri, Mounir, 'Die Entdeckung des maghribinischen Orients', in *Orientdiskurse in der deutschen Literatur*, ed. by Klaus-Michael Bogdahl (Bielefeld: Aisthesis, 2007), pp. 183–99

Fichte, Hubert, 'Ketzerische Bemerkungen für eine neue Wissenschaft vom Menschen', in *Petersilie* (Frankfurt am Main: Fischer, 1980), pp. 359–69

Fickert, Kurt, 'The Myth of America in Peter Handke's *Der kurze Brief zum langen Abschied*', *German Studies Review*, 21 (1998), 27–40

Fine, Robert, *Cosmopolitanism* (London: Routledge, 2007)

Fishkin, Shelley Fisher, *Was Huck Black?: Mark Twain and African American Voices* (New York; Oxford: Oxford University Press, 1993)

Foley, Helene P., 'Introduction', in Aeschylus, *Oresteia*, trans. by Peter Meineck (Indianapolis: Hackett, 1998), pp. vi–xlvii

Forsdick, Charles, Feroza Basu, and Siobhán Shilton, *New Approaches to Twentieth-Century Travel Literature in French: Genre, History, Theory* (New York: Peter Lang, 2006)

Foucault, Michel, 'Sex, Power, and the Politics of Identity', in *Ethics: Subjectivity and Truth*, ed. by Paul Rabinow (New York: New Press, 1998), pp. 163–73

— 'Sex, Macht und die Politik der Identität', in *Kritik des Regierens: Schriften zur Politik*, ed. by Ulrich Bröckling (Translator uncredited) (Berlin: Suhrkamp, 2010), pp. 386–400

— *The Will to Knowledge. The History of Sexuality*, 3 vols, i, trans. by Robert Hurley (London: Penguin, 1998)

Freund, Wieland, '"Eine Generation von Wallfahrern": Roadnovels – sehr europäische "Amerikanische Reisen"', in *Der deutsche Roman der Gegenwart*, ed. by Wieland Freund and Winifried Freund (Munich: Fink, 2001), pp. 45–52

Fuhrig, Dirk, 'In Gottes Überwachungsstaat', *Frankfurter Rundschau*, 23 May 2002, p. 20

Fussell, Paul, *Abroad: British Literary Travelling Between the Wars* (Oxford: Oxford University Press, 1980)

gaybooks.de, 'Geschichte der Freundschaft', www.gay-and-lesbianbooks.de/vmchk/Roes-Michael/61-Neue-Romane/1258823808-Geschichte-der-Freundschaft.html [accessed 22 March 2011]

Geertz, Clifford, *The Interpretation of Cultures* (London: Fontana, 1973; 1993)

— *Works and Lives: The Anthropologist as Author* (Cambridge: Polity, 1988)

Genette, Gérard, *Palimpsests: Literature in the Second Degree*, trans. by Channa Newman and Claude Doubinsky (Lincoln: University of Nebraska Press, 1997)

George, Roger, 'A Boat Swamped with Abstractions: Reading Raban's River', in *Temperamental Journeys: Essays on the Modern Literature of Travel*, ed. by Michael Kowalewski (Athens: University of Georgia Press, 1992), pp. 249–63

Ghirardelli, Gennaro, 'Pustelkuchen: Michael Roes am Mississippi', *Frankfurter Allgemeine Zeitung*, 21 October 2000, p. V

Gillman, Susan, *Dark Twins: Imposture and Identity in Mark Twain's America* (Chicago: University of Chicago Press, 1989)

Goldhill, Simon, *Aeschylus: The Oresteia* (Cambridge: Cambridge University Press, 1992)

Göttsche, Dirk, 'Der neue historische Afrika-Roman: Kolonialismus aus postkolonialer Sicht', *German Life and Letters*, 56 (2003), 261–80

— 'Hans Christoph Buch's *Sansibar Blues* and the Fascination of Cross-cultural Experience in Contemporary German Historical Novels about Colonialism', *German Life and Letters*, 65 (2012), 127–46

Grejda, Edward S., *The Common Continent of Men: Racial Equality in the Writings of Herman Melville* (Port Washington: Kennikat, 1974)

Grün, Max von der, *Leben im gelobten Land: Ausländer in Deutschland* (Munich: DTV, 1994)

Gutjahr, Ortrud, 'Der Entdeckungsbericht des Anderen: Erreiste Intertextualität in Felicitas Hoppes *Pigafetta*', in *Ins Fremde Schreiben: Gegenwartsliteratur auf den Spuren historischer und fantastischer Entdeckungsreisen*, ed. by Christof Hamann and Alexander Honold (Göttingen: Wallstein, 2009), pp. 239–66

Haas, Christoph, 'Die Menschenpflicht der Freude', *Süddeutsche Zeitung*, 3 August 2006, p. 14

Hage, Volker, 'Sprachlos in der Wüste', *Der Spiegel*, 25 November 1996, p. 220

— 'Die Enkeln kommen', *Der Spiegel*, 11 October 1999, www.spiegel.de/spiegel/print/d-14906942.html [accessed 26 February 2013]

Haines, Brigid, 'The reader, the writer, her narrator and their text(s): intertextuality in Christa Wolf's *Störfall*', in *Christa Wolf in Perspective: German Monitor*, 30, ed. by Ian Wallace (Amsterdam: Rodopi, 1994), pp. 157–72

Hakkarainen, Marja-Leena, 'German Home and Hybridity: Reclaiming New Cultural Identities in Selected German Migrant Narratives from the 1990s', in *Cultural Identity in Transition: Contemporary Conditions, Practices and Politics of a Global Phenomenon*, ed. by Jari Kupiainen, Erkki Sevänen and John A. Stotesbury (New Delhi: Atlantic, 2004), pp. 191–204

Hamann, Christoph, and Alexander Honold, eds., *Ins Fremde schreiben: Gegenwartsliteratur auf den Spuren historischer und fantastischer Entdeckungsreisen* (Göttingen: Wallstein, 2009)

Han, Petrus, 'Angst vor Fremden und Migrationsrealität - ein unlösbarer Widerspruch?', in *Migration und psychische Gesundheit: Belastungen und Potentiale*, ed. by Theda Borde and Matthias David (Frankfurt am Main: Mabuse, 2007), pp. 23–38

Heinrichs, Hans-Jürgen, 'Die authentische Beschreibung der fremden Kultur', in *Hubert Fichte: Materialien zu Leben und Werk*, ed. by Thomas Beckermann (Frankfurt am Main: Fischer, 1985), pp. 142–51

Heinritz, Reinhard, '"Fremde Wildnis": Über den neuen deutschsprachigen Reiseroman', *Jahrbuch Deutsch als Fremdsprache*, 17 (1991), 72–93

Henderson, Heather, 'The Travel Writer and the Text: "My Giant Goes with Me Wherever I Go"', in *Temperamental Journeys: Essays on the Modern Literature of Travel*, ed. by Michael Kowalewski (Athens: University of Georgia Press, 1992), pp. 230–48

Herrmann, Karsten, 'Ein (Werk-) Porträt des Michael Roes', http://culturmag.de/rubriken/buecher/michael-roes-im-portrat/14846 [accessed 9 June 2014]

Holdenried, Michaela, 'Ketzerische Bemerkungen zu Michael Roes' ethnologischen Roman *Rub' al-Khali*', in *Ethno/Graphie: Reiseformen des Wissens*, ed. by Peter Braun and Manfred Weinberg (Tübingen: Gunter Narr, 2002), pp. 355–66

Holland, Patrick, and Graham Huggan, *Tourists with Typewriters: Critical Reflections on Contemporary Travel Writing* (Ann Arbor: University of Michigan Press, 2000)

Honold, Alexander, 'Der ethnographische Roman am Ende des 20. Jahrhunderts: Fichte und Roes', in *Räume der literarischen Postmoderne: Gender, Performativität, Globalisierung*, ed. by Paul Michael Lützeler (Tübingen: Stauffenberg, 2000), pp. 71–95

Horrocks, David, and Eva Kolinsky, 'Living and Writing in Germany: Emine Sevgi Özdamar in Conversation with David Horrocks and Eva Kolinsky', in *Turkish Culture in German Society Today*, ed. by David Horrocks and Eva Kolinsky (Oxford: Berghahn, 1996), pp. 45–54

Hron, Madelaine, *Translating Pain: Immigrant Suffering in Literature and Culture* (Toronto: University of Toronto Press, 2009)

Huizinga, Johan, *Homo Ludens: A Study of the Play Element in Culture*, trans. by R. F. C. Hull (Boston: Beacon, 1955)

Huntington, Samuel P., *The Clash of Civilizations and the Remaking of World Order* (New York: Simon & Schuster, 1996)

Hutchby, Ian, and Robin Wooffitt, *Conversation Analysis*, 2nd edn (Cambridge: Polity, 2008)

Hutchinson, Peter, *Games Authors Play* (London: Methuen, 1983)

Jacobs, Arthur, *A New Dictionary of Music* (Harmondsworth: Penguin, 1958)

Jefferson, Ann, 'Autobiography as intertext: Barthes, Sarraute, Robbe-Grillet', in *Intertextuality: Theories and Practices*, ed. by Michael Worton and Judith Still (Manchester: Manchester University Press, 1990), pp. 108–29

Kapuściński, Ryszard, *The Other*, trans. by Antonia Lloyd-Jones (London: Verso, 2008)

Karakus, Mahmut, *Interkulturelle Konstellationen: Deutsch-türkische Begegnungen in deutschsprachigen Romanen der Gegenwart* (Würzburg: Königshausen & Neumann, 2006)

Kellett, E. E., *Literary Quotation and Allusion* (Cambridge: W. Heffer, 1933)

Kizilhan, Ilhan, 'Potentiale und Belastungen psychosozialer Netzwerke in der Migration', in *Migration und psychische Gesundheit: Belastungen und Potentiale*, ed. by Theda Borde and Matthias David (Frankfurt am Main: Mabuse, 2007), pp. 53–67

Kjeilen, Tore, 'Grand Erg Occidental: The Endless Dunes', http://lexicorient.com/algeria/g_erg_oc.htm [accessed 18 August 2011]

Koch, Manfred, 'Der kurze Sommer des Liebesglücks: Michael Roes' philosophisch-ethnologischer Roman über Männerfreundschaft', *Neue Zürcher Zeitung*, 12 October 2010, p. 17

Komar, Kathleen L., *Reclaiming Klytemnestra: Revenge or Reconciliation* (Chicago: University of Illinois Press, 2003)

Kontje, Todd, *German Orientalisms* (Ann Arbor: University of Michigan Press, 2004)

Kospach, Julia, 'Schwarz und weiss: *Haut des Südens* von Michael Roes', *Der Bund*, 10 February 2001, p. 2

Kramer, Jürgen, 'Das Verstehen fremder Kulturen: Möglichkeiten und Grenzen aus ethnologischer, hermeneutischer und psychoanalytischer Sicht', in *Fremdheitserfahrung und Fremdheitsdarstellung in okzidentalen Kulturen: Theorieansätze, Medien/Textsorten, Diskursformen*, ed. by Bernd Lenz and Hans-Jürgen Lüsebrink (Passau: Rothe, 1999), pp. 37–53

Kritzman, Lawrence D., ed., *Michel Foucault: Politics, Philosophy, Culture: Interviews and Other Writings 1977–1984* (New York; London: Routledge, 1988)

Kroß, Matthias, 'Die Poetik des Fremden', in Roes, Michael, *Perversion und Glück*, (Berlin: Matthes & Seitz, 2007), pp. 87–116

Lange, Dietz, *Erfahrung und die Glaubwürdigkeit des Glaubens* (Tübingen: Mohr Siebeck, 1984)

Langenbacher, Andreas, 'Schreiben in extremen Zonen', *Neue Zürcher Zeitung*, 6 February 2010, www.nzz.ch/nachrichten/kultur/literatur_und_kunst/schreiben-in-extremen-zonen-1.4830227 [accessed 22 February 2013]

Large, Duncan, 'Proust on Nietzsche: The Question of Friendship', *The Modern Language Review*, 88 (1993), 612–24

Leonard, James S., and Thomas A. Tenney, 'Introduction: The Controversy over *Huckleberry Finn*', in *Satire or Evasion?: Black Perspectives on* Huckleberry

Finn, ed. by James S. Leonard, Thomas A. Tenney and Thadious M. Davis (Durham NC: Duke University Press, 1992), pp. 1–11

Lester, Julius, 'Morality and *Adventures of Huckleberry Finn*', in *Satire or Evasion?: Black Perspectives on* Huckleberry Finn, ed. by James S. Leonard, Thomas A. Tenney and Thadious M. Davis (Durham, NC: Duke University Press, 1992), pp. 199–207

Lévi-Strauss, Claude, *Tristes Tropiques*, trans. by John and Doreen Weightman (London: Jonathan Cape, 1973)

Linklater, Beth, 'Germany as background: global concerns in recent women's writing in German', in *German Literature in the Age of Globalisation*, ed. by Stuart Taberner (Birmingham: University of Birmingham Press, 2004), pp. 67–88

Lisle, Debbie, *The Global Politics of Contemporary Travel Writing* (Cambridge: Cambridge University Press, 2006)

Lodge, David, *The Practice of Writing* (London: Penguin, 1997)

Luedke, Martin, 'Stachel im Fleisch', *Die Zeit*, 21 (1995), www.zeit.de/1995/21/Stachel_im_Fleisch [accessed 5 December 2011]

Lützeler, Paul Michael, 'Ein Derwisch verschwindet', *Die Zeit*, 36 (1998), www.zeit.de/1998/36/Ein_Derwisch_verschwindet [accessed 29 November 2010]

— *Postmoderne und postkoloniale deutschsprachige Literatur: Diskurs – Analyse – Kritik* (Bielefeld: Aisthesis, 2005)

— 'Macht und Gewalt: Zu Romanen über Bürgerkriege im Nahen und Mittleren Osten von Kühn, Born, Kracht und Roes', in *Gewalt und kulturelles Gedächtnis: Repräsentationsformen von Gewalt in Literatur und Film seit 1945*, ed. by Robert Weninger (Tübingen: Stauffenberg, 2005), pp. 19–37

Malaby, Thomas M., 'Anthropology and Play: The Contours of Playful Experience', *New Literary History*, 40 (2009), 205–18

Mani, B. Venkat, *Cosmopolitical Claims: Turkish-German Literatures from Nadolny to Pamuk* (Iowa City: University of Iowa Press, 2007)

Martels, Zweder von, ed., *Travel Fact and Travel Fiction: Studies on Fiction, Literary Tradition, Scholarly Discovery and Observation in Travel Writing* (Leiden: Brill, 1994)

Martin, Marko, 'Objektivität ist Lüge: Michael Roes, Völklerkundler und Literat', *Der Tagesspeigel*, 28 January 1997, p. 24

Massad, Joseph A., *Desiring Arabs* (Chicago: University of Chicago Press, 2007)

May, Yomb, 'Goethe, Islam, and the Orient: The Impetus for and Mode of Intercultural Encounter in the *West-östlicher Divan*', in *Encounters with*

Islam in German Literature and Culture, ed. by James Hodkinson and Jeffrey Morrison (Rochester: Camden House, 2009), pp. 89–107

Maze, John Robert, *Albert Camus: Plague and Terror, Priest and Atheist* (Bern: Peter Lang, 2010)

Mee, Catherine, 'European Travellers in Africa – The Negotiation of Identity', *Forum for Modern Language Studies*, 45 (2009), 378–89

Méritt, Laura, 'Fremdheit und Nähe', *Siegessäule*, 10 (2010), 40–41

Morphy, Howard, 'Proximity and Distance: Representations of Aboriginal Society in the Writings of Bill Harney and Bruce Chatwin', in *Popularizing Anthropology*, ed. by Jeremy MacClancy and Chris McDonaugh (London: Routledge, 1996), pp. 157–79

Mottahedeh, Negar, 'Images of Women: Middle East', in *Routledge International Encyclopedia of Women: Global Women's Issues and Knowledge*, ed. by Cheris Kramarae and Dale Spender, iii, *Identity Politics – Publishing* (London: Routledge, 2001), pp. 1118–20

Neumann, Peter Horst, 'Das Eigene und das Fremde: Über die Wünschbarkeit einer Theorie des Zitierens', *Akzente*, 4 (1980), 292–305

Niekerk, Carl, 'The Romantics and other cultures', in *The Cambridge Companion to German Romanticism*, ed. by Nicholas Saul (Cambridge: Cambridge University Press, 2009), pp. 147–61

Niro, Brian, *Race* (Basingstoke: Palgrave Macmillan, 2003)

Nommel, Jens, and Michael Roes, 'Im Gespräch über die eigenen Grenzen', http://handlungsreisedioalog.blogwerft.de/2007/12/13/michael-roes/ [accessed 4 November 2009]

Norbeck, Edward, 'Anthropological Views of Play', *American Zoologist*, 14 (1974), 267–73

O'Brien, Michael, *Placing the South* (Jackson: University Press of Mississippi, 2007)

Orr, Mary, *Intertextuality: Debates and Contexts* (Cambridge: Polity, 2003)

Padgett, John B., 'William Faulkner as Screenwriter', in *William Faulkner and Motion Pictures*, www.mcsr.olemiss.edu/~egjbp/faulkner/mph.html [accessed 13 August 2012]

Pascal, Roy, *The Dual Voice* (Manchester: Manchester University Press, 1977)

Pelz, Annegret, 'Alex Capus' Entdeckungen im Schreibtischgebiet', in *Ins Fremde Schreiben: Gegenwartsliteratur auf den Spuren historischer und fantastischer Entdeckungsreisen*, ed. by Christof Hamann and Alexander Honold (Göttingen: Wallstein, 2009), pp. 185–97

Pfister, Manfred, 'How Postmodern is Intertextuality?', in *Intertextuality*, ed. by Heinrich F. Plett (Berlin; New York: de Gruyter, 1991), pp. 207–24

— 'Intertextuelles Reisen, oder: Der Reisebericht als Intertext', in *Tales and "their Telling Difference": Festschrift für Franz K. Stanzel*, ed. by Herbert

Foltinek, Wolfgang Riehle and Waldemar Zacharasiewicz (Heidelberg: Winter, 1993), pp. 109–32

— 'Autopsie und intertextuelle Spurensuche: Der Reisebericht und seine Vor-Schriften', in *In Spuren Reisen: Vor-Bilder und Vor-Schriften in der Reiseliteratur*, ed. by Gisela Ecker and Susanne Röhl (Berlin: Lit, 2006), pp. 11–30

Phillips, Gene D., *Fiction, Film, and Faulkner: The Art of Adaptation* (Knoxville: University of Tennesse Press, 1988)

Pound, Ezra, 'A Retrospect', in *Poetry in Theory: An Anthology 1900–2000*, ed. by Jon Cook (Oxford: Blackwell, 2004), pp. 83–90

Praesent, Angela, 'Ein erotischer Tourist im Jemen', *Weltwoche*, 9 January 1997, p. 35

Pratt, Mary Louise, *Imperial Eyes: Travel Writing and Transculturation* (London: Routledge, 1992)

Raban, Jonathan, *For Love & Money: Writing – Reading – Travelling 1968–1987* (London: Picador in association with Collins Harvill, 1988)

Rabinow, Paul, *Reflections on Fieldwork in Morocco* (Berkeley: University of California Press, 1977)

— 'Representations are Social Facts: Modernity and Post-Modernity in Anthropology', in *Writing Culture: The Poetics and Politics of Ethnography*, ed. by James Clifford and George E. Marcus (Berkeley: University of California Press, 1986), pp. 234–61

Radisch, Iris, 'Das Ende der Spielzeit', *Die Zeit*, 4 October 1996, Section F, p. 1

Rapport, Nigel, and Joanna Overing, *Social and Cultural Anthropology: The Key Concepts* (London: Routledge, 2000)

Resch, Andreas, 'Sisyphosarbeit am Mythos', *taz*, 12 January 2010, www.taz.de/1/archiv/digitaz/artikel/?ressort=ku&dig=2010%2F01%2F12%2Fa0157&cHash=13a03790379bcd0dfa13e30908c5a59a [accessed 25 February 2013]

Rez, Helmut, Monika Kraemer, and Reiko Kobayashi-Weinsziehr, 'Warum Karl und Keizo sich nerven: Eine Reise zum systematischen Verständnis interkulturellen Missverständnisse', in *Interkulturelle Kommunikation: Methoden, Modelle, Beispiele*, ed. by Dagmar Kumbier and Friedmann Schulz von Thun (Reinbeck: Rowohlt, 2006), pp. 28–73

Ricardou, Jean, 'Terrorisme, théorie', in *Robbe-Grillet: Colloque de Cerisy*, 2 vols, i, ed. by Jean Ricardou (Paris: Union générale des éditions, 1976), pp. 10–33

Richter, Steffen, 'Das Grauen, das Grauen ... geht weiter', *Die Welt*, 15 December 2001, www.welt.de/print-welt/article493010/Das-Grauen-das-Grauen.html [accessed 25 February 2013]

— 'Rache sei dein Weg: Michael Roes reist mit der Orestie nach Algerien', *Der Tagesspiegel*, 15 March 2006, p. 32

Robben, Antonius C. G. M., and Jeffrey A. Sluka, eds., *Ethnographic Fieldwork: an Anthropological Reader* (Malden: Blackwell, 2007)

Roes, Michael, and Rachid Bouytayeb, 'Der eifersüchtige Gott: Ein Gespräch', *Merkur*, 64 (2010), pp. 228–41

Roes, Michael, 'Die Söhne haben das Schweigegebot gebrochen', *Frankfurter Allgemeine Zeitung*, 8 February 2011, p. 30, http://de.qantara.de/wcsite.php?wc_c=15900 [accessed 8 August 2011]

Romance, Joseph, 'Patriots and Philosophers: The Idea of Obligation and Race in William Faulkner's *Intruder in the Dust*', in *Democracy's Literature: Politics and Fiction in America*, ed. by Patrick J. Deneen and Joseph Romance (Lanham: Rowman & Littlefield, 2005), pp. 79–96

Rosenstock, Bruce, 'Derrida *Polutropos*: Philosophy as *Nostros*', in *Derrida and Antiquity*, ed. by Miriam Leonard (Oxford: Oxford University Press, 2010), pp. 235–66

Russell, Alison, *Crossing Boundaries: Postmodern Travel Literature* (New York: Palgrave, 2000)

Rytz, Juliane, 'Die Metaphorik der Haut in Michael Roes' *Haut des Südens*', in *Haut - Zwischen Innen und Außen: Organ - Fläche - Diskurs*, ed. by Villigster Werkstatt Interdisziplinarität (Berlin; Münster: Lit, 2009), pp. 57–67

Said, Edward, *Orientalism* (London: Penguin, [1978] 2003)

Schäffter, Ortfried, 'Modi des Fremderlebens: Deutungsmuster im Umgang mit Fremdheit', in *Das Fremde: Erfahrungsmöglichkeiten zwischen Faszination und Bedrohung*, ed. by Ortfried Schäffter (Opladen: Westdeutscher Verlag, 1991), pp. 11–42. Also available online at; ebwb.hu-berlin.de/team/.../III_19_Modi_des_Fremderlebens_Endv.pdf [accessed 11 January 2013]

Schärf, Christian, *Geschichte des Essays: Von Montaigne bis Adorno* (Göttingen: Vandenhoeck & Ruprecht, 1999)

Scherpe, Klaus R., 'Europas "rettende Liebe"? Erfundene Ethnographie von Michael Roes', in *Auslassungen: Leerstellen als Movens der Kulturwissenschaft*, ed. by Natascha Adamowsky and Peter Matussek (Würzburg: Königshausen & Neumann, 2004), pp. 109–16

Schmitt-Maaß, Christoph, '"mäandernd, ornamentalisch, ohne progression?": Intertexualität in Michael Roes' Freibeutertext *Leeres Viertel* (1996)', *Revista de Philología Alemana*, 15 (2007), 95–109

— 'Erbrechen oder Einverleiben? Zwischen eigenmotivierter Fremdforschung und Gefährdung des Subjekts: Ethnographie im Spannungsfeld von Wissenschaft, Poesie und Autobiographie', *Monatshefte*, 100 (2008), 191–212

— *Das gefährdete Subjekt: Selbst- und Fremdforschung in gegenwärtiger Ethnopoesie* (Heidelberg: Synchron, 2011)

Schneider, Peter, 'Selim blieb ein Einzelkind', *Die Zeit*, 19 (2006), www.zeit.de/2006/19/Selim_blieb_ein_Einzelkind [accessed 29 November 2010]

Schouler-Ocak, Meryam, 'Sind Migrantinnen und Migranten anders depresiv?', in *Migration und psychische Gesundheit: Belastungen und Potentiale*, ed. by Theda Borde and Matthias David (Frankfurt am Main: Mabuse, 2007), pp. 83–94

Seyhan, Azade, 'Introduction', *New German Critique*, 46 (1989), 3–9

Shakespeare, Nicholas, *Bruce Chatwin* (London: Vintage, 2000)

Sieg, Katrin, *Ethnic Drag: Performing Race, Nation, Sexuality in West Germany* (Ann Arbor: University of Michigan Press, 2002)

Silverstein, Paul A., 'Martyrs and Patriots: Ethnic, National and Transnational Dimensions of Kabyle Politics', in *Nation, Society and Culture in North Africa*, ed. by James McDougall (London: Frank Cass, 2003), pp. 87–111

Simons, Oliver, '"Amerika gibt es nicht": On the Semiotics of Literary America in the Twentieth Century', *German Quarterly*, 82 (2009), 196–211

Smith, David L., 'Huck, Jim, and American Racial Discourse', in *Satire or Evasion?: Black Perspectives on* Huckleberry Finn, ed. by James S. Leonard, Thomas A. Tenney and Thadious M. Davis (Durham, NC: Duke University Press, 1992), pp. 103–20

Smith, Sophie Catherine, *Negotiations of Masculinity in Francophone Men's Writing* (unpublished doctoral dissertation, University of Swansea, 2009)

Sölter, Arpad A., 'Die Einbeziehung des Fremden: Reflexionen zur kulturellen Fremdheit bei Simmel, Habermas und Huntington', in *Der fremde Blick: Perspektiven interkultureller Kommunikation und Hermeneutik*, ed. by Ingo Breuer and Arpad A. Sölter (Bolzano: Sturzflüge, 1997), pp. 25–52

Sontag, Susan, *On Photography* (London: Penguin, 1979)

Spurr, David, *The Rhetoric of Empire: Colonial Discourse in Journalism, Travel Writing and Imperial Administration* (Durham, NC: Duke University Press, 1993)

Statistisches Bundesamt, *Population and Employment: Foreign population. Results of the Central Alien Register* (Wiesbaden: Statistisches Bundesamt, 2007)

Steiner, George, *The Death of Tragedy* (London: Faber and Faber, 1961)

Stone, Martin, *The Agony of Algeria* (London: Hurst, 1997)

Taberner, Stuart, 'Transnationalism in Contemporary German-language Fiction by Nonminority Writers', *Seminar*, 47 (2011), 624–45

Tackach, James, 'Why Jim Does Not Escape to Illinois in Mark Twain's *Adventures of Huckleberry Finn*', *Journal of the Illinois State Historical Society*, 97 (2004), 216–25

Tassi, Marguerite A., *Women and Revenge in Shakespeare: Gender, Genre, and Ethics* (Selinsgrove: Susquehanna University Press, 2011)

Teraoka, Arlene Akiko, 'Talking "Turk": On Narrative Strategies and Cultural Stereotypes', *New German Critique*, 46, Special Issue on Minorities in German Literature (1989), 104–28

— 'Detecting Ethnicity: Jakob Arjouni and the Case of the Missing Detective Novel', *The German Quarterly*, 72 (1999), 265–89

Thiher, Alan, *Words in Reflection: Modern Language Theory and Postmodern Fiction* (Chicago: University of Chicago Press, 1984)

Thompson, Carl, *Travel Writing* (Abingdon: Routledge, 2011)

Tobin, Robert, 'Postmoderne Männlichkeit: Michael Roes und Matthias Politycki', *Zeitschrift für Germanistik*, 12 (2002), 324–33

Towner, Theresa M., *Faulkner on the Color Line: The Later Novels* (Jackson: University Press of Mississippi, 2000)

Trojanow, Ilija, 'Weltbürgertum heute: Rede zu einer kosmopolitischen Kultur', in *Ilija Trojanow*, ed. by Julian Preece (Bern: Lang, 2013), pp. 15–45

Tyler, Stephen A., 'Post-Modern Ethnography: From Document of the Occult to Occult Document', in *Writing Culture: The Poetics and Politics of Ethnography*, ed. by James Clifford and George E. Marcus (Berkeley: University of California Press, 1986), pp. 122–40

Venuti, Lawrence, *The Translator's Invisibility: A History of Translation*, 2nd edn (London; New York: Routledge, 2008)

Wallace, John H., 'The Case Against *Huck Finn*', in *Satire or Evasion?: Black Perspectives on* Huckleberry Finn, ed. by James S. Leonard, Thomas A. Tenney and Thadious M. Davis (Durham, NC: Duke University Press, 1992), pp. 16–24

Whitaker, Brian, *Unspeakable Love: Gay and Lesbian Life in the Middle East* (London: Saqi, 2006)

White, John J., *Mythology in the Modern Novel: A Study of Prefigurative Techniques* (Princeton: Princeton University Press, 1971)

Wiegandt, Kai Martin, 'Verletzt sein heißt verändert werden', *Süddeutsche Zeitung*, 23 November 2004, p. 16

Wiesner, Herbert, 'Immer bleiben Narben: Die hautnah erfahrbare Mississippi-Reise des Michael Roes', *Süddeutsche Zeitung*, 6 December 2000, Section B, p. 7

Winnington-Ingram, R. P., *Studies in Aeschylus* (Cambridge: Cambridge University Press, 1983)

Wittstock, Uwe, 'Was Wale wirklich wollen', *Die Welt*, 25 November 2000, p. 7

Young, Robert J. C., *Postcolonialism: A Very Short Introduction* (Oxford: Oxford University Press, 2003)

Youngs, Tim, 'Where Are We Going?: Cross-border Approaches to Travel Writing', in *Perspectives on Travel Writing*, ed. by Glenn Hooper and Tim Youngs (Aldershot: Ashgate, 2004), pp. 167–80

Zelik, Raul, 'Der Phallus ist Kultur', *Der Freitag*, 1 December 2000, www.freitag.de/autoren/der-freitag/der-phallus-ist-kultur [accessed 29 August 2014]

— 'Fremde Haut: Michael Roes auf Spurensuche in den USA', *Neues Deutschland*, 12 January 2001, p. 10

Zima, Peter V., *Das literarische Subjekt: Zwischen Spätmoderne und Postmoderne* (Tübingen: Francke, 2001)

Films

Someone is Sleeping in my Pain: Ein west-östlicher Macbeth, dir. by Michael Roes (not commercially available, 2001)

Timimoun, dir. by Michael Roes (Salzgeber & Co., 2005)

Index

www.ingramcontent.com/pod-product-compliance
Lightning Source LLC
LaVergne TN
LVHW022051300826
846742LV00002B/3